PENGUIN BOOKS

KILLING THE SPIRIT

Page Smith taught at UCLA and was founding
provost of the University of California at Santa
Cruz. His numerous award-winning books include
an eight-volume history of the United States, now
being published by Penguin.

KILLING THE SPIRIT

HIGHER EDUCATION IN AMERICA

PAGE SMITH

PENGUIN BOOKS

PENGUIN BOOKS
Published by the Penguin Group
Viking Penguin, a division of Penguin Books USA Inc.,
375 Hudson Street, New York, New York 10014, U.S.A.
Penguin Books Ltd, 27 Wrights Lane,
London W8 5TZ, England
Penguin Books Australia Ltd, Ringwood,
Victoria, Australia
Penguin Books Canada Ltd, 2801 John Street,
Markham, Ontario, Canada L3R 1B4
Penguin Books (N.Z.) Ltd, 182–190 Wairau Road,
Auckland 10, New Zealand

Penguin Books Ltd, Registered Offices:
Harmondsworth, Middlesex, England

First published in the United States of America by
Viking Penguin, a division of
Penguin Books USA Inc., 1990
Published in Penguin Books 1991

10 9 8 7 6 5 4 3 2 1

LIBRARY OF CONGRESS CATALOGING IN PUBLICATION DATA
Smith, Page.
    Killing the spirit: higher education in America/Page Smith.
        p. cm.
    Reprint. Originally published: New York, N.Y., U.S.A.: Viking,
1990.
    Includes index.
    ISBN 0 14 01.2183 8
    1. Education, Higher—United States. 2. Education, Higher—United
States—History. I. Title.
[LA226.S627 1991]
378.73—dc20   90–20657

Printed in the United States of America

"We must never expect to find in a dogma the explanation of the system which props it up. That explanation must be sought in its history."

—JOHN JAY CHAPMAN

To my students

ACKNOWLEDGMENTS

Honesty requires that I implicate a number of my friends and former colleagues in this work. They have been my counselors and "informants." I would like to be able to blame them for any errors or indecencies in this work, but I have not been able to figure out how to do so without exposing myself to litigation. I therefore reluctantly hold them guiltless for the views expressed herein and for any egregious errors in the text. Helpful, if innocent, were Ted Sarbin, Brewster Smith, Melanie Mayer, Bert Kaplan, Frank Barron, Dean McHenry, Grant McConnell, Robert Meister, Bruce Larkin, Richard Randolph, Marge Franz, John Dizikes, Mark Scott, Dick Davis, Dale Easley, David Gaines, Hans Huessy, Roberta Wohlstetter, George Morgan, August Frugé (especially), and, of course, my old pal, Paul Lee, who sprang me in 1973.

CONTENTS

INTRODUCTION

I think a word should be said about the genesis of this work. I spent, man and boy, some thirty years in the academic world, four as an undergraduate student at Dartmouth College, five in graduate studies at Harvard University, and twenty-one teaching on the college and university level. I left the University of California, Santa Cruz, in 1973, and for the last fifteen years I have been a somewhat bemused observer of the academic scene.

Between my years of undergraduate study at Dartmouth and my graduate studies at Harvard, I served five years in the Army of the United States, ending my military career dramatically as the victim of an enemy land mine on the slopes of Mount Belvedere in Italy.

As an undergraduate I had been drawn to a professor of social philosophy, a German émigré named Eugen Rosenstock-Huessy. Rosenstock-Huessy, who might be described as a "meta-historian," somewhat along the line of Oswald Spengler or Arnold Toynbee (his greatest work in English is *Out of Revolution: The Autobiography of Western Man*), exerted a profound influence on me. An English major, I was drawn to the grand vistas of history that Rosenstock-Huessy's writing and lectures revealed.

When the war was over, I taught at my old high school for a

year (I was on convalescent leave from the army, recuperating from my wounds) and then decided to do some graduate study in history under the GI Bill of Rights. My interest in history, awakened somewhat belatedly by Rosenstock-Huessy, had been given a special kind of urgency by the extraordinary events of the times.

I thus applied for admission to the graduate program in history at Harvard. I had done reasonably well as an undergraduate student, ending up, inadvertently, as a Rufus Choate Scholar, an honor bestowed on seniors who had straight A's in their last year of courses. I was disappointed to be turned down by the Harvard history department. To soften the blow, the letter of rejection hinted that if I applied in English, which was, after all, my undergraduate major, I might well be admitted in the English department. By that time I had it fixed in my head that I wanted to do some graduate work somewhere, so I applied in English and was admitted. The young Smith family, myself, my wife, and our two small children, arrived in Boston in the fall of 1946.

When I consulted with the English department to discover what courses I was expected to take, I was horrified to discover that Greek, Latin, Middle High German, and Icelandic were required languages for a Ph.D. in English literature. At least that was what it sounded like to me. I can't believe it was really that stringent and irrelevant. In any event, I fled to the history department and told the amiable chairman, David Owen, that he would have to let me in. I couldn't hack it with the literature people. He acquiesced but he added a strange admonition: "You won't find any of those grandiose Rosenstock-Huessy ideas here. This is a trade school preparing students for academic careers." I was a little puzzled and disconcerted by the mention of Rosenstock-Huessy. That Rosenstock-Huessy had taught at Harvard for several years I knew, but I was surprised that David Owen connected me so directly to Rosenstock-Huessy.

I later learned more of Rosenstock-Huessy's Harvard years. He had experienced the resentment and hostility of his Harvard colleagues (one of them referred to him as "that little squirt") because he refused to genuflect to two of the reigning deities of the academic world, Marx and Freud, and occasionally spoke favorably of God. Alfred North Whitehead, who found Rosenstock-Huessy a kindred spirit, teased him by saying that if he would be a "little pink" it would improve his relations with other faculty. When a senior member of the history department stated that he expected to see history become a predictive science during his lifetime, Rosenstock-Huessy vigorously dissented, infuriating the professor, who, reportedly, used his considerable influence to prevent Rosenstock-Huessy from being kept at Harvard.

As my wife says, "lap dissolve." Forty-two years later, in the summer of 1988, my wife and I attended a week-long conference at Dartmouth College on the life and work of Rosenstock-Huessy. The occasion was the hundredth anniversary of his birth. People came from all over the United States, and from Denmark, Switzerland, Germany, and Canada, to discuss Rosenstock-Huessy's work and to testify to his influence on their lives. Among those attending was a young graduate student, Mark Scott. As a high-school student, Scott had been given notes that his father, a successful businessman, had taken when he was a student of Rosenstock-Huessy many years earlier. Scott was hooked. He began reading Rosenstock-Huessy's writings. He incorporated Rosenstock-Huessy's ideas in the papers he wrote when he became a college student. His intention was to become a history professor. In pursuit of that career, he took a term's work in history at the University College London. There his professors, who had apparently never heard of Rosenstock-Huessy, expressed alarm at Scott's quotations from the German philosopher and did their best to stamp out these heresies. Scott allowed me to read the evaluations his professors had written at the end of the courses he had taken, and he has given me permission to quote from them.

Scott's professor in a course entitled "European History, 400–1200" wrote: "Perfectly able to operate within conventional structures of thought and presentation, Mark has at times chosen a highly subjective, impressionistic and emotive approach. He seems to be under the spell of one E. Rosenstock-Huessy who appears to operate within a totally subjective critique based on a celebration of the triumph of Middle-American Protestantism. Mark feels that it is a 'sell-out' to write objective history. All this apart, he has been lively in class and has provoked other students to defend their approach."

The instructor in Scott's course on "European History, 1200–1500" had strikingly similar reactions: "Intellectually, a very idiosyncratic student, though not without ability. His approach to almost any piece of work seemed to be governed by a book on what might be called meta-history by one Rosenstock-Huessy. . . . Mark found the strait-jacket of conventional history very distressing, and one felt that he was constantly wanting to revert to a field of study somewhere between poetry and history in our sense."

The professor of "Byzantine and Modern Greek Studies" reported on Scott's work in a virtually identical manner. He had found him "a most assiduous attender at the course, full of ideas and questions," but unfortunately he had "fallen victim to some rather wild notions on the meaning of history." Most alarmingly, Scott was laboring under a "theological-anthropological-sociological view of history."

When Scott's tutor came to summarize these gloomy reports, he mentioned that the young man was a member of the swimming club and the Literary Society and had made "excellent use of his time in London to broaden his intellectual and cultural horizons." Then came the chilling finale: "Minus Rosenstock-Huessy (?), he might make a good historian."

No wonder that Scott's faith in Rosenstock-Huessy was badly shaken. He felt confronted by the choice of giving up Rosenstock-Huessy or giving up his plans to become a professor of history! When I read these evaluations, written roughly forty years after I had been turned down by the Harvard history department, it came to me as a minor revelation that I had been rejected because I had been a student of Rosenstock-Huessy. His son, Hans, told me recently that his father had written a glowing letter of recommendation in my behalf to the Harvard history department and was always convinced that it was his letter that had secured my admission to graduate study in history. Actually it was that letter and the antagonism that the Harvard history faculty felt for

Rosenstock-Huessy's ideas that kept me from being accepted initially for graduate work.

The realization that my career had hung by such a slender thread startled me. And it astonished me to discover that almost forty years later another young man was in similar danger because he was attracted to ideas that had been the foundation of my own scholarly and personal life. That the academic fundamentalists had been so unrelenting in their hostility toward Rosenstock-Huessy's thought, amazed and distressed me. I felt the greatest sympathy for Scott, who was faced with the choice of giving up (or concealing) his interest in Rosenstock-Huessy's work and thought, or abandoning his hopes of a career as a history professor. It set me to thinking about the inhuman side of contemporary academic life, where only certain ideas are tolerated and those ideas seem to me, in the main, life-denying.

The reader may be interested in knowing more about this dangerously subversive character, a man so feared and hated by his colleagues that they felt no compunction about barring those tainted with Rosenstock-Huessyism from the profession. The situation was obviously somewhat different as between P. Smith and M. Scott. The members of the Harvard history department knew very well who Rosenstock-Huessy was and what a threat his ideas were to conventional notions of academic history. The faculty members at University College London into whose hands Mark Scott fell had never heard of Rosenstock-Huessy. All they knew of him was what they had learned through Scott's papers, but that was clearly enough to excite and alarm them; enough to make evident that Rosenstock-Huessy was not "the right stuff," academically speaking.

The point, of course, is not whether Rosenstock-Huessy was right or wrong in his speculations about history. The point is the instant and stony rejection of the man and his ideas; the circling of the academic wagons against him. One would think that, to arouse so much resentment, Rosenstock-Huessy would have to have been a Nazi storm trooper. In fact, he was, on one level, a thoroughly orthodox German academic. The son of a Jewish banker, Rosenstock-Huessy had become a convert to Christianity in his youth. He earned his doctorate in law and philosophy from Heidelberg and taught law at the University of Leipzig prior to World War I. During the war he served as an officer in the German army; after the war Rosenstock-Huessy passed up tempting offers from the academic and publishing worlds to work in the Daimler-Benz factory, where he laid the foundation for worker education and founded the first factory magazine in Germany. He served for some years as professor of law at the University of Breslau and, when Hitler came to power, left for the United States. After teaching at Harvard for three years on a temporary appointment and there, as we have noted, arousing the profoundest anxieties among his colleagues, he received an appointment as professor of social philosophy at Dartmouth College, and it was at Dartmouth that I fell under his influence.

I have not been alone in my admiration for Rosenstock-Huessy as a thinker, as the Dartmouth conference indicated. Among the contemporary critics who have been deeply impressed by the power and originality of his thought is the British-American poet W. H. Auden, who included a large number of quotes from Rosenstock-Huessy's work in his *Book of Aphorisms*; Auden wrote of Rosenstock-Huessy that he "continually astonishes one by his dazzling and unique insights." Auden wrote a poem, "Aubade," in memory of Rosenstock-Huessy after Huessy's death. The famous Jewish theologian Martin Buber noted that Rosenstock-Huessy had defined the "historical nature of man . . . in so living a way as no other thinker before him has done." Lewis Mumford, the authority on cities, praised his "understanding of the relevance of traditional values to a civilization still undergoing revolutionary transformations"; and added: "this contribution [Rosenstock-Huessy's *Out of Revolution*] will gain rather than lose significance in the future."

Citation from authority is a notoriously inadequate way to advance an argument. I mention these admirers of Rosenstock-Huessy not to prove the "rightness" of his teaching but simply to suggest that Mark Scott and I are not alone in believing that Rosenstock-Huessy is an important and original thinker, and that even if he weren't he and his disciples—"disciples" is certainly not too strong a word in my case—have a right to be heard in that "market place of ideas" that the university boasts of being. I can think of no more telling an index to the closed-mindedness of the American academic community than the Rosenstock-Huessy story.

I had long been a critic of many aspects of higher education, but the odd conjuncture of the Scott and Smith "cases" gave me a sense of the consequences of academic fundamentalism and provided the incentive for this work.

If the Harvard historians who rejected my application for admission to graduate study in history in the sure conviction that they were guarding the gates of academic respectability against barbarians without, could see or read me now, they would, I have no doubt, feel thoroughly vindicated in their original decision. They plainly admitted an enemy agent who has devoted an academic lifetime to subversive activities. Not only have I based my scholarly work on the alarming doctrines of Eugen Rosenstock-Huessy; I have based my teaching and personal life on his writings as well.

KILLING
THE
SPIRIT

1
MAPPING
THE DESERT

"It is easy to see that the moral sense has been bred out of certain sections of the population, like the wings have been bred off certain chickens to produce more white meat on them. This is a generation of wingless chickens. . . ."

—FLANNERY O'CONNOR

I have called this chapter "Mapping the Desert." I shall try in it to sketch what seems to me to have gone awry in the current academic scene, and in subsequent chapters to reconstruct as best I can the story of how things happened to get this way.

The major themes might be characterized as the impoverishment of the spirit by "academic fundamentalism"; the flight from teaching, the meretriciousness of most academic research, the disintegration of the disciplines, the alliance of the universities with the Department of Defense, the National Aeronautics and Space Agency, etc., and, more recently, with biotechnology and communications corporations, and, last but not least, the corruptions incident to "big-time" collegiate sports.

According to the "index of leading educational indicators," higher education in the United States has never been higher. The figures are awesome: 2,029 four-year institutions; 1,311 two-year colleges; in 1982, 865,000 instructors of various ranks and over 12,200,000 students, 7,716,000 in four-year colleges and universities and 4,531,000 in two-year colleges; over a million graduate students and 5,172,000 part-time students scattered among various categories of higher institutions of learning. The expenditures for higher education are calculated at some $95 billion each year. The average full professor's salary at private universities is in the neighborhood of $50,000 a year, an increase of $17,000 since 1980. Many academic salaries are in the $70,000-to-$80,000 range for hot professors in hot fields, and salaries above $100,000 are not unknown. Thus there are more students than ever before, more professors, more money, more research, more publications. More, pretty much, of everything, yet, looking carefully at what is actually going on, it is hard not to feel that the current situation in higher education is a classic example of the principle of "more is less."

Although small, church-related (or at least once church-related) colleges far outnumber the major (or "great" or "elite") universities, 75 percent or more of the undergraduate students in the United States attend large public universities or state colleges, which make up less than 25 percent of the total number of institutions enrolling undergraduate students. One researcher calculates the number of "top" universities at twenty to fifty. Some 280 state-supported colleges and former teachers' colleges and normal schools have been or are struggling to be upgraded to universities, and they, of course, enroll a substantial portion of that 75 percent. But it is the so-called elite universities that set the tone and, in my view, poison the springs of academic life in the United States. It is on them that this book is focused.

"Americans," wrote Herbert Croly in his enormously influential *The Promise of American Life*, "are superstitious in respect to education, rather because of the social 'uplift' which they expect to achieve by so-called educational means. The credulity of the socialist by expecting to alter human nature by merely institutional and legal changes is at least equaled by the credulity of good Americans in proposing to evangelize the individual by the reading of books and the expenditure of money and words. . . . Do we lack culture? We will 'make it hum' by founding a new university in Chicago. Is American art neglected and impoverished? We will enrich it by organizing art departments in our colleges and popularize it by lectures with lantern slides and associations for the study of its history."

More than seventy-five years have passed since Croly wrote those words, and there are signs that the long love affair that Americans have had with education—more specifically, in this instance, with higher education—may be coming to an end. Higher education has experienced a barrage of criticism in recent years. The recently retired Secretary of Education, William Bennett, has been a tireless critic of the academy. Allan Bloom's all-out attack on higher education has sold an astonishing eight hundred thousand—plus copies; a journalist named Charles Sykes has written *Profscam: Professors and the Demise of Higher Education.* Sykes writes, "In the midst of this wasteland stands the American professor. Almost single-handedly, the professors . . . have destroyed the university as a center of learning and have desolated higher education."

One of the popular terms for our era is "post-modernist." Todd Gitlin, professor of literature at the University of California, Berkeley, and a sixties activist, describes post-modernism as "indifferent to consistency and continuity. . . . It self-consciously splices genes, attitudes, styles. . . . It disdains originality and fancies copies, repetition, the recombination of hand-me-down scraps. It neither embraces nor criticizes, but beholds the world blankly, with a knowingness that dissolves feeling and commitment into irony. It pulls the rug out from under itself, displaying an acute self-consciousness about the work's constructed nature. It . . . derides the search for depth as mere nostalgia for an unmoved mover. . . . 'The individual' has decomposed, as 'reality' has dissolved, nothing lives but 'discourses,' 'texts,' 'language games,' 'images,' 'simulations' referring to other 'discourses,' 'texts,' etc." Gitlin calls post-modernism "the spiritless spirit of a global class." The experience of this class "denies the continuity of history; they live in a perpetual present. . . ." Gitlin argues that the spirit (or spiritlessness) of post-modernism is marked by a "post-1960's . . . cultural helplessness. . . . History has ruptured, passions have been expended, belief has become difficult; heroes have died and been replaced by celebrities. The 1960's exploded our belief in progress, which underlay the classical faith in linear order and

moral clarity. Old verities crumpled, but new ones have not settled in."

Sir Richard Livingstone, former vice-chancellor of Oxford University, called our time "The civilization of means without ends;
rich in means beyond any other epoch, and almost beyond human
needs; squandering and misusing them, because it has no over-
ruling ideal; an ample body with a meagre soul . . . The break-up
of the philosophy of the West is the great problem of our time,"
he added, "on which all its lesser problems depend: for in the last
resort the conduct of men is governed by their beliefs." Those
beliefs are no longer readily identifiable.

Richard Greenberg, author of the play *Eastern Standard,* which
opened recently on Broadway, commented on the plight of his
generation (Greenberg is thirty). "Most of the people I know,"
he told a *New York Times* theater critic, Mervyn Rothstein, "have
looked back at the last decade, or two or three decades, of their
lives, and have found that their premises have been faulty; the
relationships they've forged, the careers they've made for themselves, everything about the way they've lived, it's all proven inadequate. The answers they thought they'd found have been the
wrong answers. I've witnessed marriages breaking up, deep dissatisfaction, career changes, clever people and sensitive and
changeable. . . . It's been pervasive." Greenberg had grown up in
a protected, middle-class environment, "and then suddenly," he
told Rothstein, "you find yourself coming up against things that
are complex and mysterious. You come upon irreconcilable truths,
you get to the place where the keenest intellect won't go—real
life in all its complexity, moral issues, traumas, a bigger world, the
fact that we're not in a cocoon, we're not operating just between
our houses and our workplaces."

The play is the story of the journey from the glibness of the
"very fluent," who feel confident that they can respond to "any
given situation," to an understanding of the irrational or nonin-
tellectual things that hold life together. The "very fluent" are,
virtually without exception, "those who have derived their fluency
from our institutions of higher education," which are, for the most
part, blind to those "things that are complex and mysterious."

In a similar spirit, Robert Lichtman, speaking specifically of the academic world, has deplored what he called "a widespread behaviorism . . . in social thought. . . . Quality, uniqueness, creativity, and the moral dimension of existence fall before a reductive insistence upon measurement, qualification, and restrictive processes of infinitely tedious and irrelevant observation. The view of man which emerges is ahistorical, atomistic, mechanical, disjunctive, and, again, ostensibly neutral."

The critic Leslie Fiedler has expressed the same thought in a different image: "Reason, though dead, holds us with an embrace that looks like a lover's embrace but turns out to be *rigor mortis*. Unless we are necrophiles, we'd better let go."

The spiritual illness of "post-modernism," afflicting not just America but the Western world, obviously extends far beyond university walls, but it is in the university that I believe its destructive effects are most keenly felt, and it is the university, with what Alfred North Whitehead years ago called its "scheme of orthodoxies," that vastly compounds the problem. It is indeed those orthodoxies that are most troubling. There is a mad reductionism at work. God is not a proper topic for discussion, but "lesbian politics" is. The sociologist Peter Berger asks "how long such a shrinkage of human experience can remain plausible," adding, "In any case it constitutes a profound impoverishment."

Academic fundamentalism is the issue, the stubborn refusal of the academy to acknowledge any truth that does not conform to professorial dogmas. In the famous "market place of ideas," where all ideas are equal and where there must be no "value judgments" and therefore no values, certain ideas are simply excluded, and woe to those who espouse them. Such individuals are terminated, lest their corruption spread to others.

Let me cite two classic examples of academic fundamentalism. First, a course given last year at a prominent university on Gothic architecture in which the instructor discussed floor plans, stresses in arches, and innovations in building techniques but made no reference to the religious passion out of which these grand structures rose. Second, a popular and widely read work on Populism, our most radical native political movement, that made no mention of the evangelical Protestantism out of which Populism rose, and without some attention to which the movement remains uncomprehensible. When I asked the author why he had omitted any reference to the dominant religious theme, he replied that he wasn't interested in religion. He was a typical academic fundamentalist; he doubtless thought that by omitting any reference to religion he was being "scientific."

The faculties at the elite universities (and, increasingly, at those lesser institutions bent on aping them) are in full flight from teaching. This is certainly not a new development. It has been going on, in varying degrees, since the rise of the modern university, when teaching "loads" began to be reduced so that research-oriented professors could pursue their researches.

During the student rebellion of the 1960s and early '70s, the trend to less and less teaching was briefly interrupted, since one of the principal complaints of students was that their professors paid little attention to them. So sustained was such criticism that a long-time university watcher, David Riesman, expressed his concern lest "publish or perish" be replaced by "teach or perish" and the research mission of the university be thereby compromised.

In many universities, faculty members make no bones about the fact that students are the enemy. It is students who threaten to take up precious time that might otherwise be devoted to research. I have heard colleagues boast of having infrequent office hours at awkward times to avoid contact with students outside the classroom; these same professors discharge their formal teaching obligations as cheaply and expediently as they can, usually by reading ancient notes to large classes of passive students two or three times a week, with "sections," if there are any, conducted by dedicated but inexperienced graduate assistants who also read and grade the students' papers and examinations.

I recently encountered a professor I know. To my query as to how she was, she replied enthusiastically: "Wonderful. I'm not teaching this quarter." And her husband (also a professor)? Even better. He had been on leave all last year and was, at that very moment, writing an application for a grant that would relieve him of all teaching duties for the next year.

The point I wish to make is a simple one. There is no decent, adequate, respectable education, in the proper sense of that much-abused word, without personal involvement by a teacher with the needs and concerns, academic and personal, of his/her students. All the rest is "instruction" or "information transferral," "communication technique," or some other impersonal and antiseptic phrase, but *it is not teaching* and the student is not truly learning.

By and large the word "research" is its own justification. It is a magic word that has no referent in the real world. "Research" is a word without soul or substance, as broad as the ocean and as shallow as a pond. It covers a multitude of academic sins and conceals a poverty of spirit and a barrenness of intellect beyond calculating.

The argument that will be made here can be simply stated. It is that the vast majority of the so-called research turned out in the modern university is essentially worthless. It does not result in any measurable benefit to anything or anybody. It does not push back those omnipresent "frontiers of knowledge" so confidently evoked; it does not *in the main* result in greater health or happiness among the general populace or any particular segment of it. It is busywork on a vast, almost incomprehensible scale. It is dispiriting; it depresses the whole scholarly enterprise; and, most important of all, it deprives the student of what he or she deserves—the thoughtful and considerate attention of a teacher deeply and un-equivocally committed to teaching; in short, it robs the student of an education for which the student is required to pay a very large sum of money (and often to mortgage his/her future). Indeed, one reason higher education is so outrageously expensive is that, the less teaching professors have done, the higher their salaries have risen. It is not unusual for a professor whose salary is in the $70,000–$80,000 range to teach only two or three courses a year.

If the professors teach less in the name of research, who takes up the slack? The answer is a new academic underclass described as "part-time instructional staff." This part-time staff includes "teaching assistants," graduate students who do a major part of the undergraduate teaching in order to help pay their way through graduate school. They are supplemented by individuals, many of them with Ph.D.'s, who have not been able to secure regular full-time employment. A recent study by Howard Rothman Bowen and Jack A. Schuster found their use to be "very extensive." At one community college, 79 percent of the faculty were part-time. "In no instance was it claimed that part-time faculty were integrated into the academic departments to which they were assigned or into campus life. . . . [T]he overall conclusion was inescapable. Typically the part-timer is viewed as an expedient, and the part-timer's understandable response is a minimal commitment to the institution."

Another category that Bowen and Schuster identified on most campuses is the "nomads"—i.e., men and women who held full-time but strictly limited appointments, often filling in for faculty away on leave. They had little time for students; they were "invariably spending much of their energy trying to find new jobs to go to when their current appointments expired." Many of the "nomads" were fully as capable as their regularly employed colleagues, as both teachers and researchers. They had been victims of the buyer's market, of the fact that there were too many well-qualified prospective professors for the available openings. One heard horror stories of dozens of young Ph.D.'s from high-ranking graduate schools applying for every available position in overcrowded fields. A Berkeley-educated classicist filling in for a year at a Southern university said: "So far as I know, I've been iced. I thought I could succeed, if I did it professionally."

Bowen and Schuster found wherever they looked a "renewed emphasis on scholarship"—or, it might better be put, an "increased emphasis," since the insistence on publish-or-perish had never notably diminished. The reasons were, in part, competition for higher ranking among universities and a buyer's market as the result of a shameless overproduction of young Ph.D.'s; since large graduate departments brought generous funding, more students had been admitted in the period from 1960 to 1985 than jobs could be found for. The researchers found much discontent among older faculty members. "Not infrequently they expressed outrage about market-driven compensation, differential pay policies which they considered unjust and even humiliating." Such policies favored not only "the new breed of self-centered young faculty" but also the "high-demand academic fields."

Having strongly endorsed research as the most appropriate criterion for promotion, Bowen and Schuster had second thoughts. "In the groves of academe, to question the importance of research approaches heresy. Still, we cannot help but wonder whether the stampede toward scholarship—or what passes for scholarship—serves the nation's needs or the long-run interests of those campuses which historically have been strongly committed to excellent teaching. We fear that the essential balance between teaching and scholarship has been lost, that the scales are tipping too far toward the latter in many institutions."

The strange thing about the existing system is that the men who invented it (there were, it is agreeable to report, virtually no women involved during the years when the system developed in its most brutal and inhuman form) suffer from its irrationality more than anyone else and give occasional rather weak signals that they would like the nightmare to end. The professors have, in effect, created a classic Frankenstein monster, who now rules over them, controlling their careers through their fear of not being promoted (and thus having no opportunity to enjoy the rewards of their ingenuity in creating a notably self-indulgent "life-style").

Closely related to the whole research issue is the general demoralization of the standard nonscientific academic disciplines—the so-called social sciences (which, it is increasingly evident, are not "scientific" in any real sense of the word) and the humanities (which are not very humane). My admittedly casual inquiries in these fields have revealed a startling degree of disarray. Fields have fragmented into more and more subfields, so that it is hard to get an intelligible account of what is going on in any particular discipline: it depends, in large part, on whom you talk to. Allan J. Lichtman wrote in 1974 that "as disciplines become increasingly technical they tend to devolve into competing subgroups, scarcely able to communicate with each other, much less the reading public."

Sir Walter Moberly reported that the president of a "great American university" told him some years ago that "the members of his teaching staff had practically nothing to say to one another, for they had nothing in common. They had no common core of culture, no common frame of reference or stock of fundamental ideas." In the words of Irving Babbitt, the members of a "modern college faculty sometimes strike one in an Emersonian phrase, as a collection of 'infinitely repellant particles.' "

A recent study done for the Carnegie Foundation for the Advancement of Teaching underlines the lack of loyalty among faculty toward the college or university that employs them, and toward their students. The authors of the report write: "The seemingly limitless supply of research funds, consulting opportunities, easy promotions, and dazzling offers, has been around for some time now. There is a whole generation of able young faculty members who never knew a time when affluence did not prevail. Thus it is hardly surprising that a few of them exhibit an opportunism that startles their elders. Some of these heavily-bid-for young people appear to have no institutional loyalty whatever and simply follow the offers where they lead. . . . In their view, students are just impediments in the headlong search for more and better grants, fatter fees, higher salaries, higher rank." The study proposed the establishment of "ethical standards to curb the crassest opportunism in grantsmanship, job-hopping, and wheeler-dealing." The call for—what?—rules?—to prevent the "crassest opportunism" seems a bit odd. Would "crass opportunism" go unpunished? Does not the system that promotes and rewards such behavior need far more than a code of ethics?

The problems of the university do not stop with the scandalous neglect of teaching or the absurd inflation of research; the universities are tied to the military-industrial complex by financial bonds that I suspect can never be broken. Today 90 percent of all federal research funds come from the Nuclear Regulatory Commission, NASA, and the Department of Defense. Can we really speak of the independence of the university in the face of that statistic? The best we can say is that so far the federal government has been relatively restrained in using its power as the dispenser of enormous sums of money to bend universities to its will. Perhaps that is because the universities are so compliant rather than because the government is so restrained. Certainly the desire to tap into government largesse has played a major role in determining the composition and character of university faculties. Many professors have been appointed to important chairs primarily because they had reputations for attracting large government grants. Government is interested in education primarily, in the words of Sebastian de Grazia, "as a means to other ends." Indeed, how could it be otherwise?

Under the title "Biotechnology: Big Money Comes to the University?" James Rule, professor of sociology at the State University of New York at Stony Brook, raises, in a recent issue of *Dissent*, the question of the effect on what's left of the independence of universities of the alliances between universities and companies engaged in various forms of genetic engineering. The case, as between Department of Defense funding for defense-related research projects and contractual relationships between such firms as Monsanto and Allied Corporation, would seem all in the latter's favor. At least firms involved in genetic engineering do not have as their goals improved means of killing human beings. Their professed aims have to do with fighting disease and prolonging life while making enormous profits. But the growing involvement of corporations with universities, wherein the universities' research in bio-whatever is funded by corporations that market the results and divide the profits with the affiliated universities, raises serious ethical and moral problems. Washington University in Saint Louis signed an agreement with Monsanto Company in 1982 under the terms of which Monsanto gave $23.5 million to the university's medical school to fund research "leading to marketable biomedical discoveries." Monsanto holds half the seats on the board that approves research undertaken under the terms of the grant. The company also has the right to delay announcement of the results of all joint projects for up to four years, in order, obviously, to exploit the market for new products resulting from research.

A professor at the University of California at Davis signed a similar contract with Allied Corporation in 1981 for $2.5 million with the understanding that the firm would have patent rights over the results of the professor's researches. Rule mentions such beneficial discoveries as genetically produced insulin and the alteration of "crops and livestock to fit human needs and environmental constraints." Aside from the fact that many thoughtful persons have strong reservations about such tampering with nature, the vast sums of money involved cannot help corrupting the process and pushing university researchers toward profit-making projects.

When Harvard was approached in 1980 to become involved with a biotechnology company founded by a faculty member, the university backed off and President Bok issued a self-righteous statement: "The preservation of academic values is a matter of paramount importance to the university, and owning shares in such a company would create a number of potential conflicts with these values." But in 1988 "these values" are not so highly regarded. After eight years of playing coy, Harvard has undertaken to raise $30 million to form a partnership "to exploit the ideas of its medical school faculty."

Even *The New York Times* questioned the entanglement of the universities for profit with corporations. An editorial on September 19, 1988, begins: "Oscar Wilde could resist everything except temptation. University presidents, it seems, can resist everything except money. . . .

One Harvard faculty member defending the new venture insisted to a reporter that "the good judgment of administrators and faculty" would insure that research would not be skewed toward profit-making projects. This poses the interesting question: can a soul once sold be sold again?

The fact that corporate largesse descends disproportionately on the "bio" field—biochemistry, biology, and biophysics—causes tension and jealousies between scientific fields and, perhaps even more, between the sciences and the nonsciences, the latter feeling more and more like stepchildren in the academy. In an age when bumper stickers proclaim "The One Who Dies with the Most Toys Wins," those fields shut out from federal and corporate toys feel neglected. One is reminded of Brooks Adams' observation in *The Theory of Social Revolutions* that "capital" owns the universities "by right of purchase." The association between the universities and agrobusiness has been a long and, on the whole, fruitful one, although serious questions have been raised recently about the role of the university in the development of a farm economy that, while highly profitable to the large corporate farmers, depresses, where it does not actually endanger, the lives of farm workers. One must ask if the university can, in the long run, preserve its freedom to carry on "pure" science in the face of such shameless huckstering. Who pays the piper calls the tune. There is no reason to believe that the university is immune to that law.

Since universities sold their souls some time ago, when they began accepting enormous federal grants to do work for the military-industrial complex, the corporate connection in the biotechnology-computer realm was a natural and probably inevitable next step. Let us pray that one consequence will be that we will hear no more pious pronouncements about the universities' being engaged in the "pursuit of truth." What they are clearly pursuing with far more dedication than the truth is big bucks.

When Brooks Adams described the American university in 1912 as owned by capital and used for its purposes, he was thinking primarily of the university's tendency, clearly marked even then, toward specialization. But the university is a capitalistic institution in ways that Adams failed to mention. It is intensely individualistic and highly competitive. Student is pitted against student through the grading system, and faculty member against faculty member for promotion and other academic favors. Most professors, at least at the "great universities," are liberal in inclination; many are vaguely "socialistic." It will doubtless disconcert them to hear themselves described as "rugged individualists" in the classic mold of Social Darwinism, men and women in merciless competition with each other and, odder still, with their students. Since the academic world is so bewitched by "models," let us try the model of the ambitious academic who competes at every level of the academic process from high school through graduate school. He or she "invests" in an academic specialty. The time taken to acquire a Ph.D., a time quite out of proportion to anything it is essential to learn in a specific field, is the graduate student's "capital." With some skill and considerable patience, it can be turned into the lifelong meal ticket called tenure. He/she thus guards that investment of time jealously, fends off intruders, and does his/her best to improve the return on his/her investment through the various career strategies that we are familiar with.

In view of the seriousness of the charges made here against the academic world, it may seem merely frivolous to add a complaint against "big-time" university athletics. The charge can be simply made. Intercollegiate athletics are riddled with unethical, unprincipled, hypocritical, often illegal acts and policies. Hardly a week passes without some new revelation of skulduggery. This morning's paper tells of the coach of a Texas football team that is alleged to have paid $4,000 in bribes to a former player as "hush money" to keep him from recounting illegal payments to other players. A football scandal at another Texas university involved several regents and the governor of the state. Texas A&M, which has hardly recovered from a two-year ban on post-season "bowl" games, is being investigated once more, with rumors that the head coach will be forced to resign. The University of Oklahoma has been penalized for a number of rules infractions. The Southeast Conference is the greatest offender. In the last years, five Texas universities have been charged with violations of National Collegiate Athletic Association rules.

Even when there are no specific scandals, the system itself is scandalous. I have been connected with four "major" colleges or universities with big-time sports programs over my academic career—Dartmouth, Harvard, William and Mary, and UCLA—and only Harvard failed to have a football scandal during my years there. Dartmouth and Harvard both had relatively low-intensity big-time athletic programs, but Dartmouth in the era of Earl Blaik came dangerously close to crossing the line between a legitimate and an illegitimate football program.

College football coaches are under tremendous pressure (typically from alumni) to turn out winning football teams. Their success depends largely on recruiting outstanding high-school or junior-college players. The competition for such players is, in consequence, merciless, often corrupting to the young men recruited, demeaning to the recruiters and to the institutions with which they are associated, and, as we have noted, not infrequently illegal.

Anyone who has been in a major university for any length of time can tell countless tales of chicanery, manipulation of the educational process, and illegal payments to football players and their families.

In collegiate basketball the situation is just as bad. Today's paper tells me that Jerry Tarkanian, coach of the basketball team at the University of Nevada at Las Vegas, has received a verdict from the Supreme Court of the United States that his constitutional rights were not violated when the university suspended Tarkanian for two years because of rules infractions. Needless to say, he is still coaching.

One of the most conspicuous bizarreries of modern academe is the fact that the majority of the big-sport athletes and virtually all of the "stars" are black. Basketball is almost wholly "black," football predominantly so. In football the most dramatic positions are virtually monopolized by superb black athletes—running backs, wide (pass) receivers, and the corner backs who defense against them. Most of the candidates for (and most of the winners of) the Heisman Trophy, awarded each year to the outstanding football player in the nation, are black. Until a few years ago, the critically important position of quarterback was reserved for white players. This year the quarterbacks on six of the top-ranked teams in the nation were black, and one suspects that before long black quarterbacks will be as common as black wide receivers.

The crowning irony is that, in states where blacks were only a few years ago barred from voting, the majority of football and basketball players are black. When Georgia, let's say, plays Alabama in football or basketball, black players dominate—if not in numbers, in performance (of course, collegiate basketball has become virtually a black monopoly from Mississippi to Arizona and points north and south). On every campus I visit I see a little band of black students (they are especially conspicuous on campuses in states where there are few black residents, such as Utah, Nevada, Nebraska, Colorado). There are the mammoth black students— basketball forwards and centers, the football tackles, linebackers,

and defensive ends—and the small black students—the fleet backs
and pass receivers. They mix very little with white students. They
are the classic black entertainers. It is for their exploits that arenas
of white students shout themselves hoarse. The cultural discon-
tinuity is staggering, the irony beyond articulation.

Doubtless the reason that faculty members are indifferent to
the corruptions of big-time athletes on their campuses is a kind
of "bread-and-circuses" mentality. The undergraduates are indulged in these spectacles in order that the faculty be left free to
pursue their researches.

Faculty members go on about their business as if this corruption
at the heart of their universities were none of *their* business. It is,
like bad weather, or the poisoning of the environment by industrial
chemicals, something regrettable but about which they feel no
responsibility. The football field or the basketball court is not in
their field. When a particularly lurid scandal hits the institution
that employs them, some of them rise at faculty meetings to ex-
coriate the culpable individuals and demand reform, but reform
never comes. Big-time intercollegiate football is to institutions
that claim to be dedicated to the pursuit of truth and, at least at
commencement time, speak of the noble ideals of higher education, as the CIA is to a country that professes some modest degree
of public morality.

The perpetual revolving (and revolting) big-time sports scandals
inevitably direct our attention to the alumni. In the words of Nevill
Sanford, author of *The American College*: "a close look at college-
educated people in the United States is enough to dispel any
notion that our institutions of higher learning are doing a good
job of liberal education." A colleague of Sanford's was driven to
distraction at having to work with a group of alumni from the
college at which he taught. "He came quickly to the conclusion
that these products of his and his colleagues' labors had no respect
for learning, understood nothing of the conditions necessary to
it, and were quite willing to sacrifice fundamental freedom of the
mind to the interests of expediency."

In Robert Hutchins' words, the alumni play "a weird and often-
times a terrifying role." The noise that certain alumni made was

"in inverse proportion to the amount they give to the university." If alumni behave in such a manner, as Hutchins notes, it is "too much to expect that citizens who never went to college can understand what a university is when those upon whom the blessings of the higher learning have been showered understand it less well than anybody else." When the Yale football coach Harry Hickman, who gave up coaching for ranching, was asked how he liked his new occupation, he replied: "Fine, the cattle don't have any alumni." It is easy to make light of the matter, but the odd antics of the alumni of American colleges and universities constitute the heaviest cross many university presidents have to bear. It is not clear what, if anything, can be done to remedy the situation. It is one of those cases where one can only hope that some general elevation of social consciousness will have a civilizing effect on alumni. Perhaps alumnae will bring a degree of rationality into the picture.

Quite aside from the question of how well the university is performing its primary task of teaching undergraduate students, or its secondary one of producing genuinely significant research, there remains the basic question of whether it can continue to live off the federal grants and corporate contracts while engaging in the most sordid and immoral practices *re* big-time sports and still call its soul its own. Must there not be some modest ethical standards and a twinge of morality now and then? The future of the American university does not, I suppose, depend on removing these cancers from its collective body, but cancers they are, and as long as they persist, any profession of exalted ideals by the university will have a hollow ring. Hypocrisy is one of the least appealing human traits. The modern university is knee-deep in it.

We often talk of the "academic community," whereas there is no community but only atomized individuals known as specialists who hardly talk to each other, let alone to their colleagues in other fields. The restoration of community would, of course, necessitate constant friendly intercourse, both intellectual and social, between colleagues in various fields of study, and, equally important, contact of faculty with students. Short of those two bonds (or ties), there is and can be no community, however often and piously we may use the word. It is simply absurd (and self-deceiving) to speak of a modern university as an "academic community." The lack of any real academic community was underlined dramatically in the Vietnam War era, when tens of thousands of students abandoned college campuses to found their own communities—or "communes," as they preferred to call them—so great was the need for community. Recently a young faculty member at a major university complained of the "briefcase mentality" she had encountered on her campus. "There's never any time to talk. It's all like an ad from *The New Yorker*. The ideal setup seems to be a townhouse in Santa Barbara, a BMW to take you back to the campus to dispense your wisdom and then as quickly to whisk you back home to your word processor. The new faculty are very detached and cynical. It all gives me physical discomfort in the gut."

A major development in the world of higher education that merits attention is the widespread effort of state colleges and teachers' colleges or "normal schools" to upgrade themselves to university status. No longer satisfied with their original mission—to train elementary, high-school, and, in some cases, junior-college teachers, these public institutions yearn for the status of the "great universities." Many faculty members in state colleges are products of essentially the same inferior graduate education as their counterparts (and sometimes fellow graduate students) at high-status universities, making the inequities more galling. The movement, though understandable, is nevertheless regrettable. It can only accelerate the decline of higher education.

A straw in the academic wind is the formation a few months ago of the National Association of Scholars, a group of some three hundred professors of "the old school" which has announced its determination to "reclaim the academy." *The New York Times* of November 15, 1988, reports that the "scholars" (the word is significant) lament the "revolutionary transformation of university life." They take as their text Allan Bloom's *The Closing of the American Mind*. Alan Kors, a history professor at the University of Pennsylvania and a speaker at the group's first convention in New York City, drew fervent applause when he declared, "The barbarians are in our midst. We need to fight them a good long time. Show them you are not afraid, [and] they crumble."

The special target for the "scholars" were the new programs for women and members of minority groups, which, the professors averred, had contaminated "objectivity on decisions about curriculum, promotion and academic discourse." From which one naturally suspects that the dissenters are the beleaguered champions of "scientific objectivity."

As readers of this work will discern, I have a mild degree of sympathy for the members of NAS. Things certainly are out of sync in the academic world, but a rear-guard action in the name of "objectivity" is clearly not the path to enlightenment. The members of the National Association of Scholars who lament the politicizing of university issues that in their view were once decided "objectively" fail to realize that the "old" curriculum they so miss was as political in its own way as the new. It was the politics of the *status quo,* which, by its studied neutrality, ratified "things as they are," and rendered the university a cipher on the most critical issues of our time.

Before I cease mapping the desert, I must include some oases (every respectable desert has some oases). Even in the elite universities there are, here and there, brave souls who either have already won tenure or are willing to risk their academic lives, and who teach fully and responsibly.

Then there are, of course, the hundreds upon hundreds of small, obscure colleges, denominational and nondenominational, whose faculties teach devotedly and whose students learn happily and well.

Finally, and most important in the context of this work, there are community colleges, where thousands of able and intelligent men and women take their teaching opportunities with the greatest seriousness and give more than value received. These institutions, with close ties to their parent communities, free for the most part of the snobbish pursuit of the latest academic fads that so warp their university counterparts, and free also of the unremitting pressure to publish or perish, are, I believe, the hope of higher education in America. Unheralded and scorned or patronized by "the big boys," they carry out their mission with spirit and élan. There are, I am sure, indifferent community colleges as well as good ones, but the ones I have visited have all charmed me, and I am pleased to have an opportunity to express my gratitude for the lively times and good spirit I have experienced in my visits.

If the flight from teaching is the most serious charge against the American university, along with the pedestrian (or worse) research that results from the flight, the spiritual aridity of the American university is, for me, the most depressing aspect of all. By 1900 the university had cast out every area of investigation and every subject that could not be subsumed under the heading "scientific" and had made all those that remained (like literature and philosophy) at least profess to be scientific. Excluded were such ancient and classic human concerns as love, faith, hope, courage, passion and compassion, spirituality, religion, fidelity—indeed, one is tempted to say, anything that might be somewhat encouraging to young people eager to receive some direction, or, in the words of a student survey form, develop "a philosophy of life." If love could not be discussed, sex, of course, was a lively topic. My morning paper informs me that "Scientists Focus on the Components of Sexual Desire." Experiments have revealed to prominent psychologists that "the sex hormone testosterone is a genuine aphrodisiac." It promotes desire, but it is less potent in enhancing performance. "Sexual desire," we are told, "yields its secrets to the cold eye of science." Among the revelations awaiting us: Men have stronger sexual drives, generally speaking, than women (have we heard this before?). Many men would like to have sexual intercourse at least twice a day. Most women, presumably busier, would be content with once a day. Such fascinating and novel information has been gleaned by giving experimental subjects levers to press while viewing pornographic movies or listening to pornographic readings. Is this the kind of research that professors scant their teaching for?

The German philosopher Karl Jaspers wrote: "Once the substance of education has become problematic, the faith in it wavering, the question as to what are the aims of education poses itself. It is a hopeless undertaking, however, to seek such ideals in a manner that ignores the actual historical situation and our own real aims, if, in short, one seeks these ideals in isolation from our own lives." It is for this reason, Jaspers continued, "that such educational slogans as . . . development of special aptitudes, moral improvement, broadening one's frame of reference, character building, national pride, strength and independence, ability to express oneself, development of the personality, creation of a unifying sense of common cultural tradition, etc. don't amount to much." This is of course the problem of our time. The aims of education seem problematic indeed. When we are in such an era, the temptation is invariably to redouble efforts that have already proved inadequate or illusory. Thus the clearer it becomes that most research is carried on in a deadening and routine way, the louder become the exhortations to do more such work, as though salvation were to be achieved by mere volume. The last thing anyone wishes to do is to stop and try to think about the validity of what has become a kind of reflex. That, nonetheless, is my intention, and the method is of course historical. So we must go back to our educational beginnings, to, as the Founding Fathers were fond of saying, "first principles," and try to trace the strange history of higher education in America.

2
THE BEGINNING

The three aims of education: "Erudition which aims at man's reason, moral education which aims at man's character and independence, and piety which aims at his understanding of God."

—COMENIUS

The Protestant Reformation was the spiritual parent of the British colonies of North America. Martin Luther and John Calvin were the principal prophets of the Reformation. They shared a conviction that the Christian faith rested ultimately on individuals, the saints, who made up the Reformed congregations of the faithful, a "priesthood of believers" who were the keepers of their own consciences and the managers of their own ecclesiastical affairs. John Calvin put forth his views in his mammoth *Institutes of the Christian Religion,* which came to rank just below the Bible for those of his followers who made up the "Calvinist" branch of the Reformation. Calvin insisted that there was a direct and essential relationship "between the knowledge of God and the knowledge of ourselves." Moreover, "the mind of man was naturally endowed with the knowledge of God." "We lay it down," Calvin wrote, "as a position not to be controverted, that the human mind, even by natural instinct, possesses some sense of a Deity." A proper understanding of God's intentions for human beings was only to be discovered by the individual believer's attention to the Scriptures. In this system priests, as the custodians of the sacred mysteries, were to be replaced by preachers, ministers, and teachers whose function it was to help explicate the Scriptures for the faithful.

Most important of all, the faithful should have sufficient education to read and reflect upon the Scriptures and their relevance in the life of the individual. Such doctrine was, in a real sense, the seed of *individualism*. It was also the ground for the passion of the New England colonists for education.

While we are on the subject of Calvin, it is well to note another of his revolutionary principles. In his discussion of the nature of "civil government" he advocated obedience to lawful authority, but when such authority becomes tyrannical and oppressive, it must, Calvin declared, be resisted. "I am," he wrote in the final pages of the *Institutes*, "so far from prohibiting them [the subjects of a tyrannical king], in the discharge of their duty, to oppose the violence or cruelty of kings, that I affirm, that if they connive at kings in their oppression of their people, such forbearance involves the most nefarious perfidy, because they fraudulently betray the liberty of the people, of which they know they have been appointed protectors by the ordination of God." I do not think it is going too far to say that in that passage is to be found the basic rationale, at least for pious New Englanders, of the American Revolution, some two hundred years after the publication of the *Institutes*.

It was Calvin's doctrines that inspired the Pilgrims (or Separatists) to make the perilous journey from Holland to the shores of a *New* England, as it inspired the more prosperous and better-educated Puritans who followed them to establish the Massachusetts Bay Colony. A number of the Puritan leaders were graduates of one of the Cambridge colleges, for Cambridge was a hotbed of heretical Protestantism in the eyes of the Church of England, the state church set up by Henry VIII when he toppled the Catholic Church from power.

If the inspiration of the Massachusetts Bay Puritans to found a college was essentially Calvinistic, the form was that of the Oxford and Cambridge colleges, and Oxford and Cambridge in turn had their roots in the medieval tradition of learning. The Seven Liberal Arts, established in the medieval university, were the Trivium (grammar, rhetoric, and logic) and the Quadrivium (music, arithmetic, geometry, and astronomy). In the twelfth century there was a revival of learning, during which great numbers of classical manu-scripts were introduced into the universities as textbooks. "[C]lassical antiquity," Samuel Eliot Morison wrote in his account of the founding of Harvard, "was studied in a true humanistic spirit, for the sweetness that it gave to life." Logic became all the rage, and other studies were abandoned. A poet of the day made fun of logic's claims. "Dame Logic" assures a student "that she could make him fly / Before to walk he 'gan to try." The result was "Scholastic Philosophy," a grand system of thought that offered an integrated vision of man and the universe.

The education provided by Cambridge and Oxford for the largely upper-class young men who matriculated was intended, in Samuel Eliot Morison's words, to "develop the whole man—his body and soul as well as his intellect. It must teach manners to the boy of gentle or wealthy birth, and prepare him to take his place in the governing class. . . . Latin and Greek literature remain central because they breed statesmanship, nobility, *virtus.*" It was, in essence, this educational ideal, overlaid with the Protestant passion for the redemption of Christendom, that the leaders of the Massachusetts Bay Colony wished to plant in the New England wilderness.

John Eliot, the Apostle to the Indians, appealed to an English Puritan to contribute to the establishment of Harvard "not only for the common wealth sake; but also for Larnings sake, which I know you love, & will be ready to furder . . . for if we norish not Larning both church & common wealth will sinke. . . ."

An account of the founding of Harvard, sometimes attributed to Henry Dunster, first president of the college, told the story of its beginnings: "After God had carried us safe to *New England* and wee had builded our houses, provided necessaries for our liveli-hood, rear'd convenient places for Gods worship, and setled the Civill Government: One of the next things we looked for, and looked after was to advance *Learning* and perpetuate it to Posterity; dreading to leave an illiterate Ministery to the Churches, when our present Ministers shall lie in the Dust. And as wee were thinking and consulting how to effect this great Work; it pleased God to stir up the heart of one Mr. *Harvard* (a godly Gentleman,

and a lover of Learning . . .) to give one halfe of his Estate . . .
toward the erection of a Colledge; and all his Library. . . ."

The admission standards were simple enough.

1. When any Scholar is able to Read Tully or such like classical Latin Author *ex tempore,* and to make and speak true
   Latin in verse and prose . . . and decline perfectly the
   paradigms of Nouns and verbs in the Greek tongue, then
   may he be admitted into the College, nor shall any claim
   admission before such qualifications.
2. Every one shall consider the main End of his life and
   studies, to know God and Jesus Christ which is Eternal
   life.

A number of rules governing the behavior of students followed,
among them: "They shall be slow to speak, and eschew not only
oaths, lies, and uncertain rumors, but likewise all idle, foolish,
bitter scoffing, frothy wanton words and offensive gestures." One
of the severest rules was that "Scholars shall never use their
Mother-tongue except . . . in the public exercises of oratory or
such like. . . ." Requirements for graduation were as simply stated
as those for admission: "Every Scholar that on proof is found able
to read the original of the Old and New Testament into the Latin
tongue, and to resolve them logically withal being of honest life
and conversation," and having the approval of the overseers and
the head of the college, could receive his degree.

Harvard was followed in 1695 by the College of William and
Mary in Virginia. Yale, founded in 1701, trod in Harvard's foot-
steps, teaching Greek, Latin, classical literature, the sciences, and
moral philosophy.

If the first wave of college-founding (if we can call three colleges
a wave) was motivated by the desire to preserve learning in church
and state, the second was the result of one of those periodic
"awakenings" that, in one form or another, have marked American
society throughout much of its history. The Great Awakening
swept through the English colonies (or at least those north of
Mason's and Dixon's Line) like wildfire. The prophets of the Awak-

ening declared that the guardians of the faith had grown cold and formal in faith and practice. The passions aroused by the preaching of men like George Whitefield and Jonathan Edwards brought thousands of conversions and split the religious establishment into New Lights and Old Lights. The New Lights, rebuffed at Harvard and Yale, began to found their own "log Cabin Colleges," where enthusiasm for the renewed life of the faithful could be freely expressed.

Princeton was the most notable educational by-product of the Great Awakening. Its charter authorized the establishment of the College of New Jersey, "wherein Youth may be instructed in the learned Languages, and in the Liberal Arts and Sciences. . . ." The charter also specified that "no Freeman within the said Province of New Jersey, should at any Time be molested, punished, disquieted, or Called in Question for any difference in opinion or practice in matters of Religious Concernment. . . ." All students should have "free and equal Liberty and Advantage of Education in Said College any different Sentiments in Religion *notwithstanding.*"

The provision was less a measure of religious tolerance than an admission that the Protestant churches had experienced so many schisms that it was impossible to prefer one denomination over another without embroiling the college in the conflicts that raged between (and within) the denominations. The College of New Jersey had from the start a strong Presbyterian bent, as contrasted with the Congregational leanings of Harvard and Yale, and the Church of England influence at William and Mary.

Although tolerance of religious differences was plainly stated, it was equally clear that the major motivation of the College of New Jersey was "the great Scarcity of Candidates for the *Ministerial Function* . . . the Colleges of New-England, educating hardly a competent Number for the Services of its own Churches." Like its New England counterparts, the College of New Jersey was careful to stress that, "in Proportion as Learning makes its Progress in a Country, it softens the natural Roughness, eradicates the Prejudices, and transforms the Genius and Disposition of its Inhabitants. . . . Public Stations are honourable fill'd by Gentlemen who have received their education here [the College of New Jersey]. . . ." The author of an appeal for funds from "the Pious and Benevolent in *Great-Britain*" expressed the conviction that "the Happiness of Multitudes in sundry Colonies, and their numerous Posterity, in the present and future Ages, far distant," depended on the generosity of benefactors across the ocean.

Whereas the older colleges found themselves under strong pressures to adopt more liberal policies in regard to the admission of students of varied religious affiliations, colleges founded under denominational auspices did not hesitate to enforce their own orthodoxies. In addition to such institutions, often hardly more than a few dozen students and three or four minister-teachers, the decades prior to the American Revolution saw a spate of colleges founded along more liberal lines: King's College, later Columbia; the College of Philadelphia (later Pennsylvania); the College of Rhode Island (Brown); and Queen's College, which became Rutgers.

These largely urban colleges, started by upper-class colonists, were far more susceptible to the ideas of the Enlightenment, which were so evident on the Continent and in Great Britain. The Anglican Church had always considered itself an island of ecclesiastical rationality surrounded by an ocean of enthusiastic sects. The Ur-church of New England Calvinism, the Congregational Church, experienced a constant erosion of its severer tenets until a schism produced Unitarianism, the most "rational" of the major denominations.

The Anglican Church, the Church of England, which in the United States became the Episcopal Church, was the agency, as we have noted, for the transmission of as many Enlightenment ideas as its ecclesiastical polity and doctrine could tolerate. It drew on the writings of such men as Richard Hooker, who wrote in the sixteenth century, "laws they are not which public approbation hath not made so," a revolutionary notion at the time Hooker announced it.

It is at this point that I wish to stress the convergence of two currents, the radical Protestantism of New England (and to a lesser degree of the middle colonies) and the more "rational" and "enlightened" doctrines of the Church of England. Radical Protestantism provided most of the impetus for the initial resistance to the Crown; the far more conservative Anglican tradition contributed a strong sense of political order in the form of a steady adherence to the theory of natural law, derived from the theories of Saint Thomas Aquinas as they had been passed down through a succession of Anglican theologians, Richard Hooker being the most famous.

Radical Protestantism, with its disposition to fragmentation—Baptists, Methodists, New and Old Light Presbyterians, and on almost *ad infinitum*—affected American education most dramatically in the founding of hundreds and eventually thousands of denominational colleges, many of which proved highly ephemeral.

The ten-year interval between the Stamp Act crisis in 1765 and the outbreak of armed conflict gave the English colonies time to search through the whole of history, from classical Greece and Rome to Montesquieu and the political philosophers of the Scottish Common Sense School, for arguments in support of their determination not to yield their liberties to the British Parliament.

After Lexington and Concord, Americans began to consider the principles upon which a new government would best be established. The Federal Constitution was the fruit of practical experience in governing, or participating in the governing of, the individual colonies, and of a formidable mustering of political theory. It was the end product of what I have called the "Classical Christian Consciousness," a set of identifiable ideas or propositions about the nature of man and society. First there was the conviction that the universe, earth, and heaven itself were governed by "natural laws." There were laws governing the physical world, the epitome of which was Newton's law of gravity; there were also laws governing human beings. God Himself was governed by laws of His own ordaining. Perhaps the most eloquent statement of the relation of natural law to the affairs of men was that of the Massachusetts patriot James Otis. His pamphlet *The Rights of the British Colonies Asserted and Proved,* published in 1765, challenged its readers on the nature of authority. It was true the wealthy man had power, although he might not have "much more wit than a mole or a musquash." But it did not follow from this that "government is rightfully founded on property, alone." Nor is it "founded on grace. . . . Nor on force . . . Nor on compact? Nor property?" Had it, then, any "solid foundation? and chief corner stone, but what accident, chance or confusion may lay one moment and destroy the next?"

It was Otis' view that it had "an everlasting foundation in the unchangeable will of God, the author of nature, whose laws never vary. The same omniscient, omnipotent, infinitely good and gracious Creator of the Universe, who has been pleased to make it necessary that what we call matter should gravitate, for the celestial bodies to roll around their axes, dance in their orbits and perform their various revolutions in that beautiful order and concert, which we all admire, has made it equally necessary that . . . the different sexes should sweetly attract each other, form societies of single families of which larger bodies and communities are as naturally, mechanically and necessarily combined, as the dew of Heaven and the soft distilling rain is collected by all the enliv'ning heat of the sun." Government was, in short, a divine ordinance founded "on the necessities of our nature. It is by no means an arbitrary thing, depending merely on compact or human will for its existence." It was this faith in an ordered universe that gave the Founding Fathers the confidence to undertake to write a constitution for the new nation.

The Founding Fathers were all more or less orthodox Christians, the majority of them Episcopalians. They believed in the Bible not as an infallible document but as the word of God revealed throughout the history of the Jews and, most clearly and explicitly, in the teaching of Jesus Christ in the New Testament. The Bible was the progressive revelation of God's will, but its meanings were illuminated by reason. The revelation was ongoing, and the challenge to human faith and reason was to understand God's teaching better as time passed. Revelation was itself "progressive." Since they were children of the Enlightenment, the Founding Fathers had hope of progress through the use of reason, but it was a cautious hope. History was filled with instances of the collapse of empires made weak and impotent through arrogance and "luxury." They accepted Jeremiah's statement that "the heart is deceitful above all things, and desperately wicked," and of course they held to the doctrine of original sin in the sense that they believed that man- and womankind had innate inclinations to vice. Many of the Founders, tracing the rise and fall of great nations, were not sanguine about the chances that the new republic could survive for many generations, and some, of a millennial turn of mind, suspected that the drafting of the Constitution might mark the last step in human history before Christ returned to earth to reign a thousand years. Philip Freneau, "the poet of the Revolution," wrote a poem along those lines.

For individuals who fell under the spell of one of the three main Enlightenments (Scottish, English, or French), the promise of progress through the use of human reason was intoxicating. They eagerly embraced the maxim of Rousseau that the voice of the people was the voice of God. Jefferson (who was not a member of the Federal Convention; he was in Paris during the Convention) was a spokesman for the French Enlightenment in America. He believed as devoutly in reason, science, and progress as any *philosophe*. The Enlightened consciousness in America I have called the "Secular Democratic Consciousness." It was suspicious of authority, believed, for the most part, in unrestrained democracy and in majority rule. As opposed to the doctrine of original sin, it believed in the natural goodness of man once he was free from superstition/religion. Many Americans who aligned themselves in politics with the Secular Democratic Consciousness also held fast to most of the tenets of Protestantism and were quite unaware that there was any conflict between the faith they avowed in church and the political principles that guided them at the polls.

The Classical Christian Consciousness, having drafted the Constitution, the culmination of some two thousand years of political theory and practice, was soon forced into the background, politically and ideologically. That was not surprising if one keeps in mind that most of the representatives of Classical Christian Consciousness were members of a highly educated, sometimes self-educated "elite," as we would say today.

The enthusiasm of the common man for democracy could not be gainsaid. With the skillful encouragement of Jefferson, the Secular Democratic Consciousness became the predominant consciousness, leaving the avatars of the old order to grumble about the pretensions of the great unwashed, or the only slightly washed.

The conflict between the old consciousness and the new revealed itself quite clearly in an often acrimonious debate about the aims of education, specifically who should get it and how. It was not long before the common man made it clear that if he could not gain admission to the gentlemanly cloisters of Harvard or Princeton he would start his own colleges. The president of Dickinson College in Carlisle, Pennsylvania, newly arrived from Scotland, voiced a typical complaint: "Everything here is on a dead level," he wrote. ". . . Our gentlemen are all of the first edition [the new upwardly mobile]; few of them live in their father's house. . . . In a republic the demagogue and rabble drivers are the only citizens that are represented or have any share in the government. . . . Americans seem much more desirous that their affairs be managed by themselves than that they should be well managed. . . ."

Jefferson had his own plan for a democratic education. The Virginian proposed to divide every county into five school districts "and in each of them to establish a school for teaching reading, writing and arithmetic." Every family in a particular district would be entitled to have their children go to such a school for three years at no charge. Each year the brightest boy whose parents could not afford to pay for further education would be chosen to go to one of twenty grammar schools in the state, where he would learn "Greek, Latin, Geography, and all the higher branches of numerical arithmetic." After two years in grammar school, "the best genius of the whole [would be] selected, and continued six years, and the residue dismissed. By this means twenty of our best geniuses will be raked from the rubbish annually and be instructed, at the public expense." At the end of six more years, one-half would be dismissed and the rest, "chosen for the superiority of their parts and disposition," would be sent on to the College of

William and Mary to spend three years in the study of "such sciences as they shall chuse."

Jefferson was confident that such a system would draw "Worth and genius . . . from every condition of life, and [render them] completely prepared by education for defeating the competition of wealth and birth for public trust." It was a classic Enlightenment vision: an aristocracy of intellect rather than of social rank. It was the scheme of a man with unquestioning confidence in reason and science. Those who fell by the wayside were dismissed as "rubbish," hardly a democratic sentiment. Jefferson would not expose young children to the demoralizing effect of the Bible but would emphasize instead "the useful facts of Grecian, Roman, European and American History." Children should be taught "the first elements of morality" so that they might learn that happiness, the pursuit of which Jefferson had guaranteed them in the preamble to the Declaration of Independence, "does not depend on the condition of life in which chance has placed them, but is always the result of good conscience, good health, occupation, and freedom in all just pursuits." Elementary-school students should be trained principally in history, because "history by apprising [the pupils] of the past will enable them to judge of the future; it will avail them of the experience of other times and other nations; it will qualify them as judges of the actions and designs of man; it will enable them to know ambition under every disguise it may assume; and knowing it, to defeat its views."

Noah Webster, the father of the American dictionary, and Dr. Benjamin Rush, often called the father of American medicine, were both deeply interested in the education of the youths of the new republic. Although Rush was in favor of an education that emphasized the practical, he believed "Religion is necessary to correct the effects of learning. Without religion I believe learning does real mischief to the morals and principles of mankind." Rush protested John Adams' concern with classical learning. To Rush, Greek and Latin served little purpose other than to perpetuate class distinctions. Elementary and secondary education should be compulsory. In addition to a system of state colleges, Rush wanted "one federal university under the patronage of Congress, where the youth of all the states may be melted (as it were) together into one mass of citizens after they have acquired the first principles of knowledge in the colleges of their respective states." The federal university would be charged with teaching "the laws of nature and of nations, the common law of our country, the different systems of government, history and everything else connected with the advancement of republican knowledge and principles. . . . This plan of general education alone will render the American Revolution a blessing to mankind."

Students should also be taught "simplicity in writing" their own language, which would "probably be spoken by more people in the course of two or three centuries than ever spoke one language at one time since the beginning of the world." French and German should be taught, as well as "all those athletic and manly exercises . . . which are calculated to impart health, strength, and elegance to the human body." Scholars should be sent abroad to gather all the latest knowledge in the fields of "agriculture, manufactures, and commerce. . . ." Others should be assigned to explore the "vegetable, mineral and animal productions of our country . . . procuring histories and samples of each of them. . . .".

A university established on such a plan would "begin the golden age of the United States," Rush wrote. While European scholars were engaged in "disputes about Hebrew points, Greek particles, or the accent and quantity of the Roman language," young Americans would be learning "those branches of knowledge which increase the conveniences of life, lessen human misery, improve our country, promote population, exalt the human understanding, and establish domestic, social and political happiness."

Noah Webster was another advocate of practical education. Like Rush, Webster believed Greek and Latin should be replaced by more practical subjects. It was the role of education to "not only diffuse a knowledge of the sciences, but . . . implant in the minds of the American youth, the principles of virtue and liberty; and inspire them with just and liberal ideas of government." It seemed to Webster that "what is now called a *liberal Education* disqualified a man for business. . . . The method pursued in our colleges is better calculated to fit youth for the learned professions than for business." Since the virtues of men were "of more consequence to society than their abilities . . . the *heart* should be cultivated with more assiduity than the *head*."

A Massachusetts farmer, William Manning, who himself had had no more than three years' schooling, wrote what was perhaps the most striking essay of the era combining the major themes of the Classical Christian Consciousness with those of the Secular Democrats. Manning was inspired by the Jay Treaty in 1798 to commit his thoughts to paper. He is especially valuable because he represents that strain of radical Protestantism which, on many social and political issues, was virtually indistinguishable from ardent believers in reason, science, progress, and the French Revolution. "Larning," in Manning's view, was the key to political power, or at least to participation in the "process." It was therefore an area where "the Few" did their best to close out "the Many." "Larning," he wrote, "is of the gratest importance to the seport of a free government & to prevent this the few are always crying up the advantages of costly collages, national acadimyes & grammar schooles, in ordir to make places for men to live without work, & so strengthen their party." In Manning's opinion, such institutions were strongholds of reactionary politics. If this were not so, "we should not be stunded with Exhibitions in favour of Monocyes & running down Republican prinsaples as we often be." Manning plainly had Harvard, where students and faculty were predominantly Federalist, in mind. Every state should "maintain as many Coledges in conveniant parts thereof as would be attended upon to give the highest Degrees of Larning," and this in "the cheepest & best manner possible." Education should be compulsory, "for the publick are as much interested in the Larning of one child as an other."

Not surprisingly, Manning was on the side of a practical education, "For their is no more need of a mans having knowledge of all the languages to teach a Child to read write & cipher than their is for a farmer to have the mariners art to hold a plow." With all his advanced political notions, Manning was an orthodox Calvinist: "Men," he wrote, "are born & grow up in this world with a vast veriaty of capacityes, strength & abilityes both of Body &

Mind, & have strongly implanted within them numerous pashions & lusts continually urging them to fraud vilence & acts of injustis toards one another." The individual had planted in him "a desire of Selfe Seporte, Selfe Defence, Selfe Love, Selfe Conceit, Selfe Importance, & Selfe agrandisement, that it Ingroses all his care and attention so that he can see nothing beyond Selfe. . . ."

Perhaps the most striking exchange on the subject of the aims of education was that between John Adams and Thomas Jefferson. When the two old men renewed their friendship after years of coolness, Jefferson chided Adams for opinions on education imputed to him by an inquiring reporter. Adams, Jefferson wrote, had been quoted as advocating "a steady adherence to the principles, practices and institutions of our fathers" as "the consummation of wisdom and akme of excellence." Modern times would "produce nothing more worthy of transmission to posterity, than the principles, institutions and systems of education received from our ancestors." Jefferson was convinced that Adams must have been misquoted. "You possess, yourself, too much science not to see how much is still ahead of you, unexplained and unexplored," Jefferson wrote. No, Adams had been quoted correctly. "Checks and Ballances, Jefferson . . . are, our only security, for the progress of the Mind, as well as the Security of the Body." The "*general principles* of Christianity: and the general principles of English and American Liberty" must be preserved and passed on to the rising generation.

The exchange between the two Revolutionary leaders helps to define the two kinds of consciousness that I have proposed, the Secular Democratic (Jefferson), with its faith in limitless progress through science and reason; and the opposing view, that the best thought and experience of the race was a precious heritage that must be preserved as a vital part of the consciousness of the new nation, the Classical Christian Consciousness (Adams). That debate has, indeed, been continual throughout the history of the republic and goes on with scarcely diminished ardor to this day.

An excellent index of the relationship between democracy and education might be found in the number of new states that included provisions in their constitutions for state colleges or soon started colleges. North Carolina, Georgia, Tennessee, and Vermont all started state-supported institutions before 1800. The spirit that prevailed in the new state colleges was decidedly secular, a fact that often provided a spur to the rapidly proliferating sects and denominations to start their own institutions, where true doctrine could be taught without compromise.

3
THE NEW REPUBLIC

"Every society is burdened with the task . . . of creating an
order that will endow the fact of its existence with meaning in
terms of ends divine and human."

—ERIC VOEGELIN

From 1800 to the outbreak of the Civil War, higher education in
the new republic was distinguished by four major trends. Religious
orthodoxy was constantly challenged on the older campuses, the
debate over classical versus practical education went on as con-
tentiously as ever, the founding of new "colleges" that were often
little more than academies continued unabated, and a modest beginning was made in providing higher education for women.

Colleges like Yale and Harvard became battlegrounds where
the champions of religious orthodoxy warred against more liberal
ecclesiastical views. Where the liberal forces won, their conservative adversaries often went elsewhere and founded new citadels
of orthodoxy. At Yale, Schubael Conant spoke for many similarly
beleaguered faculty members when he complained of "a Den of
Narrow-Spirited Bigots, who strain up the Calvinistic Doctrines
to the highest Pitch, and interpret *moderate, catholick Calvinism,*
to be a Defection from the Standard-Faith; whose Narrowness,
and Haughtiness is such, that they can't bear that Others should
depart a Hair's-Breath from their Sentiments. . . ."

The Yale Report of 1828 announced that Yale's purpose was
not to teach that which is peculiar to any one of the professions,
but to "lay the foundation which is common to them all." "Classical

discipline" constituted "the best preparation for professions of divinity and law. . . ." It was "especially adopted to form the taste, and to discipline the mind, both in thought and diction, to the relish of what is elevated, chaste, and simple." But that argument had its critics, who believed that "classical discipline" was just another name for a snobbish and "aristocratic" education designed for the sons of gentlemen rather than for workingmen or "mechanics."

In the debate about practical versus classical education, classical education, at least in the older colleges of the East, maintained a decided advantage, although some bold innovators, like Francis Wayland of the College of Rhode Island, energetically espoused a mixture of the two. Wayland wished, in the democratic spirit of the age, to make the college curriculum more useful to "merchants, farmers and manufacturers." In his opinion, undergraduates should learn "a *smaller* number of things *well*. By learning one science well, we learn *how to study*," he wrote, "and how to master a subject. Having made this attainment in one study, we readily apply it to all others."

The struggle over whether to have a "classical" curriculum or one oriented more directly toward the practical was in large part a class, as well as a sectional, struggle. The defenders of the educational *status quo* were usually the defenders of the social and political *status quo* as well. But it must be kept in mind that, when someone like Benjamin Rush or Francis Wayland urged the practical, he had in mind a course of study like that outlined by Rush for the projected federal university. Such "practical" curriculums were what became in most institutions the standard liberal-arts education. What was missing primarily was the study of Greek and Latin, which, even in those institutions publicly committed to the "classical discipline," had come to be more honored in the breach than the observance.

In the opinion of the more orthodox, the 1820s saw a startling rise in "atheism" and "radicalism" of one kind or another. Philip Lindsley, who had graduated from Princeton and was president of the University of Nashville, deplored the spread of "abolitionism, and radicalism, and agrarianism, and ultraism and amalgamationism, and Loco-Focoism, and Lynchism, and Fanny-Wrightism," which were "all the rage."

Hardly a week passed in which a new denominational college was not started. They followed the line of frontier settlement as it moved westward. Yale was an especially fertile breeder of denominational colleges as devout Congregational graduates of Yale went west to found, with missionary zeal, colleges modeled on their alma mater.

In the twelve-year period prior to 1838, the ratio of college students to the population at large had grown substantially. In 1838 one in every 1,294 youths had gone to college. By 1840 there were 119 colleges scattered about the country and forty-four schools of theology. Zeal for education was strongest wherever New Englanders went. In the midst of a desperate struggle for dominance against Southerners as determined to make Kansas a slave state as their New England rivals were to have it free, eighteen universities and ten colleges were incorporated in the state from 1855 to 1860. Only three of the twenty-eight survived (one of those was the University of Kansas), but by the 1890s Kansas had over fifty seminaries, colleges, and universities founded by seventeen church denominations.

A problem that plagued most colleges, particularly the smaller denominational institutions, was the large number of students who failed to complete their course of studies and receive a degree. At Iowa State University in the 1860s only fifteen students graduated out of six hundred who entered. At Harvard some 20 percent graduated.

In the state of Tennessee in 1848 there were twenty-five "colleges" and "universities" authorized to award degrees. Many were simply diploma mills where degrees were, in the words of one indignant observer, "bought and sold on the open market." Ten years later there were only six still in existence. Much the same could be said of other states. It is not going too far to describe the situation in higher education in the decades prior to the Civil War as chaotic.

A German traveler in the United States in the 1850s, Moritz Busch, noted that there were four business schools and five denominational colleges in Cincinnati. The president of one such college wrote that "the legislatures of the country have never done for even professional education one tithe of what has been done by the various denominations of Christians among us. In many cases the state has done nothing; at best it has done but little. . . ."

Especially active in college-founding was the radical wing of Protestantism that espoused reform causes, from temperance and women's rights to abolition. Such colleges were animated by the Protestant passion for the redemption of the world. The centerpiece of their curriculums was a course on "Moral Philosophy," often taught by the president of the institution, who was almost invariably a minister. Moral philosophy typically explored the implications of such social ills as drunkenness, slavery, and discrimination against women, immigrants, and the disadvantaged generally. They did so, of course, in conventional Christian terms of good and evil, sin and redemption. In the words of a modern author, the students "might consider both the deepest spiritual questions and the most pressing social problems."

Charles Grandison Finney, a famous evangelical minister who adapted the revival meeting to the uses of Midwestern Protestantism, joined with the Tappan brothers to establish the Lane Theological Seminary in Cincinnati. Lyman Beecher, described as "the most prominent, popular and powerful preacher in our nation," and the father of the extraordinary Beecher brood, was the first president. One of the students at Lane was young Theodore Weld, who organized a series of debates on the slavery issue. They lasted for nine consecutive nights. Most of the students and many of the faculty were converted to the cause of immediate abolition. Although Beecher himself was opposed to slavery, he was alarmed that Weld's activities would wake "the slumbering demon of pro-slavery fanaticism." When the trustees of Lane forbade any more discussion of the slavery issue by students, the entire senior class of forty students withdrew from the seminary and with the support of Arthur Tappan transferred to the new institution at Oberlin. Tappan and his brother, Lewis, stipulated that to a life of "special devotion to church and school, and . . . earnest labor in the missionary cause" be added the clause "the broad ground of moral reform, in all its departments, should characterize the instruction in Oberlin Institute." The college which had opened its doors to men and women and blacks in 1834 was soon turning out a steady stream of students who became leaders in the abolitionist movement, among them Theodore Weld, Lucy Stone, and Antoinette Brown, who became leaders in the women's rights movement as well as in the anti-slavery cause.

Throughout our era, science was definitely the poor relation on college campuses, and much of the instruction in all subjects was deadeningly routine. George Templeton Strong, the New York lawyer and diarist, alarmed that Columbia was falling behind in the sciences, proposed that "professors be prevented from degenerating into drones . . . by requiring of them to accomplish something every year or six months, making it a condition of holding office that at certain periods they produce some essay, memoir, or investigation in their respective departments. . . ." When Strong's effort to have a first-rate chemist appointed to the Columbia faculty (Strong was a graduate of Columbia) was blocked because the individual was a Unitarian and the trustees were Episcopalians, Strong noted in his diary that Columbia was apparently doomed to be "a sleepy, third-rate high school for one or two generations more." Strong was not encouraged by the so-called Columbia Report of 1853, a portion of which was entitled "The Establishment of a University System." According to a subsection headed "The Mission of the College," its mission was "to direct and superintend the mental and moral culture. . . . Mental and moral discipline, it is agreed, is the object of collegiate education. The mere acquisition of learning, however valuable and desirable in itself, is subordinate to this great work. . . . The design of a college is to make perfect the intellect in all its parts and functions; by means of a thorough training of all the intellectual faculties, to attain their full development; and by the proper guidance of the moral functions, to direct them to a proper exertion. To form the mind, in short, is the high design of education as sought in a College Course."

What this passage seems to mean, so far as it means anything at all, is that the writer has only the vaguest notion of the "mission" of a college, unless it is to instill sound moral principles in its students. Unfortunately, the Report continues, this exalted goal does not entirely satisfy recent critics of a college education. "On the contrary, the demand for what is termed progressive knowledge . . . and for fuller instruction in what are called the useful and practical sciences, is at variance with this fundamental idea. The public, generally unaccustomed to look upon the mind except in connection with the body, and to regard it as a machine for promoting the pleasures and the conveniences, or the comforts of the latter, will not be satisfied with a system of education in which they are unable to perceive the direct connection between the knowledge imparted, and the bodily advantages to be gained. For this reason, to preserve in some degree high and pure education and strict mental discipline, and to draw as many as possible within its influence, we must partially yield to those sentiments which we should be unable wholly to resist." In other words, compromise was called for, if anything was to be salvaged in terms of a moral education. The proposed solution was "parallel courses," a traditional moral education and a more practical "progressive" one.

Impressive as the ideal of "mental and moral discipline" sounded, the facts were, for the most part, quite otherwise. The conventional college curriculum was dreary in the extreme. It was much as Charles Francis Adams, Jr., had described his Harvard education in the 1850s. "In one word," Adams wrote of the Harvard of his undergraduate days, "the educational trouble with the Harvard of my time was the total absence of touch and direct personal influence between student and instructor. . . . It was not good form—was contrary to usage—for the instructors and the instructed to hold personal relations. Our professors in the Harvard of the 'fifties' were a set of rather eminent scholars and highly respectable men. They attended to their duties with commendable assiduity, and drudged along in a dreary humdrum sort of way in a stereotyped method of classroom instruction. But as for giving direction to, in the sense of shaping, the individual minds of young men in their most plastic state, so far as I know nothing of the kind was even dreamed of; it never entered into the professorial mind. This was what I needed, and all I needed—an intelligent, inspiring direction; and I never got it, nor a suggestion of it. I was left absolutely without guidance. . . . No instructor produced, or endeavored to produce, the slightest impression on me; no spark of enthusiasm was sought to be infused into me." The passage is especially striking in that Harvard's deficiencies were just those elements ("guidance" perhaps most conspicuous among them) which the champions of the "classical" education claimed distinguished the traditional education that they believed threatened by "practical and progressive education."

We do not have to rely solely on the testimony of Charles Francis Adams, Jr., although he was unusually perceptive. There are a number of other witnesses and intelligent observers with testimony to the same effect, among them Charles Francis' brother Henry, who taught at Harvard for several years. "No one," Henry Adams wrote, "took Harvard College seriously. . . . [A]s far as it educated at all, [it] was a mild and liberal school, which sent young men into the world with all they needed to make respectable citizens, and something of what they wanted to make useful ones." But four years of Harvard produced "an autobiographical blank, a mind on which a water-mark had been stamped. . . . [I]t taught little and it taught that ill. . . ." Adams' own classmates seemed to him "aggressively commonplace," men without enthusiasm. It seemed easy to "stand alone . . . when one has no passions; easier still when one has no pains."

The fact was, science was frustrated at every turn, relegated to a subordinate role in academe, interrogated as to its beliefs, chastised for presuming to dispute the hegemony of a classic education.

It is interesting to note that students from urban high schools, particularly those of New England, often left high school better educated than many college graduates. A Russian visitor noted that in the boys' and girls' high schools in Boston the "young people are taught . . . ancient geography, general history, algebra, geometry, trigonometry as applied to measurement, surveying, navigation, astronomy, more on the United States Constitution, bookkeeping, drawing, French and Spanish." These were all included in a three-year program. Students who remained an extra year could take mechanics, logic, philosophy, and "engineering and higher mathematics."

By the Civil War a new element in the debate over the proper curriculum had been introduced by graduates of American colleges who went to Germany to study in universities where "scholarship" was rigorously pursued simply for the sake of knowledge. George Ticknor and George Bancroft went to Göttingen and there acquired a whole new vision of what academic activity might be. Ticknor had written to Jefferson as early as 1815, when Jefferson was planning what would become the University of Virginia, that scholarship had advanced the German universities as far in forty years "as other nations have been in three centuries . . . & which will yet carry them much further." Ticknor wrote of "the unwearied & universal diligence among their scholars—a *general* habit of laboring from fourteen to sixteen hours a day—which will finally give their country an extent and amount of learning of which the world before has had no example." It was a remarkably shrewd observation for a young American to make, and history proved its soundness. The German university became the foundation of modern Germany in a way that was certainly without historical precedent unless it might be the role of the medieval university in creating a common European culture.

When Ticknor returned to the United States and to Harvard to take a chair in Spanish literature and write a classic work on that subject, he was determined to try to reform Harvard along German lines. The tutors who taught traditional subjects in, at least to Ticknor, a lackadaisical manner should be replaced by lecturers who must be the outstanding scholars in their fields. There must be departments of specialized study such as mathematics and literature. George Bancroft, while in general agreement with Ticknor (he wanted to introduce German historical scholarship, "which had made the darkest portions of history become almost transparent"), was wary of the lack of moral grounding in German scholarship. It seemed to Bancroft too sealed off and self-contained to suit the American temperament. If German scholarship could be transplanted, "if we could engraft on a healthy tree, if we could unite it with a high moral feeling, if learning could only go to school with religion," he wrote, it would indeed become a blessing. It had been astonishing to observe what "German perseverance" could accomplish when joined with "reason and acuteness. . . . [E]very author is read, every manuscript is collected, every work perused, which can be useful, be it dull or interesting, the work of genius or stupidity . . . the most trifling coins and medals, the ruins of art. . . ." Bancroft was describing the painstaking thoroughness that came in time to distinguish all modern scholarship, especially, one must note, the indiscriminate examination of every available bit of evidence, be it "the work of genius or stupidity." Since stupidity far outweighs genius, it could be argued that a disproportionate amount of the modern scholar's time is taken up with the "dull" and the "stupid" and that this, in time, has taken its toll on the imaginative capacities of that same scholar.

Soon all aspiring young scholars considered it essential to go abroad to one of the great German universities. In Josiah Royce's words, the American student "could hear and read his fill in a world of academic industry, and amid elsewhere unheard of treasures of books. The air was full of suggestion. . . . [It] seemed one of absolute blessing and power. One went to Germany still a doubter as to the possibility of the theoretic life," Royce wrote; "one returned an idealist, devoted for the time to pure learning for learning's sake, determined to contribute . . . to the massive store of human knowledge, burning for a chance to help build the American University."

Francis Lieber, a student of the great German historian Barthold Niebuhr, came to the United States as a political refugee in 1827. Lieber's comments on German scholarship provide an interesting supplement to Bancroft's. Lieber, considered the father of political science in America, believed that the achievements of scholars in his homeland were due to the fact that "the German's life is entirely within him." Since political activity was forbidden, he must turn his energy and intelligence inward, into a "private" world of scholarship, "because almost the only field of ambition of a German, I mean the ambition which looks beyond the life of the individual and seeks for another distinction than that of wealth and titles, is science. . . ." It was a penetrating insight. For an ambitious young German not born to "wealth and titles," the career that promised the greatest success and prestige was that of a scholar and university professor. Lieber's comments help to account for the highly individualistic and competitive nature of German scholarship. It was, in essence, a self-contained enterprise, with little or no reference to the broader world except in the hard sciences, where the collaboration between the universities and industry was to make Germany the world leader in industrial technology by the middle years of the century.

The dominant intellectual current of the time was Transcendentalism, a credo of which Ralph Waldo Emerson was the principal prophet. Emerson, who lectured in cities and towns all over the country, was a kind of one-man religion. Starting as a Congregational minister, Emerson abandoned the Trinity for the Over-Soul. Transcendentalism, with its mild religious or "spiritual" element, provided a transition from the rigors of orthodox Calvinism to a more secular view of the world. The principal rival of Transcendentalism and, even more, of Protestant Christianity was Darwinism. In 1859 Charles Darwin published *On the Origin of Species by Means of Natural Selection,* a book that put forth in dramatic form the argument for the evolution of the planet and life on earth. Darwin's propositions about natural selection and the survival of the fittest were a direct challenge to the description of the creation of the universe in the Book of Genesis. Equally significant, the Englishman Herbert Spencer invented Social Darwinism, which applied evolutionary principles to human society and, in doing so, reinforced the older Enlightenment faith in science, reason, and progress. According to the doctrines of the Enlightenment, progress was to be achieved primarily by the use of reason (and that form of reason called science).

Darwinism was welcomed by the Secular Democratic Consciousness as an ally in the fight against religion and in behalf of science. It appeared to give solid scientific support to the basic propositions of the Enlightenment. Whereas the Enlightenment philosophers placed their trust in the rather uncertain hope of reason, Social Darwinism argued that progress was in the "process," so to speak. It was part of the material structure of the world, resulting from the continual refinement of species, human as well as animal, by natural selection. Science, elevated to a new importance, would preside over these developments, guiding them, when the opportunity offered, in a socially desirable direction. Prior to the Civil War, the old order held fast to the seats of academic power. The war was an intellectual as well as a political, social, and economic watershed. In the years immediately following, the old centers of resistance toppled, one after another.

Religion, Protestantism specifically, suffered a serious erosion. Educated young men like Oliver Wendell Holmes announced their skepticism. When Holmes, a Union officer, was badly wounded, he felt tempted to "a deathbed recantation," but his "Philosophy" came to his rescue. He reaffirmed his faith that "whatever shall happen is best—for it is in accordance with a general law. . . ." Charles Francis Adams, Jr., read John Stuart Mill on Auguste Comte and "emerged from the theological stage, in which I had been nurtured, and passed into the scientific"—i.e., became a Darwinian.

His brother Henry confessed "his aching consciousness of a religious void" in his life and wondered whether "any large faction of society cared for a future life, or even for the present one. . . . Not an act, or an expression, or an image, showed depth of faith or hope. . . . Of all the conditions of his youth," Adams wrote in the third person in his *Education,* "which afterward puzzled the grown-up man, this disappearance of religion puzzled him the most. . . . That the most powerful emotion of man, next to the sexual, should disappear," Adams added, "might be a personal defect of his own; but that the most intelligent society, led by the most intelligent clergy, in the most moral conditions that he ever knew, should have solved all the problems of the universe so thoroughly as to have quite ceased making itself anxious about past or future . . . seemed to him the most curious phenomenon he had to account for in a long life."

Henry Adams called himself a Darwinist because "it was easier to be one than not," despite the fact that, to Adams, Darwinism seemed absurdly unscientific. "Unbroken Evolution under uniform conditions," Adams wrote, "pleased everyone except curates and bishops; it was the very best substitute for religion; a safe, conservative, practical, and thoroughly Common-Law deity. . . . [T]he idea was seductive in its perfection; it had the charm of art. . . . In geology as in theology," it could only be proved that "Evolution did not evolve; Uniformity . . . was not uniform; and Selection did not select." The Darwinians' "Natural Selection seemed a dogma to be put in place of the Athanasian Creed; it was a form of religious hope; a promise of ultimate perfection," an up-to-date version of natural law. Finally, Adams wrote, "He was a Darwinian for fun."

Later Adams, in his bitter, jesting way, called himself a "Conservative Christian Anarchist." His experience of the loss of faith was the experience of his class. It was of men like Adams that Max Weber was thinking when he called the loss of religious faith by Western intellectuals in general "the disenchantment of the world."

4
THE EMERGENCE
OF THE UNIVERSITY

"Bliss was it in that dawn to be alive,
But to be young was very heaven."

—WILLIAM WORDSWORTH

Three conditions existed in the post–Civil War era that made possible or, perhaps, inevitable the emergence of the modern university.

First, talk of graduate studies was in the air. Pioneer scholars like George Bancroft and George Ticknor trekking to Germany to pursue graduate work were followed by dozens and then hundreds of young Americans eager to drink from the fountains of German scholarship. Before long it became a virtual requirement for prospective academics. William James and Josiah Royce were only among the more famous who made the intellectual pilgrimage to Heidelberg, Leipzig, Breslau, and Göttingen.

Second, the accumulation of vast fortunes by the robber barons, the railroad and mining and steel and lumber tycoons, provided capital for the first significant steps in the process of establishing graduate study.

Finally, there was the general American notion, described by Herbert Croly, that education was "a good thing." The Puritans believed that an educated ministry was essential to the spiritual health of the congregations/towns of New England. Moreover, as we have noted, they believed in "learning," in the study of the classics and of moral philosophy as the basis of a pious and useful life. That belief underlay the founding of innumerable denominational colleges as the nation spread westward. But now Americans were seized by the conviction that education was "a good thing" in and of itself. Above all, it was a way to "get ahead" in the unremitting race of life. Education became, increasingly, a *personal* matter. Education was an entrée to better things. In the words of John Jay Chapman, "The terrible, savage hordes of Americans waked up in 1870 to the importance of salvation by education. . . ."

The problems of instituting graduate programs were suggested by the fact that, when Harvard did so in the academic year of 1869–70, the college had to employ "outside" lecturers, among them John Fiske, Charles Sanders Peirce, and Ralph Waldo Emerson. Only three regular students attended all the lectures and took the examinations.

Johns Hopkins earned undying fame by being the first tycoon to take advantage of the interest in graduate study. It was Hopkins' inspiration to start a university devoted exclusively to graduate studies. Johns Hopkins University thus became the model and prototype for American universities in general. All wished to rival (and the bolder, to exceed) Hopkins in the development of graduate work.

Before we tell the story of Johns Hopkins' early years, it is necessary to set the social and political scene in which the expansion of the university took place.

In tracing the history of ideas, intellectual historians are often inclined to treat ideas as though they were, somehow, self-contained and autonomous. That is to say, as if they had a life of their own that existed more or less independently of the social context in which they were to be found. The shortcomings of such an approach are obvious. If ideas influence human behavior, they are also formulated not in the abstract but in response to events in the real world. This was certainly the case during the period following the Civil War.

The most dramatic (and traumatic) events of the post-war era had to do with a desperate struggle by workingmen and -women to share in the burgeoning prosperity of the nation. By the end of the war, real wages had shrunk by one-third from 1860. The Order of Saint Crispin, which might be fairly described as a Christian evangelical union movement, was founded in 1867. The period from 1866 to 1878 was one of constant strikes, many of them prolonged and violent, and of attempts by workers to form unions. Most such efforts were ruthlessly suppressed by employers. Union membership, which reached three hundred thousand by the early 1870s, had dropped to some fifty thousand by 1877. A depression, which reached its nadir in 1876, caused widespread unemployment and heavy cuts in already meager wages. One result was the Great Strikes of 1877. Beginning in western Maryland, railroad workers paralyzed many railroad lines. The strikes spread to workers in other industries, practically shutting down Baltimore, Chicago, and New York. For days the threat of revolution hung in the air. In Baltimore, militia, sent to suppress the riots, were attacked by angry mobs. Federal troops were dispatched by President Hayes to restore order in Martinsburg, West Virginia, one of the railroad towns where the strikes had their origin. More than fifty people lost their lives, and thousands were injured in bitter fighting between workers and law-enforcement officers before order was restored.

It is impossible, at this distance, to capture the alarm that the Great Strikes caused, but in 1900 John Swinton, the editor of a labor journal, looked back on the strikes as the most significant event between the end of the Civil War and the end of the century.

The immigrants who poured into the United States in the aftermath of the Civil War brought with them an inventory of revolutionary creeds. The Marxian Socialists, who split with the Anarcho-Communist followers of Mikhail Bakunin, established the American headquarters of the First International in New York City in 1872, began organizing as the Workingmen's Party, and then changed its name in 1877 to the Socialist Labor Party. This infusion of "Red" European radicalism was a major cause of concern, and many Americans attributed the Great Strikes to "foreign agitators."

The intellectual and literary consequences of the Great Strikes were notable. Not only did the Great Strikes raise in dramatic form the whole question of the nature of capitalism and, for some, the necessity of revolution; they focused attention on the very notion of progress itself. Henry George, reflecting on the paradox of poverty in the midst of plenty, wrote his famous *Progress and Poverty*, which was published in 1879. The Knights of Labor, like the Order of Saint Crispin an evangelically inclined labor movement, was organized in 1869 by Uriah Stephens and then headed by Terence Powderly: a combination of a revivalist and a unionist. The Knights grew spectacularly to a membership of some seven hundred thousand in less than ten years.

The Haymarket Massacre in Chicago in the spring of 1886 gave impetus to the organization of the American Federation of Labor, a "trade" union as opposed to the "industrial" union of the Knights of Labor. In 1892 the Homestead Massacre resulted from the effort to form a union in the Carnegie Steel plant at Homestead, Pennsylvania. Two years later the Pullman Strike paralyzed the nation's railroads for almost four weeks.

These were only the most spectacular episodes in the merciless and bloody war between capital and labor (the mercilessness was on the side of capital, the blood on the side of labor). That war produced a substantial number of political tracts in the form of utopian novels as well as what came to be called in the 1930s "proletarian novels," novels sympathetic to the cause of workingmen and -women, and a national best-seller by the philanthropist-reformer Henry Demarest Lloyd entitled *Wealth Against Commonwealth*, a blistering indictment of the crimes of capital against labor, a work sometimes identified as the opening gun of the muckrakers.

On top of the general miseries of workingmen and -women came the terrible depression of 1893, whose most dramatic event was the march of Coxey's army of unemployed to the nation's capital.

The political consequence of these events was the formation of the Populist Party, the most radical political party in our history, whose heart and soul was the radical, evangelical, fundamentalist Protestantism of the farmers of the Midwest. The demise of the Populist Party was as swift as its rise had been spectacular. Its successor as a reform movement was the quite different Progressive Party, whose strength lay among middle-class reformers and professionals.

This mini-history of the "war between capital and labor," as it was generally called, is necessary if we are to understand the history of higher education in the period between the end of the Civil War and the first decade of the twentieth century, the era in which the modern university took form.

There was constant discussion of the mechanics of revolutionary or peaceful social change, and there was general agreement that things could not go on indefinitely as they were, with the nation divided into what often seemed hostile armed camps. The hope of the middle-class intellectuals, of the Christian Socialists and reformers lay in utilizing the new scholarship in the service not simply of reforming the American economic system but of radically altering it to make it a more just and equitable society, and to do this through democratic means.

The inheritors of the Secular Democratic Consciousness could hardly have failed to notice that the progress that was supposed to result from the application of reason and "science" to the problems besetting human societies had been uncertain at best. Darwinism promised that evolution to higher human and societal forms through natural selection and survival of the fittest was "scientifically" inevitable. For the more politically advanced, Marxism promised a similar outcome to human history, the withering away of the state and a secular millennium.

By the 1870s any notion of peaceful progress toward "heaven on earth" seemed questionable, to say the least. Wherever one looked there was corruption, municipal, state, and federal, not to mention greater exploitation of the poor and weak by the strong and powerful. Darwinism as the vector of progress seemed illusionary. Marxism predicted "scientifically" that there must be a violent upheaval as a prelude to the workers' millennium. For thousands of idealistic young men and not a few young women, the new scholarship promised an alternative. Perhaps the trouble with the old "Enlightenment" reason was that it rested more on visionary dreams than on scientific research. A new scholarship, combining the old visions with rigorous "scientific methodology," must, finally, bring the long-hoped-for transformation of society.

The notion was as old as George Bancroft's dream of combining the thoroughness of German scholarship with the "religious" feelings of Americans for redeeming humanity.

If Johns Hopkins' first stroke of genius was his notion of an institution devoted to graduate studies on the Germanic model, his second was in his choice of Daniel Coit Gilman to be its founding president. Gilman, president of the recently founded University of California, was committed to building up the sciences and to attracting to Hopkins the most outstanding scholars in every academic field. The head of each department should, Gilman believed, be left free to "determine what scholars he will receive & how he will teach them; that advanced special students be first provided for; that degrees be given when scholars are ready to graduate, in one year or ten years after their admission." In the words of Frederic Howe, an early student, Gilman "selected as instructors men of enthusiasm, of independence, of courage," such men as are required in every bold new venture. The university and the students themselves were "very badly housed in a group of old lofts and residences on Howard Street, close by the business section of the city." There were no fraternities, playing fields, or organized sports. Instead of the conventional rows of chairs with passive students facing a "pedantrifying" professor, the teacher and his students sat in comfortable old chairs around a long table. "Teachers and students alike felt a dignity and enthusiasm in their work." We "wondered at the intimacy between professors and students, at the possibility of meeting distinguished teachers as human beings." Ira Remsen was a famous chemist; Herbert B. Adams, one of the country's foremost historians; Basil Gildersleeve, a renowned Greek scholar; and Woodrow Wilson, a respected political scientist. Students compared Johns Hopkins to the famous medieval universities of Paris, Padua, and Bologna, and not inappropriately.

Hopkins became the immediate beacon for every bright and ambitious would-be scholar. Josiah Royce, a product of the University of California, Göttingen, and Leipzig, was among the new university's first students. "Here at last," he wrote later, "the American University had been founded. The academic life was now to exist for its own sake. The 'conflict' between 'classical' and 'scientific' education was henceforth to be without significance for the graduate student. And the graduate student was to be, so we told ourselves, the real student. . . . The beginning of the Johns Hopkins University was a dawn wherein ' 'twas bliss to be alive.' Freedom and wise counsel one enjoyed together."

To Royce, Hopkins proved that "the academic business was something more noble and serious than . . . 'discipline' had been in its time. The University . . . preached to [its students] the gospel of learning for wisdom's sake, and of acquisition for the sake of fruitfulness. One longed to be a doer of the word, and not a hearer only, a creator of his own infinitesimal fraction of a product, bound in God's name, to produce it when the time came." The words "wisdom" and "God's name" represent Royce's conviction that the two traditions could be united; the result would be a new morality, the morality of the wise "doer," trained in all the new methods for tracking down the truth. "New" became a magic word; new information, new methodologies, new theories would free mankind from manifold ancient woes. "Original work," as Royce put it, done "in God's name," was to be the hallmark of the new era. Royce was candid enough to confess that the new scholarship exacted a "great price." One was exposed to the often severe and wounding criticism of one's peers. It was hard, he wrote, "to learn to bear criticism . . . without feeling wounded."

Frederic Howe came back from a year of study in Germany more convinced than ever that the future lay with "my own kind of people . . . educated, university people who read books and talked about them." It was still a highly moral world, though formal religion was lightly regarded when it was not actively resisted. "I got its new moralities, the moralities of educated men, of scholars, of intellectual reformers. . . . The people were hungry for guidance; on that we were clear—guidance that we, the scholars, alone could provide. . . . The Johns Hopkins motto was *Veritas Vos Liberabit* [the truth shall make you free]. Through the truth we would redeem the world. . . . I was initiated into a new order; the order of scholars whose teachings had changed me, would change the world. . . . This was the priesthood of my service."

From Richard Ely, a political economist and a Christian socialist, Howe learned of the exploitation of laborers by capitalists. Ely was born in a small town in upstate New York in 1854. After graduating from Columbia, he spent three years studying economics at several German universities. When he returned to the United States, he was appointed to the faculty of Johns Hopkins at the age of twenty-eight. Ely attacked the laissez-faire economics of the day, which had taken the line that the economy worked according to certain laws, laws not too different from the laws of nature in their operation, and that to interfere with them was to invite disaster. One of the "laws" was that capital should never pay labor a cent more than was needed to hire the necessary labor force. Economic principles were not immutable, Ely argued. Economic policies could and often should be altered to meet the evident needs of a society.

Ely became a champion of a wide variety of reforms, among them the supervision of factories to guard the life and health of those who worked in them, since it was abundantly evident that the manufacturers were often indifferent to the safety and well-being of their employees.

To Frederic Howe, Ely was the exemplification of the maxim "Putting mind to work in the service of society." The idea that scholarship in the United States might become a great engine for social reform seemed to men like Howe to fulfill the dream of progress that had inspired reform-minded individuals since the dawn of the Enlightenment. From Ely, Howe learned "that the industrial system was not what I had assumed it to be in Meadville [the Pennsylvania town in which Howe had grown up]. . . . Employers, I now learned, were capitalists. They exploited their workers. In the new world that took shape for me at the university, industry was a grim affair of miners and mills, trusts and monopolies. . . . Little children were slaves in cotton-mills and sweat shops. . . . There was menace in the industrial system; there was need of change. . . . I came alive. I felt a sense of responsibility in the world. I wanted to change things. I was not very clear what

I wanted to change or how I should go about it. It had to do with politics."

The immediate results of a Johns Hopkins education seemed to bear out Howe's and Royce's dreams of a world redeemed from coldness of heart and injustice by a new cadre of scholars dedicated to reform. Johns Hopkins graduates became presidents of universities, powerful heads of academic departments, pioneers in new fields of study. They numbered in their company reform-minded journalists, notable scholars, diplomats, liberal politicians, and, perhaps above all, like Howe himself, municipal reformers. Charles Homer Haskins became dean of the Harvard Graduate School. Charles Hazen was a history professor at Columbia. Edward Alsworth Ross became a pioneer sociologist at the University of Wisconsin, the home of the new scholarship, where liberal professors put their talents at the service of Robert La Follette's Progressive Party. Walter Hines Page distinguished himself as a journalist and diplomat.

Other graduates were John Dewey, Thorstein Veblen, Joseph Jastrow, James Cattell, and Newton D. Baker.

Following the success of Johns Hopkins University, it seemed as though every tycoon wanted one of his own. Universities became more popular than yachts or Newport mansions (and much more expensive; colleges were passé or for lesser tycoons). Vanderbilt University was started in 1875 by a gift of $1 million by the Commodore. Jonas Gilman Clark founded Clark University in 1887 at Worcester, Massachusetts, on the model of Johns Hopkins. Clark was almost as fortunate in his choice of his university's first president as Hopkins had been. He chose G. Stanley Hall, a leading psychologist, and Hall gathered a brilliant young faculty. Like Gilman, Hall believed in leaving his faculty and students to their own intellectual devices. An early student, L. M. Terman, wrote: "no professor, so far as I could see, kept a class list. Attendance records were, of course, unheard of. No marks or grades of any kind were awarded. . . . The student was allowed to take his doctor's examination whenever the professor in charge of his thesis thought he was ready for it. No examination except the four-hour doctor's oral was ever given. . . . A professor lectured only three or four times a week on whatever subject he pleased. . . ."

Ezra Cornell, a tycoon who had started life as a carpenter, then became a financier and, finally, founder of Western Union, hired Andrew D. White as head of *his* new university, founded on progressive principles with a grant of $500,000. Cornell's intention was to turn out men who would become leaders of the nation as well as engineers and inventors. He also wanted his university to devote part of its energy to investigating the social problems that mocked the nation's pretensions to be a progressive and enlightened republic. "I would found an institution," Cornell wrote, "in which any person can find instruction in any study."

Stanford, founded by the rapacious rail baron Leland Stanford, opened in 1891, funded by a gift of $20 million. John D. Rockefeller gave somewhat in excess of $30 million to get the University of Chicago going in 1892. Rockefeller chose William Rainey Harper as the first president of *his* university. Harper was a case, as they say. His first act was to raid other universities for their most noted scholars. The university opened with 328 undergraduates, 210 graduate students, and 204 divinity students. The "stolen" faculty numbered 120. The university's purpose, Harper announced, was "to make the work of investigation primary, the work of giving instruction secondary."

Although Harper was something of a nut in his pride in ceaseless work, he was also thoroughly American, and he reminds us of one of the less agreeable aspects of the philosophy, spoken or unspoken, that underlay much of American educational psychology: education was intended to form the student's—more specifically, the male student's—character by setting him difficult, laborious, and unrewarding tasks to perform and insisting that he carry them out properly and, above all, punctually. Punctuality was of the essence. Lateness was more apt to be punished than mere dullness, which was, after all, unavoidable and evident enough in the curriculum itself.

Harper set an example by the mad whirl of activity that marked his waking hours. He rose and dictated to his poor secretary at five in the morning. He announced to one visitor proudly, "I have forty points to be discussed this morning." A friend, not surprisingly, suspected that "there was something of exhibitionism in his industry. . . . He liked to make appointments at obscene hours."

The attitude of the universities toward the denominational colleges can perhaps be gauged by Harper's statement that there were too many of them; their numbers should be greatly reduced and many of them be assigned the rank of high schools.

In the new universities as well as the old, the clergy, who had dominated the boards of trustees of colleges, were replaced by businessmen, lawyers, bankers, and railroad tycoons. Ezra Cornell was proud that his university at the time of its founding counted on his board of trustees three "mechanics," three farmers, one manufacturer, one merchant, one lawyer, one engineer, and one "literary gentleman." Twenty years later there were five bankers, three lawyers, two manufacturers, two judges, and an editor.

Scientists and practical men also replaced clergymen as heads of institutions founded or funded by wealthy businessmen. Daniel Coit Gilman had been professor of physical and political geography at Yale's Sheffield Scientific School. David Starr Jordan, president of Stanford, was a biologist, and F. A. P. Barnard, the president of Columbia during the years when that institution emerged as one of the country's major new universities, had been professor of chemistry and mathematics.

It turned out that the tycoons who wanted universities also wanted football teams, and that meant undergraduate students. Hopkins reluctantly added undergraduates before the end of the century, and Clark followed suit.

Daniel Coit Gilman's most famous follower was Charles W. Eliot, the president of Harvard who set out to make Harvard rival or exceed Hopkins as a center of graduate students. It was no contest. As a fund-raiser and an academic imperialist, Eliot was without rival. By the end of the century Johns Hopkins lagged far behind. When Eliot was made president of Harvard in 1869, there were twenty-seven faculty members and sixty-seven instructors and administrators. When he retired in 1909, the faculty and staff had grown to seven hundred. By the 1890s, the open spirit that had characterized Johns Hopkins in its early years had given way to a growing list of requirements. The virtually unlimited freedom was gradually circumscribed. The students, in the words of Ira Remsen, Gilman's successor, "would fly from one thing to another. . . . There was a good deal of what I might call puttering." The decision was made to "offer something in order to keep [the] students in line. The Ph.D. degree was the next thing after the A.B. degree and we recognized that we must offer this in order to keep that body of workers in line, and that, in order to secure the results we wanted, it was also necessary to require a piece of research for that degree. . . . We thought, at first, we might avoid it, but we found that we must adopt it." The tone was reminiscent of that used by industrialists to describe measures required to keep *their* workers in line.

5
THE STATE UNIVERSITIES

"The justification for the privileges of universities is not to be found in their capacity to take the sons of the rich and render them harmless to society or to take the sons of the poor and teach them how to make money."

ROBERT HUTCHINS

It could be argued that the principal beneficiaries of the spectacular burgeoning of graduate study were the state universities, especially those of the Midwest. The state colleges (or universities, as the case might be), had gotten a tremendous boost from the first Morrill Act, passed in 1862 and signed by Lincoln (his predecessor, James Buchanan, had vetoed an earlier version), which provided for grants of federally owned land to the states, the income of which was to be used to help fund state colleges. Every state was to receive thirty thousand acres of land for each senator and congressman. States were required to found at least one college within five years of the passage of the bill. At the time of the passage of the act, as the reader may recall, a number of states had already established colleges, among them Wisconsin, Minnesota, Missouri, Georgia, North Carolina, and Tennessee. In 1866, when 240,000 acres of federal land were given to Wisconsin, the university entered a period of remarkable expansion.

In 1890 the Morrill Act was extended, providing more funding for state universities at a critical period in their transition from small provincial institutions to major universities. It was almost as though the state colleges had been waiting in the wings to assume their dominant role in American higher education.

J. B. Angell, president of the University of Michigan, declared there was "no more conspicuous feature in the history of America . . . than the rapid and brilliant development of state universities. From Ohio to the Pacific, from North Dakota to Texas, nearly every State has established or is preparing to establish a university on the foundation of the United States land grants. . . ."

The State University of Iowa when Roger Galer went there was small, shabby, and poor, but "in all the great essentials of a liberal culture, the University gave us excellent facilities with as good results, as have been attained with all the vast array of buildings, apparatus, books, museums, and specialized instruction of these later years," Galer wrote. Twenty years later Iowa was a flourishing modern university.

At the University of Nebraska, Alvin Johnson recalled, there was a student "who had walked in from Loup City, a hundred and fifty miles, with a broken ankle, to save a few dollars on railway fares." A decade later (1910) the student body had changed markedly. "All the students had money and bicycles," Johnson wrote, "and here and there one had a 'buzz wagon,' a primordial automobile that would carry a crowd of laughing boys and girls to the near woods." Fraternity life became the center of college education for most undergraduate students, sororities for the women.

Different as they were in many ways, the emerging state universities shared with places like Johns Hopkins and Clark University the exhilarating sense of a great new venture. They also shared the vision of mind as being in the service of society, although they were also more practically oriented in terms of careers. At the same time, they were careful to put more than geographical distance between themselves and their Eastern cousins. The Wisconsin State Senate Committee on Education School and the University Lands stressed the uniqueness of the Western notions of higher education: "We are done with the conservatism of the past. We draw our inspiration from our present principles and build our hopes upon the future. . . . It is not by poring over the dreamy and mystical pages of classical lore that the student is to develop the energy of character and strength of purpose to enter manfully into the great battle of life—to storm nature in her vastness, and to unlock her treasures; but by obtaining a thorough knowledge of physical sciences, following nature into her great laboratories, and discovering her chemical secrets; learning the nature of the air we breathe, the water we drink, and the food that nourishes our system. . . . Give, then, to the *whole* people of the State an educational institution suited to their wants. . . ."

The citizens of Wisconsin expected that the university "shall primarily be adapted to popular needs, that its courses of instruction shall be arranged to meet as fully as possible the wants of the greatest number of our citizens. The *farmers, mechanics, miners, merchants* and *teachers* of Wisconsin, represented in this legislature, have a right to ask that this bequest of the government shall aid them in securing to themselves and their posterity, such educational advantages as shall fit them for their pursuits in life, and which by an infusion of intelligence and power, shall elevate those pursuits to a social dignity commensurate with their value."

Angell of Michigan was one of the founding generation of powerful university administrators. On the University of Kansas' twenty-fifth anniversary in 1891, Angell was invited to make the principal address. He reminded his audience that it was a "marvel . . . that so early in the hard and troubled life of this State the institution opened her hospitable doors and invited the youth from all parts of this broad State to enter and receive a college education almost without money and without price. . . . At its very birth, the storm of the great Civil War broke upon its head, and deluged all this border, including this fair town [Lawrence] itself, with blood." The state universities, Angell declared, "very early . . . began to show a broader and more liberal spirit in the arrangement of their curricula of study than the colleges which were modeled on the New England type. They made ample provision for instruction in science and the application of science to the arts. . . . They founded schools of engineering, pharmacy, medicine, dentistry and law. They opened their doors at an early day to both sexes" and, finally, "attained a development almost unprecedented in the history of colleges and universities." Angell congratulated his audience on the fact that 56 percent of the students at the University of Kansas came from families where the father earned his living by manual labor, most typically, of course, by farming.

"Wise is the State which by timely generosity to its universities," Angell continued, "has touched with such an uplifting power the mind and heart of every child within its borders. Rich with a wealth transcending that of forests and mines, of flocks and herds, is a State filled with noble women and noble men thoroughly furnished by a sound and generous education for all the demands and opportunities of our Christian civilization of the nineteenth century." Angell had faint praise for the small denominational colleges—"a limited number of them can and do discharge a useful function"— but there was "great danger to education itself" in their tendency to "multiply . . . unnecessarily." Angell believed that "it would be better for higher education if not another college were established east of the Rocky Mountains for at least a generation to come." The state universities, Angell argued, had not only "uplifted" the high schools to a notable degree; they had lifted "all the colleges throughout the Western States."

A good part of Angell's address was devoted to assuring his audience that state universities were no threat to the religious convictions of their students. The regents were well aware "that our citizens, with almost no exception, desire that the conditions of college life should be helpful, rather than harmful, to the religious development of their children." The university faculties, Angell assured his listeners, "are made up of men who, with almost no exceptions, are earnest, reverent, God-fearing men."

Finally, Kansans were exhorted to support their university as generously as possible. "In the fierce competitions of these days," Angell concluded, "those communities and those States which produce the largest intelligence, the energetic and noble character, will push to the front."

When Charles R. Van Hise was inaugurated as president of the University of Wisconsin in 1904, he reviewed the relationship of the university to the high schools and the citizens of the state. Certificates of graduation from high school were accepted by the university. Soon after the university opened its doors, departments of law, agriculture, and engineering were started. When funds from the land grants under the Morrill Act proved inadequate, the state began in the 1870s to fund the university to the extent of $10,000 per year (Wisconsin had started in 1854). After twenty years there were twenty-nine faculty members and 310 students. In the next thirteen years the faculty almost doubled and the student body increased to 505. There were three "resident graduate" students in 1887. By 1892 a science building was completed and more than a thousand undergraduate students were enrolled. The number of graduate students had risen to twenty-two, and the university was organized into Colleges of Letters and Science, Engineering, Agriculture, and Law.

"A score of years ago," Van Hise declared, "it could not have been said of any state in America, that it had shown willingness to support a university of the highest class; but now several state institutions are recognized as standing in the first group among American universities. These institutions are mainly supported through taxation imposed by a democracy upon itself, for the sons and daughters of the state, poor and rich alike. . . . A state university can only permanently succeed where its doors are open to all of both sexes who possess sufficient intellectual endowment, where the financial terms are so easy that the industrious poor may find the way, and where the student sentiment is such that each stands upon an equal footing with all. This is a state university ideal, and this is a new thing in the world." It was "one of the highest functions of a professor in the class-room and in the laboratory" to be a "comrade" to his students. Included in Van Hise's remarks was a plea to private donors to contribute money for the building of residence halls and a dining commons.

Like Angell before him, Van Hise could not forbear to point out to his audience that, at least in regard to the sciences, the "East" had lagged conspicuously behind the West: "For a long time in the east science was regarded as an intruder, and was only slowly and partially admitted to full fellowship with the studies of the old curriculum. . . . No one now doubts the right of pure science to full admission in the list of subjects which may be pursued for a liberal education. Not only so, but it is recognized that the scientific spirit has permeated and vivified the studies of the old college course."

The interesting consequence of the admission of "pure science" to the university, Van Hise pointed out, "was the rapid growth of the applied sciences. . . ." The most prominent were agriculture, engineering, and medicine. "The people of the west," Van Hise noted, "went even further than this and demanded that language, mathematics, political economy and history should be so taught as to serve the man of affairs." This principle had led to the establishment at Wisconsin of a "school" of commerce, or, as it has since more forthrightly been called, a business school. It would be easy to show, Van Hise told his audience, that the "discoveries at the University of Wisconsin bring vastly more wealth to the state each year than the entire expenditure of the institution. . . ." Van Hise did not hesitate to add architecture, sculpture, painting, and music as subjects of equal value to engineering or "pure science." The fact was that in its practice and appreciation of the arts the United States was, compared with Europe, in a state of "semi-barbarism." "If the university does not become the center for the cultivation of the highest capacities of the human mind, where is the work to be done in this country?" Van Hise asked rhetorically.

Van Hise attributed the rise of "the great groups of studies classified under political economy, political science, sociology, and history" to academic respectability to the fact that university men were trained, in those fields, "to regard economic and social questions as problems to be investigated by the inductive method, and in their solutions to aim at what is best for the whole people. . . . Such of these men as are filled with a burning enthusiasm for the advancement of the race are capable of great accomplishment, for they possess the enlightenment upon which wise action can be based. Already men who have studied history, economics, political science, and sociology in the universities have achieved large results in the formulation and enforcement of the written law, and in the growth of a healthy and powerful public sentiment." Before long "such men" would "be found in every city and hamlet leading the fight against corruption and misrule, and, even more important and vastly more difficult, leading in constructive advance." Social problems "scarcely less momentous than that of slavery" confronted the nation, and only trained intelligence could hope to solve them.

By 1902 the faculty at the University of Wisconsin numbered 180 and the undergraduate student body counted 2,877 with 115 graduate students. Perhaps a third of the undergraduate student body were enrolled in courses in applied education, preparing to be teachers in the state's primary and secondary schools.

The overall rate of growth in higher education was astonishing. In 1870 there had been 52,000 candidates for the bachelor's degree in 563 "institutions of higher learning," as the census termed them. They constituted 1.1 percent of college-age youth. By 1900 the numbers had risen to 235,000, 2.3 percent of those of college age. In 1900 some 22,000 bachelor degrees were awarded, 5,237 to women (there were thus roughly four times as many degrees awarded to men as to women). At the same time, of 392 Ph.D.'s awarded in 1900, only twenty-three went to women.

The 1890 census listed approximately a thousand colleges and universities, but ten years later the number had dropped to 977, most, doubtlessly, victims of the depression of 1893. A significant change occurred in the composition of faculties. Whereas the census of 1890 listed 7,358 men and 4,194 women faculty members, a difference of less than two to one on the male side, twenty years later the number of men had increased to 19,151 as opposed to 4,717 women. In other words, the number of male faculty members had multiplied by almost two and a half, while women faculty had only increased by some five hundred. Men now outnumbered women by better than four to one. The enormous growth in the size of universities and the emphasis on scholarly researches had been a male-driven and -dominated movement. The cry for "professionalism," and the increasing length of time needed to acquire an advanced degree, worked to the disadvantage of women. In addition, the development of departments was a deterrent to women, because it effectively placed the control of faculty appointments in the hands of the department chairmen rather than in the hands of the presidents and trustees.

Most women faculty were to be found in women's colleges and in state universities. In the latter institutions they were usually in the newly created departments of physical education, domestic science, and public health, although there were important exceptions. Women faculty members in the older private men's colleges and universities were the rarest exceptions. It might thus be said that the first victims of the new scholarship were women. Jews, for different reasons, soon found themselves virtually barred from university teaching.

In the single decade between 1890 and 1900, the number of university teachers increased by almost 100 percent, giving rise inevitably to the question of how capable people could have been recruited in such a short time. Some professors advanced from high-school teaching after brief periods of graduate work. Not a few Protestant ministers, many of whom had experienced doubts in an age when religion appeared in sharp decline, secured university appointments, most typically in sociology.

One of the most striking aspects of the new learning was that it was, perhaps above all, a youth movement. Since the Ph.D. had not yet been established as a requirement for employment, graduation from a reputable graduate program, or, preferably, several years of study in a German university, was sufficient. Many young instructors were full professors by their mid-thirties. When Edward A. Ross, who had gone to Germany to do graduate work in economics, returned to the United States in 1891, he was amazed to find that most of the fellow economists whom he encountered at a meeting of the American Economic Association were, like Ross, in their thirties. He got a position at Indiana State University and soon thereafter received offers from Cornell and Stanford. So rapid was his advance up the academic ladder that two years after receiving his Ph.D. he was a full professor. His salary rose as rapidly as his rank.

State universities and denominational colleges were radicalized by the Populist movement of the 1890s. Institutions like the University of Kansas and Iowa College, later Grinnell, were hotbeds of Christian Socialism. The Society of Christian Socialists was founded in 1889 by, among others, Richard Ely and Washington Gladden. Christian Socialist evangelists like George Herron traveled about the country lecturing to large crowds of students. At

the University of Michigan in 1894, Herron addressed the largest
audience that had ever gathered on that campus. When Populism
waned, many of the denominational colleges swung sharply to the
right, but the state universities of the Midwest were once again
radicalized, by the Progressive movement, with the University of
Wisconsin, under the influence of Robert La Follette, placing itself
in the forefront of the reform movement. Professor John R. Common, an ally of Ely and a professor of economics at Wisconsin,
was an ardent spokesman for what he called "utilitarian idealism,"
which he compared to "esthetic idealism." Both had the same goal:
"the perfect product." "I do not see," Commons wrote, "why there
is not as much idealism in breeding a perfect animal or a Wisconsin
No. 7 ear of corn . . . as there is in chipping out a Venus de Milo
or erecting a Parthenon." Wisconsin agricultural students were, in
fact, required to begin their studies by imaging an "ideally perfect
cow." Commons was tired of hearing the Greek ideal exalted above
modern principles. Wisconsin researchers had made "a science
and an art out of what to the Greek was degrading toil" typically
performed by slaves.

John Dewey with his dedication to "problem solving" was an
even more prominent spokesman for the notion that the immediate goal of education should be the improvement of society.

Emma Goldman testified to the spirit of the University of Wisconsin. "Professors and students," she wrote, "were vitally interested in social ideas. . . ." The professors "were progressive, alive
to the problems of the world, and modern in the interpretation
of their subjects." The Wisconsin of Robert La Follette was akin
to the early Johns Hopkins in its zeal for reform. But the zeal was
short-lived. When Goldman returned to Wisconsin a year later,
she found the professors less "reckless." The legislature was considering the university's appropriation, and it was considered un-
wise to espouse radical notions. Much the same thing had
happened at the University of Kansas, recently a "stronghold of
free thought," now treading cautiously.

It is necessary to say something about the experience of undergraduate students (the term "undergraduates" did not come into

existence until there were graduates). There has been, so far as I have been able to determine, no golden age of teaching, certainly not at the better-known institutions. The testimony of graduates of even the most prestigious colleges and universities is almost uniformly disheartening. Charles Francis Adams, Jr., was a student at Harvard in the 1850s. As he describes it, it sounds very much like Harvard in 1989. It was thus not so much that graduate studies ruined a flourishing enterprise; they simply made a bad situation worse.

Josiah Royce, perpetually optimistic, was confident that the university would never neglect its undergraduate students. The mission of the university was training "the mind of the nation," Royce wrote. There need be no fear that undergraduates would be neglected in the enthusiasm for graduate study. Royce was confident that "the numbers and the large significance of the undergraduates in every university insure and always will insure the closest attention to their needs and interests." Indeed, the undergraduate could only profit by his "years of intercourse . . . with elder men and progressive scholars." They will be "possible future colleagues . . . beginners in constructive wisdom. . . . For what is scholarship but spiritual construction."

But that was hardly the way things turned out. When Charles Francis Adams, Jr., sat down to write his autobiography, it seemed to him that the Harvard of the turn of the century was, if possible, more disheartening than the Harvard of his youth. Charles W. Eliot had, to be sure, greatly increased enrollment and endowments and added, with great fanfare, "electives" to relieve the lockstep of the old curriculum, but he had also introduced what Adams considered premature specialization, a consequence more of a desire to conform to the narrowly specialized interests of the faculty than to promote sound undergraduate education. Adams added: "I only know that so far as producing the ideal results in individual minds standing in crying need of direction, the system . . . was very bad fifty years ago, and I have every reason to believe that the system now in use is yet worse."

That Harvard students suffered from the lack of any real contact with faculty was plain to John Jay Chapman. The students of William James and undergraduates majoring in philosophy were the most notable exceptions. James and his colleagues in philosophy, Hugo Munsterberg aside, considered close relations with their students inseparable from true teaching and true learning. So many students had breakdowns of various kinds, including suicides, during Chapman's time that emergency measures were considered necessary. The authorities decided that the heart of the problem was a lack of simple human contact. Since the professors remained determinedly aloof, it was decided to give weekly teas for the undergraduates at Brooks Hall, "to ask everyone, to get ladies from Boston, Bishops from anywhere, social people at any cost, social talent to bridge the gulf between instructors and instructed. Nobly they labored. It was shoulder-to-shoulder, never say die, love one, love all, more tea, more ladies. . . . [I]t was a real dawn, somewhat grotesque and naive. . . . [B]ut Harvard has been a more human place ever since. Indeed, what Harvard truly needed was the outside world—ladies, Bishops and tea."

The aspect of Harvard that most impressed Oswald Garrison Villard, the son of the great railroad tycoon Henry Villard and grandson of the abolitionist William Lloyd Garrison, was its snobbishness. It was an attitude shared by faculty and students alike. Villard was flattered when the famous historian Albert Bushnell Hart singled him out to be his assistant, but he was profoundly disillusioned when Hart told him he had been selected because "of my social standing, the fact that I wore nice clothes, and was a member of a couple of good clubs. He was tired, he said, of having to pick 'greasy grinds,' . . . because they often lacked the appearance and ability necessary to win the respect of their students." It is reassuring to learn that there were at least some "greasy grinds." Again, according to Villard, most of the students had little interest in anything outside their immediate field of vision. They were ignorant of goings-on in the larger world beyond the Harvard Yard and enrolled, so far as they could, in "snap" courses.

When young Lincoln Steffens entered the University of California, Berkeley, the first American university to place a major emphasis on science, he experienced little care or attention from the eminent faculty. "No one," he wrote, "ever developed for me the relation of anything I was studying to anything else, except, of course, to that wretched degree. Knowledge was absolute, not relative, and it was stored in compartments, categorical and independent. The relation of knowledge to life, even to student life, was ignored, and as for questions, the professors asked them, not the students, and the students, not the teachers, answered them—in examinations. . . . It was not assumed that we had any curiosity or the potential love of skill, scholarship, and achievement or research."

Steffens' fellow journalist Ray Stannard Baker, the friend and biographer of Woodrow Wilson, had much the same experience. "Why had they [these professors] not told me about, or at least referred me to, books that would have helped me in understanding the things I was seeing."

The reformer Frederic Howe attended a typical small denominational "liberal-arts" college in Pennsylvania. His five years there were "very nearly barren. . . . The inflexible pattern of American collegiate life left almost no impression on my mind. It had neither variety nor inspiration. . . . What was offered was not what I wanted. . . . My real life was outside the classroom, in politics, fraternity life, in journalism and ephemeral college activities. . . . Professions of faith were rather more important than scholarship." The professors were pious and well meaning, many of them retired ministers or missionaries. "None of the subjects stirred in me the least enthusiasm," he recalled.

Besides being an indefatigable fund-raiser, extracting millions from millionaires susceptible to his considerable charm, Charles W. Eliot revolutionized undergraduate education by introducing the "elective" system, which allowed undergraduates to select their own courses without having to follow a prescribed curriculum. Enthusiasm for the elective system was far from universal. Benjamin Ide Wheeler, president of the University of California, had little patience with an elective system, declaring that "life has no . . . easy-going elective system, and colleges ought not to have [one]. Life wants men to do things . . . because it's their duty to do them, not because they elect to do them." Wheeler was certainly right in criticizing the excessive individualism that characterized the educational experience of most students. "We have got to share our lives with others," he wrote, "in order to have them normal. Ultra-individualism means isolation. . . ."

Woodrow Wilson, president of Princeton, convinced that the balance had swung too far in the direction of electives, pressed for required courses in American political and institutional history to present "the common experience, the common thoughts and struggles, the old triumphs and defeats of . . . men . . . in the past." A student wrote Wilson: "Before I came to Princeton I had heard much of Princeton democracy, but after I came I soon found out generally speaking democracy applied . . . only to athletes. . . . To make a good club a man can't . . . entertain ideas much in advance of, or much different from, those generally entertained by the student body, or his social aspirations will have vanished forever." He had to be constantly on his guard "not to deviate in the slightest degree from the smooth, somewhat monotonous, affable acquiescent manner and thought which is required as the standard for club-making."

The typical student at Yale was described as "a careless boy-man, who is chiefly anxious to 'have a good time,' and who shirks work and deceives his instructors in every possible way." Dean Briggs of Harvard believed "Social ambition is the strongest power in many a student's college life, power compared with which the rules and the threats of the Faculty, who blindly ignore it, are impotent, a power that robs boys of their independence, leading them to do things foolish or worse. . . ."

At the end of the century, John Jay Chapman wrote: "Our colleges perform a wonderful social service; they are boys' clubs and men's clubs. Educationally they are nearly extinct as far as the old humanities go." Chapman was dismayed to see Eliot running after tycoons of the Jay Gould stripe to finance his ambitious building plans. It would be left to the next generation to "pick up the pieces and reconstruct the idea that the university is a place of thought, truth, religion."

Conscious of the incongruity of undergraduate instruction and graduate work, a number of "institutes" were started in the 1890s, the Massachusetts Institute of Technology, the California Institute of Technology, and the Carnegie Institute prominent among them. While most of these institutes admitted specially promising undergraduates with strong science backgrounds, they eschewed the more juvenile aspects of undergraduate life.

It can be argued that the principal beneficiaries of the elective system were professors. It meant that they could "follow their bents, gratify their own curiosity, and offer courses in the results," in Robert Hutchins' words.

Critics denounced the elective system as the academic equivalent of capitalism's laissez-faire and a craven capitulation to students' whims, but university after university followed suit. The elective system accommodated neatly to the increasing specialization in scholarly studies. It also pitted department against department in competing for student favor.

By the first decade of the new century, the situation could be fairly described much as follows. In order to mount and support graduate-degree programs, the state universities had to admit large numbers of more or less indigestible undergraduates. Since the professors at such institutions were preoccupied with their graduate students and research activities, the undergraduates got only the most cursory attention and an inferior education. The trade-off was that the undergraduates were given virtually free rein to enjoy themselves. Fraternities, sororities, football games, proms, and hops were the principal foci of undergraduate life. The professors were glad to have the students off their hands and out of their minds. The system, in practical fact, encouraged a casual, self-indulgent, often overtly anti-intellectual atmosphere. The father of Dan Quayle, the current Vice-President of the United States, unselfconsciously described his son in his undergraduate days as interested primarily in "booze and broads," interests common to his type in state universities all across the nation. Not surprisingly, relatively few undergraduate students in the "great universities" went on to do graduate work. Without the "farm system" of small, independent, originally denominational colleges scattered about the country, the great universities would have been hard pressed to find graduate students. To put the matter as simply as possible, in the state universities the undergraduates "paid" for graduate studies with the tacit understanding that they would not be subjected to more education than they could tolerate. In Woodrow Wilson's words, "The work of the college, the work of the classrooms and laboratories, has become the merely formal and compulsory side of its life, and . . . a score of other things, lumped under the term 'undergraduate activities,' have become the vital, spontaneous, absorbing realities for nine out of every ten men who go to college."

By the end of the century the neglected undergraduate had forced himself/herself on the attention of university administrators and trustees, less by silent suffering, as in the case of Chapman's Harvard, than by riotous and scandalous behavior (one riot may be taken to equal several hundred cases of severe depression in catching the attention of university administrators).

The solution was a combination of parental authority (*in loco parentis*) and bread and circuses, in the form of fraternities and sororities plus big-time sports. Benjamin Ide Wheeler probably represented the apogee of paternalism when he exhorted freshmen entering the University of California to bathe daily; "washing the parts conventionally exposed to the weather" was not sufficient, he warned. He also warned against "sexual uncleanliness."

A conspicuous recanter of old sins was Andrew White, who as president of Cornell had made it a standardbearer of the new scientific, graduate-oriented education. Where he had formerly "rather pooh-poohed the talk about culture" as "mainly cant," he had undergone a conversion. He now believed, he told parents and students, "that, whatever else we do, we must . . . not only . . . make men and women skillful in the various professions and avocations of life but . . . cultivate and bring out the best in them as men and women."

Culture, as it turned out, was closely related to discipline. There was a general feeling that the lack of supervision had encouraged some of the less admirable qualities of the young. There was widespread agreement that in the concentration on graduate education the neglected undergraduates had run somewhat wild. Again in White's words, a "refreshing series of ethical waves" were needed to set things right.

6
GROWING PAINS

"The actual teaching is . . . selected and controlled . . . by the
business interests playing on the vested academic interests."

—J. A. HOBSON, 1909

It soon became evident that the owners of the new universities
had no interest in seeing them used as engines of reform. The
owners were content with things as they were. Any substantial
changes were apt to be to their disadvantage. They had not contributed their millions to raise up a nest of academic vipers ready
to bite the hand that fed them. There was a brief struggle. At
Chicago, Edward Bemis, an economist who advocated public own-
ership of municipal utilities and such "natural" monopolies as tim-
ber and minerals, found himself in hot water with William Rainey
Harper, the president of the University of Chicago. Bemis, who
had been a student of Ely at Hopkins, taught a course entitled
"The State as an Agent for Social Amelioration," which appeared
to the trustees as nothing more than outright socialism. Walton
Clark, general superintendent of the United Gas Improvement
Company, a subsidiary of Rockefeller's Standard Oil, was said to
have told Bemis soon after his appointment, "If we can't convert
you we are going to down you. We can't stand your writing. It
means millions to us." Harper did his best to persuade Bemis to
resign, but Bemis stood fast. When Bemis attacked the use of the
injunction to break the Pullman Strike, Harper told him: "it is
hardly safe for me to venture into any of the Chicago clubs. I

propose that during the remainder of your connection with the university you exercise great care in public utterances about questions agitating the minds of the people." The head of the economics department wrote to Harper, noting that he was aware that Bemis was "making very hard the establishment of a great railroad interest in the University. I know you have done what seemed best to stop him. . . . I do not see how we can escape . . . except by letting the public know that he goes [is fired] because we do not regard him as up to the standard of the University in ability and scientific methods." The key phrase was "scientific methods." Any expression of a strong political opinion was clearly unscientific. "Scientific" meant "objective, dispassionate, neutral." It was clear that Bemis had to be sacrificed to the "capitalists," whose largesse was essential to the operation of the university. A colleague told Bemis that he had no quarrel with his scholarship but that Bemis had seriously compromised the university with his outspoken political opinions. The colleague told Bemis that he himself had given up any discussion of politics and was lecturing on transcendental philosophy "so as to be as far as possible from these reform movements and establish the scientific character of my department." Here "scientific" obviously meant staying out of trouble by not discussing controversial political issues. When Bemis remained recalcitrant, Harper warned him not only that he risked being fired if he persisted in speaking out, but that he would be blacklisted and unable to get another academic post.

Apparently in an attempt to establish a rationale for firing Bemis, Harper gave a talk entitled "The Public Work of Professors." In it he argued that a professor was bound to teach a subject, "not his opinions. . . . He must stand above party lines, and be independent of party affiliations." Above all he must not confuse "popular pleading [with] scientific thought." Harper's doctrine became the rationale for discouraging professors everywhere from speaking out on controversial topics and for punishing those who did. Advocacy of reform in virtually any form was branded as "unscientific." On the other hand, those who opposed reform were commonly applauded for their "objectivity." The safest stance was a strict neutrality, or simply lying low, like Bemis' colleague who took refuge in transcendental philosophy. To be called "unscientific" was the equivalent of being called, in an earlier era, "irreligious" or "immoral." The academic fundamentalists were quick to excommunicate heretics.

The firing of Bemis stirred up something of a fuss. Lyman Abbott, pastor of the famous Plymouth Congregational Church in Brooklyn, New York, wrote: "The money power is not to be permitted to control our great universities, or their teaching. . . . It is impossible to maintain freedom of research and teaching without touching what are called 'burning questions'. . . . Freedom of teaching, in our judgment, is absolutely essential to the higher life of our universities, and colleges; to their vitality, their progress, and their integrity." George Gunton, spokesman for the Rockefellers and editor of a magazine (*The Social Economist*) underwritten by the Rockefellers, undertook to answer Abbott's criticism. "Why," he asked, "should an institution pay a professor to teach social doctrines which are contrary to the consensus of the opinions of the faculty, the supporters of the institution, and of the general community?" As though to conclude the discussion, Rockefeller gave $1 million to the university's endowment with the promise of another $2 million in matching funds. President Harper announced a holiday. The vice-president of the trustees attributed the university's good fortune to the Almighty, declaring: "There was a man sent from God whose name was John." The liberal Chicago *Chronicle* described the episode as pouring "Standard Oil upon troubled waters." The firings for heretical political opinions went on.

Professor Henry Carter Adams was bounced from Cornell for publicly taking a strong pro-labor position. E. Benjamin Andrews was fired from Brown for supporting William Jennings Bryan on the ground that Andrews held "unsound financial opinions" that his students should not be exposed to. In this instance, Rockefeller withheld a large contribution until the trustees did their duty.

J. Allen Smith was an advocate of Henry George's single-tax scheme (he had read George's great work while a student at the University of Missouri, despite a warning to students not to read it). Smith went on to do graduate work at the University of Michigan, where he fell under the influence of Richard Ely and John R. Commons. After getting his degree, he took a position at Marietta College in Ohio, where he ran afoul of the trustees by announcing his support for Bryan. The trustees promptly sacked him (he described them as "partisan Republicans . . . interested in gas and other monopolies [who] would like to see the teaching in this college subordinated to their own private interests").

Edward Alsworth Ross, a graduate of Johns Hopkins, was given a job teaching economics at the newly founded Stanford University. There his inclination to liberal causes aroused the ire of Jane Lathrop Stanford, widow of the railroad tycoon after whom the university was named. She had him fired, whereupon seven other faculty members resigned, among them Arthur Lovejoy, a promising young philosopher and a former student of William James.

Richard Ely, inspirer of Frederic Howe, Edward Bemis, and numerous other reform-minded young scholars, found he was no more immune to persecution for his political opinions than his students. When Ely went from Hopkins to the University of Wisconsin in 1892, he was thirty-eight years old, founder of the school of "new economics" as well as one of the founders of the American Economic Association and president of that body. That did not save him from attack at Wisconsin, where he had come as a recruit to the forces of Progressive reform led by young Robert La Follette. La Follette, in the spirit of Johns Hopkins, had enlisted the brightest young professors at the university in his program of reform. Oddly enough, the campaign to fire Ely was led by the editor of the nominally liberal *Nation,* E. L. Godkin. Godkin called Ely "a practical ethical socialist" and called for his dismissal. The regents appointed a committee to look into the charges. Ely was exonerated and continued to operate as one of La Follette's closest advisers.

Despite the clearing of Ely's name, the firing of professors who espoused ideas considered dangerous (in the main, any idea having to do with state or federal intervention in or control of the economy) continued. Although many professors played an active role in reform politics, the lesson taught by the cases of Bemis, Andrews, Smith et al. was not lost on the professoriate, not a notably bold bunch at best. The ideal of "scientific detachment" was an attractive alternative for many in the profession, and it seemed to grow more so with every passing year.

One of the plainest statements of the academic facts of life was by an officer of the Western Railroad Association who was a trustee of Northwestern University. He wrote: "As to what should be taught in political science and social science, they [the professors] should promptly and gracefully submit to the determination of the trustees when the latter find it necessary to act. . . . If the trustees err it is for the patrons and proprietors, not for the employees, to change either the policy or the personnel of the board."

Trustees at Chicago, Yale, Princeton, Columbia, and Johns Hopkins agreed with their Northwestern counterpart. It was up to the trustees to determine, in the final analysis, what should be taught, or at least from what perspective a politically sensitive subject should be taught. Many endowers of chairs insisted on their right to interview prospective holders of said chairs to make sure their views were thoroughly orthodox. Ezra Cornell poked about his campus, quizzing students and faculty alike on their opinions, until one student protested: "If Mr. Cornell would simply stand upon his pedestal as our 'Honored Founder,' and let us hurrah for him, that would please us mightily; but when he comes into the laboratory and asks us gruffly, 'What are you wasting your time at now?' we don't like him so well." Andrew White declared: "I lay much stress on good physical health as well as intellectual strength. I want no sickly young professors if I can avoid them."

At the very moment (1906) when the American University, as Josiah Royce had termed universities collectively, was in a dizzying spiral of growth and accumulating power, professors were raising their voices against tyrannical university presidents, stifling academic bureaucracies, and meddling boards of trustees. Needless to say, those in the forefront of such criticisms were graduates of Johns Hopkins. Joseph Jastrow was a professor of psychology at the University of Wisconsin. Jastrow charged that any faculty member who questioned the authority or the policies of the administration was subject to various subtle forms of punishment, from the "Impatient frowning down of any questioning" to discrimination in matters of leave and promotion. Increasingly, professors were viewed not as they were in most European countries, as companies of scholars who in large part ran the universities whose reputations they adorned, but as employees of business-dominated boards of trustees and regents. Jastrow insisted that "our autocratic methods of university management would be nothing less than intolerable to the German scholar"—not, of course, to mention those in the privileged sanctuaries of Oxford and Cambridge.

The trustees were the special villains. "A non-professional body of citizens" with often only the most superficial notion of what a university was about, in Jastrow's view, had final say in matters far beyond their competence. Worst of all, as we have noted, most boards of trustees did not hesitate to say what should and should not be taught in the universities under their control.

Jastrow described the new tycoon-type university president as someone of great personal ambition, "a secretive habit of mind, a protective insensibility, a pseudo-diplomatic behavior, and a love of war that seems to come with the executive title. . . ." The result was a situation that varied from "the ridiculously irritating to the sublimely intolerable." There was much truth in his observation that it was "nothing short of absurd to withdraw from faculty discussion all the real education issues, and expect a company of scholarly men to grow enthusiastic over the privilege of wearily debating" rules governing student behavior.

One of the most remorseless critics of the new university was one of its greatest luminaries. Thorstein Veblen, a classic Minnesota hayseed of Norwegian ancestry who held up his socks by pinning them to his trousers, was a shrewd observer of the American nouveau riche. He also turned his acidulous pen on university presidents and their trustees. Between them, he argued, "they had turned the university in all its bearings into a mechanistic, statistical consistency, with numerical standards and units; which conduces to perfunctory and mediocre work throughout, and acts to deter both students and teachers from a free pursuit of knowledge." At the same time, "the system" encouraged "volubility, tactful effrontery, conspicuous conformity to the popular taste in all matters of opinion, usage and conventions." Veblen called university presidents "Captains of Erudition," as in Captains of Industry. Of one such nameless enemy, he wrote that he had "stifled all manly independence and individuality wherever it has exhibited itself. . . . All noble idealism, and all the graces of poetry and art have been shriveled by his brutal and triumphant power." The result of his twenty-five-year incumbency (was it Eliot?) was a faculty that had become "a byword of nugatory intrigue and vacant pedantry."

It was the business of the president, Veblen pointed out, to exhort his charges constantly by delivering "quasi-scholarly homiletical discourse, frequent, voluminous, edifying and optimistic"; as well as presiding over "ritualistic solemnities, diverting and vacant; spectacular affectations of (counterfeit) scholastic usage in the way of droll vestments, bizarre and archaic; parade of (make-believe) gentility; encouragement and (surreptitious) subvention of athletic contests; promulgation of (presumably ingenuous) statistics touching the volume and character of the work done." "Under such a scheme of standardization, accountancy and control," Veblen wrote, "the school becomes primarily a bureaucratic organization, and the first and unremitting duties of the staff are those of official management and accountancy."

One of the most frequently mentioned faculty complaints was the inadequacy of professors' incomes. Joseph Jastrow was only one of many professors who complained that they could not live on their academic salaries and were forced to various undignified expedients to provide for their families. William James felt that his work at Harvard had been constrained and his health impaired by the necessity of augmenting his salary. Grudging and meager pay was particularly resented when it was contrasted with the great wealth and extravagant style of living of the trustees themselves. As businessmen they operated on the principle that they followed in their own businesses: pay no more for work than the market requires.

Almost as galling as their lack of voice in their own affairs and their low salaries was the capriciousness of the system of appointment and promotion that prevailed in most universities (Harvard and Cornell were notable exceptions). Presidents commonly decided such matters without consultation with the faculty; faculty members of the same rank and with similar duties often received quite different salaries, according to the whims or prejudices of the president. Such "Jupiterian" behavior (it could hardly be called policy) invited "despair" in some faculty members, while in others it encouraged the most egregious careerism, wherein a professor "degenerates into a professorial *commis*, keen for the main chance, ready to advertise his wares and advance his trade, eager for new markets, a devotee of statistically measured success." One of the most eminent scholars of Jastrow's acquaintance, an individual of "national reputation," had confessed to him that "in any true sense we had no true universities in [America], and certainly no academic life. . . ." The success of his own career, he told Jastrow, "was probably due to his yielding to influences that his ideals condemned."

A consequence of the pervasiveness of the business ethos in the universities was the intense spirit of rivalry that developed between universities. In a bitter Darwinian struggle, each institution competed for dominance. The tycoons who set about to drive competitors into bankruptcy or create monopolies of dubious legality carried the same practices to their function as trustees, or, even more strikingly, as founders. John D. Rockefeller was determined that his university should outshine that of Jonas Gilman Clark or Ezra Cornell in lists of eminent scholars as well as eminent football players. John Jay Chapman deplored Eliot's cultivating of millionaires. "The chest-thumping, back-slapping, vociferous and cheap emotionalism, done to get money . . . is too much like everything else. . . . Everything seems to be a baseball team-jollying, tough good feeling, and thorough-going belief in money and *us*. . . . Harvard is a baseball team, and they'll bid high to get the best man, even if they have to outbid the Sioux City Nine." Eliot's philosophy, like that of his counterparts in other universities, was, in Chapman's words, "boom, boom, boom." New lecture halls, new gymnasiums, new laboratories must go up each year, and new students must be found to fill them or else the dreadful suspicion would develop that University X or Y was falling behind in the universal Darwinian academic struggle for survival. Chapman decided it was no one's fault; it all had a mad momentum of its own. "Eliot in his financial rhapsodies drew golden tears down Pluto's cheeks . . ." Chapman wrote. "The music was crude; it was not Apollo's lute; it was the hurdy-gurdy of pig-iron and the stock-yard." "They done the best they knew," he wrote William James wryly.

Thorstein Veblen's observations were similar. The universities did their best, in his view, to encourage "sentimental chauvinism" and "boyish emotions of rivalry and clannish elation." Students, alumni, and benefactors alike gloried in holding up "convincing statistical exhibits showing the greater glory of '[their] own' university, whether in athletics, enrollment, alumni, material equipment, or schedules of instruction. . . ."

Professors were forced, in the opinion of Jastrow, to become hucksters themselves. They were valued for the weighty books they wrote, but equally for their ability to attract large numbers of students to their courses and thus swell enrollments. The competitive fever, Jastrow wrote, "sets departments to devising means to outrank in numbers the devotees of other departments; it makes the student feel that he is conferring a favor upon the university by coming, and then upon the professor by choosing his class. . . . [I]t contaminates the academic atmosphere so that all life and inspiration go out of it, or would, if the professor's ideals did not serve as a protecting aegis, to resist, often with much personal sacrifice, these untoward influences."

It was not so much the poverty associated with the academic life that discouraged young men "of power and ambition" from becoming professors as the prospect of a life of "servitude" under the control of an imperious board of trustees who considered the professor a mere employee. "A happy academician," Jastrow concluded, "must be sought by the despairing light of a Diogenes lantern. . . ."

The American University, then, became an intricate bureaucracy. Administrators and their staffs multiplied faster than instructors. People began to talk about "ratios," how many professors to how many students, how many administrative staff to how many faculty members. The administrators and their staffs were referred to as "instructional support." It was rather like the ratio between combat troops in modern warfare and their "support" in the rear echelons. The larger the support forces grew, the less the teachers taught. For one thing, much of their time and energy was spent contending with the administration and trying to wrest a degree of power from authoritarian presidents and chancellors, who often viewed their faculties as contentious and unruly children. David Starr Jordan advised against calling the Stanford faculty members together more than once a year.

Any discussion of the growth of graduate studies in the United States must include attention to the looked-down-upon denominational colleges. They were the farm system of the universities. Institutions like Harvard or the University of Wisconsin did not draw their graduate students so much from the ranks of their undergraduates as they did from the small liberal-arts colleges (as the denominational colleges were increasingly referred to).

Thorstein Veblen stressed that relatively few undergraduates at universities with ambitious graduate programs went on to do graduate work. The universities drew most of their students from "the smaller and less businesslike colleges." The small liberal-arts colleges, most of them denominational in their origins and still clinging to many of the ideals of a classical education, honored teaching above research and encouraged close relations between students and teachers. It was in such obscure and modest institutions that students received the stimulus and encouragement to continue their studies at universities. A strange anomaly thus developed. While the universities had, in the main, a condescending attitude toward the small "liberal-arts" colleges scattered throughout the hinterland, they clearly depended on them for a disproportionate number of their ablest graduate students.

Many towns started colleges in the hope of strengthening marginal economies. Mastersville, Ohio, had fewer than a thousand residents, but it could count three colleges within a radius of seven or eight miles from the town. One was Church of Christ, one Methodist, one Presbyterian. Athens, the Presbyterian college, had a strict classical curriculum requiring four years of Greek and Latin. In the words of John Holmes, who grew up in the town, the college "turned out some great men, preachers and school-teachers, and mathematicians who prepared text books used all over the Middle West." Scio, the Methodist college, required two years of Greek and four years of Latin. Scores of Methodist ministers graduated from Scio during its relatively brief life. Newell Sims, making a study of "Hoosier Village," a town in Indiana, noted that after several efforts to start a college in his pseudonymous Aton, a teachers' college was finally founded that drew most of its student body from the town itself. Its ideal, Sims wrote, was "a narrow utilitarianism that sacrificed academic thoroughness" and put "a premium . . . on certain qualities of character, such as religious devotion, moral rectitude, and 'servicefulness.' " Many of the graduates went into social service and reform. Of 394 graduates prior to 1910, eighty had become ministers, missionaries, and "reform workers." The "modern view of the world in philosophy and science," Sims wrote, "is combatted with religious zeal." The student was "trained for political, religious, moral and intellectual conservatism and bias." A serious intellectual atmosphere prevailed. "Social equality is inculcated and practiced," Sims noted. "The poorest and humblest student is quite as much at home in the atmosphere as any other. The spirit of the institution is a democratizing force, and its operation is manifest in the life of Aton."

R. H. Knapp and H. B. Goodrich, in their study of the *Origins of American Scientists,* found that the colleges that produced the highest proportion of scientists were virtually all "founded by Protestant denominations for the training of ministers and teachers." In its initial form the college was invariably small with a predominant religious commitment, "its social and moral standards severe, its curriculum classical, and the position of the science not yet secure." This phase, in the words of the authors, "gave way to a second state, which might be characterized as the period of 'first secularization.' In this second stage, religious preoccupations began to lose their hold, the curriculum was usually modified to provide for specialization, secularization of student interests became clearly manifest, and the sciences moved into a position of great prestige and popularity. . . . Gradually this second stage gave place to a third, in which the processes of secularization proceeded to a point at which sectarian commitment became virtually indiscernible. . . . Urbanity and cosmopolitanism grew apace, and the sciences suffered a comparative decline as other fields of interest such as medicine, law, and managerial vocations attracted increasing adherence."

Knapp and Goodrich pointed out that the denominational colleges of the Midwest and Far West had a much higher "productivity index"—that is, turned out far more scientists in proportion to their total graduates than the state universities and the "great universities" of the East.

Much the same could doubtless be said of the other academic disciplines. It is clear, for instance, that a number of Ph.D.'s in the social sciences had small-town origins and had done their undergraduate work in denominational colleges. It is also interesting to note that a large number of scientists were the sons or grandsons of Protestant clergymen, Unitarians and the Congregationalists primarily. Knapp and Goodrich speculate that individuals from small towns "possess in common certain distinguishing attributes of character, among them strong individualistic incentives to achievement, pragmatism . . . democratic ideology, rationalism and empiricism of outlook, and frequently sobriety, thrift and other fundamental Protestant virtues."

A somewhat "coeval" group of small-town youth went into the field of engineering in large numbers. Herbert Hoover was the prototype of such ambitious, upwardly mobile young men; there were thousands like him.

The thousands (including those that fell by the wayside) of small denominational colleges across the country performed, in the aggregate, a critically important service to the nation. However bleak and austere many of them doubtless were, however limited in intellectual range and aesthetic sensibilities, the young men and women that they turned out decade after decade were individuals with, as we say today, strongly internalized values. They were the "inner-directed" individuals that David Riesman wrote about in *The Lonely Crowd,* men and women confident of their ability to remake the world, starting with the United States. They were the radicals, the reformers, the Populist politicians, state legislators, the enemies of the railroads and the mine owners, the lumber barons, the exploiters. They were the friends of the free blacks and the Indians, the champions of women's rights, the laborers for Christ in foreign lands as well as in "domestic missions" among the urban poor and the newly arrived immigrants. Their Eastern upper-middle-class counterparts were found in the women's colleges that sprang up in the post–Civil War era.

John R. Common was a graduate of Oberlin, and he often avowed that the religious training he had received there was a central element in his zeal for reform. Frederic Howe made a similar confession. Emphatically as he rejected what appeared to him the narrow and inhibiting character of Allegheny College, the religious spirit of the institution found expression in his "priesthood of service" at Johns Hopkins.

7

THE EDUCATION
OF WOMEN

"[W]omen's college education should be the same as men's
. . . because men and women are to live and work together as
comrades and dear friends and lovers."

—M. CAREY THOMAS,
PRESIDENT OF BRYN MAWR COLLEGE

The passion for education that seized the nation at the end of the
Civil War did not overlook the issue of the education of women
and their participation in the process of higher education. An
ardent advocate of women's rights, Alba Woolson, wrote in 1873:
"All the fervent discussion of the present day concerning women,
so earnestly written and so eagerly read, only proves a universal
conviction that there is something wholly wrong about her as she
is; and not only this, but that society is suffering sadly in consequence, and crying aloud for deliverance. It can never be set right
till she is released from the tutelage she is so fast outgrowing, and
led by man to take her place as an honored companion and equal."

In 1860 there had been fifteen women's colleges in the United
States, many of them little more than high schools. Fifteen more
were founded prior to 1880, and an additional twenty-seven in
the decades prior to 1900. By 1930 there were seventy-eight
women's colleges, exclusive of Catholic institutions. A number of
the women's colleges were in the South, few in the Midwest, where
women were admitted to most public colleges and universities.

Mary Lyon had started the Mount Holyoke Female Seminary
in South Hadley, Massachusetts, in 1837. Modeled on Amherst
College, Mount Holyoke stressed plain living and high thinking

and, above all, Christian service. Generation after generation of Mount Holyoke graduates went into the missionary field and carried the word of salvation around the world, especially to women in the ancient cultures of the East, to India, China, and the Middle East and later to Africa and Japan.

The most significant development in higher education for women in the post–Civil War period came in the founding of what we might call the women's Ivy League—Vassar, Smith, Wellesley, and Bryn Mawr.

Vassar College was founded by a millionaire brewer, an English immigrant named Matthew Vassar, who contributed $800,000 to launch it. When it opened its doors in 1865, it was dedicated to the most advanced notions of the healthy and useful life. The arts were emphasized long before they received attention in men's colleges. Vassar College offered students courses in music and in art appreciation. Catharine Beecher, sister of Harriet, had made the improvement of women's health her major crusade, and she, more than anyone else, may be taken as the "mother" of physical-education programs for women. Vassar, following Beecher's lead, established one of the first collegiate programs in physical education and trained hundreds of young women, who planted the seeds of physical education in institutions of higher learning all over the country. Vassar stressed "euthenics," the science of wholesome living: proper diet, exercise, comfortable clothes, dance, and music.

When Sophia Smith, a spinster, inherited a fortune from a miserly brother, she decided, on the advice of her pastor, John Morton Graves (who first tried to get her fortune for his alma mater, Amherst), to leave her estate for the establishment of a women's college. The result was Smith College at Northampton, Massachusetts, which opened for business in 1875.

Wellesley College opened the same year as Smith. It, too, was notably progressive, combining Christian piety with the newest ideas in education. It led its sister colleges in the development of the sciences and offered its students well-equipped laboratories. Wellesley had a graduate school of physical education and boasted of an art building, a museum, a chapel, and an impressive library.

The founder of Wellesley was Henry Fowle Durant, a notable eccentric, born Henry Welles Smith in Hanover, New Hampshire. A graduate of Harvard, Smith/Durant became a successful lawyer, then was born-again as a devout Christian (which he apparently felt was inconsistent with being a successful lawyer), changed his name with his change of faith, became an evangelical minister and a dedicated abolitionist. Like many male abolitionists, he was also a champion of women's rights, among them the right to higher education. He was the college's first president, and when he died in 1881, he was succeeded by Alice Freeman, making Wellesley one of only two colleges with female presidents, Mount Holyoke being the other. Alice Freeman was a graduate of the University of Michigan and had been head of the Wellesley history department. In 1887 she resigned as president of Wellesley to marry George Herbert Palmer, a Harvard professor of philosophy and natural religion.

A life of Christian service was stressed at Wellesley, whose motto was *Non Ministrari sed Ministrare,* "Not Being Ministered Unto, but to Minister." One graduate, Eleanor Franzen Churchill, wrote years later: "As I look in my mirror of memories, I see myself, the daughter of a Swedish Lutheran minister, entering Wellesley as a timid, shy, reserved, 'greasy-grind' type of introvert, and leaving it four years later, an idealistic extravert, committed to giving my life to the betterment of the people of the world." Eleanor Franzen's way was to go to Bombay, India, as Congregational "teacher-missionary." Later, in Berea, Kentucky, she and her husband started the Churchill Weavers to provide jobs for the young men and women from the hills and hollows of Appalachia who were attending Berea.

Wellesley College, like a number of its sister institutions, took special pains to enroll black students and students from the Far and Middle East. Marguerite Stitt Church recalled: "The outlook was broad, the vision high, as our sights were raised to help us become useful citizens in an unfolding world. I have always been proud, for instance, that it was daily contact with black, yellow and white fellow students . . . which taught me that everywhere and forever 'people are people,' wherever you find them. And

Wellesley's nearly all-woman faculty included giants in their day. Their influence lasts."

A Japanese student, Tamali Uemura, returned to Japan and founded the Kashiwago Presbyterian Church. She subsequently conducted Bible studies for the royal family and attributed to Wellesley "the new sort of womanhood, which I made my own . . . during my four years of study there."

Ellen Fitz Pendleton, president of Wellesley for twenty-five years, was "concerned that vast areas of the world—Asia, Africa, Latin America—were technically not part of our cultural tradition and could therefore quite respectably be neglected. . . ." Pendleton tried to compensate in various ways to make Wellesley students more aware of other cultural traditions. One measure was the establishment of ties with a sister college in China, the Women's College of Yenching University (started by missionary women). There was an exchange of faculty as well as students between the two colleges. Mayling Soong returned to China to become a leader in a number of reform causes, among them legislation to abolish child labor and improve the status of women, and to marry Chiang Kai-shek, Generalissimo of Nationalist China. A British visitor to Wellesley was impressed by the academic achievements of the students but, he added, "how does it affect their chances for marriage."

Bryn Mawr College, in the Philadelphia suburbs, was opened in 1888. It was modeled after Johns Hopkins in its commitment to public service, and soon it began to offer advanced degrees, one of the first women's colleges to do so.

The Ivy League women's colleges performed an important function in developing new areas of the curriculum. They were centers of intellectual life and educational innovation. Most were far stronger in the arts than their male counterparts. What we call today the "health sciences" were also much emphasized. Nutrition was a field developed almost exclusively in women's colleges. Hygiene and euthenics were also stressed (euthenics became "domestic science" and then "home economics"). These fields were avenues of access into colleges and universities for thousands of professionally oriented women. What developed as a "women's curriculum" was, in fact, more intelligent, humane, and "progressive" than the curriculum in such places as Yale and Princeton.

The intellectual stimulus and excitement in the women's colleges were in large measure generated by the conviction on the part of the students that they were engaged in a great new venture. To them, women's colleges were an important if not essential aspect of God's plan for the emancipation of their sex and the redemption of the world. The three principal channels into which the energies of women college graduates flowed were: domestic reform, most strikingly perhaps in the "settlement houses" for immigrants in most large cities modeled on Jane Addams' Hull House in Chicago, but in literally dozens of other reform movements as well; foreign missionary work; and school and college teaching (especially in the South and Midwest).

The significance of work in the missionary field is one that has been largely neglected by historians. India and China were the main areas of American missionary activity. By 1890 women predominated in every mission field. In the Near East women missionaries outnumbered men by a margin of almost two to one. In Japan women outnumbered men 283 to 146. Almost without exception, missionary women were college graduates. Many of them established schools for native women. Since they did not have to deal with conservative male school boards, they were able to introduce the most advanced pedagogical methods and subjects to their pupils. The ideas of John Dewey, who hated religion, were carried to remote missionary schools around the world by eager young women, lately of Wellesley or Smith.

At an intercollegiate meeting of Christian women, Isabel Trowbridge Merrill addressed "The College Girls of America," assuring them that "the life of a missionary is the happiest, most joyous, most satisfying one I know. . . . A college girl's whole training is toward activity and what else can give her so much pleasure and satisfaction as to be in an environment that calls out all her powers and gives her a chance to live a vital life that tells? Oh, girls, it pays so many times over. And if *we* do not take Christ to the women and girls in Turkey, *who will?*" The simple fact is that American women college graduates played the major role in improving the often wretched condition of women in many foreign lands. The irony was that in the missionary field they enjoyed far more freedom, and indeed power, than they could have expected to exercise in their own country.

In 1934 a student at Mount Holyoke College, one of the greatest producers of women missionaries, wrote a poem about the college's missionary band:

> *Abigail Moore went out to India*
> *A century ago, and Susan Waite*
> *To China, and Fidelia Fiske embarked*
> *For Persian cities, from South Hadley Town.*
> *(South Hadley Town, where fertile seed was sown)*
> *And all across the world to desolate lands,*
> *And lands most desolate with humanity,*
> *They took their sisterhood, from northern ports*
> *Up the earth's slope to sea-surrounded reefs,*
> *Down the earth's curve to wave-embattled capes,*
> *To Egypt and Japan and Labrador,*
> *Hawaii, Turkey, and Colombia*
> *Yearly they went, not yearly to return—*
> *And not all to return at any time.*
>
> *Why did you go, Theresa, Abigail?*
> *God knows! Had you not faith? He knew indeed*
> *Who sent you, why a fire was in your hearts*
> *Burning for all the anguish of mankind,*
> *A torture and a light, until you took*
> *The cross upon your shoulders and went out*
> *To weep, and solace weeping and hunger; to feed*
> *Your thousands by the sea; forget your dreams*
> *And learn the truth of God, and finally*
> *To die worn out with fever, or dispatched*
> *With one neat flashing of a Chinese sword—*
> *So death was conquered and you might go home.*

The women's colleges preserved the ideal of Christian service long after it had faded from their male counterparts. The graduates of Johns Hopkins and its successors longed to "put *mind* in the service of the society." That was the loftiest dream of the Secular Democratic Consciousness. The women partook of the Classical Christian Consciousness. They wished to devote their *lives* to the service of the Lord, in the United States or in foreign lands. At the same time, they pursued their goal in the most enlightened spirit of the age, the best "science" married to the old Protestant dream of redemption.

One of the most burning educational issues in the post-war era was "coeducation," the admission of both men and women to a single institution. The Reverend John Todd spoke for the skeptics when he asked: "Must we crowd education on our daughters, and for the sake of having them intellectual, make them nervous, and their whole earthly existence a struggle between life and death?" The fact was, of course, that it was the radical evangelical denominational colleges that had pioneered coeducation. The rationale was simple enough. If blacks and whites were equal in the eyes of the Lord, it must be equally the case that men and women were. As we have noted Oberlin opened its doors to blacks and women. "Women are to be educated because we choose civilization rather than barbarism," a young Oberlin instructor announced. A visiting Scotsman, David Macrae, expressed the opinion that women benefited from being educated with men both intellectually "and in some respects morally." Concerned that coeducation might impair "the delicate modesty and refinement which constituted the opposite sex's greatest charm," he queried a young Oberlin graduate, who admitted that "the idea of kissing a girl who had studied anatomy, and knew quadratic equations, alarmed me at first, but after making the experiment, I found the kiss the sweetest I have ever got in my life."

The traditional concerns about male and female roles were never far from the surface. The story was told of an Oberlin student who, reporting exceptionally high grades to her father, asked if he was proud of her. He replied: "Yes, indeed, and if your husband happens to know anything about housekeeping, sewing and cooking, I am sure your married life will be very happy."

Antioch College in Yellow Springs, Ohio, was, like Oberlin, a strong abolitionist institution, and it, too, admitted women from its inception. Knox College at Galesburg, Illinois, which opened its doors in 1841, was also coeducational.

By 1872 there were ninety-seven coeducational colleges and universities in the United States, the great majority of them, like Oberlin, Antioch, and Knox, denominational institutions. Of the ninety-seven, sixty-seven were in the Middle and Far West and seventeen in the South. New England counted only five.

The lead in private universities was taken by Cornell, where women were given equal status with men in 1872. Before women were admitted, however, the president, Andrew White, made an informal survey of existing coeducational institutions to determine whether coeducation produced "strong-minded" women and "unmanly" men. Oberlin and Antioch were of special interest to White. They had been admitting women for a generation. Presumably, if there were hazards in coeducation, they would be apparent at those institutions. White came back reassured that coeducation failed to make male students effeminate. "[F]rom no Colleges," he assured nervous trustees, "did a more hardy, manly, brave body of young men go into our Union armies than from Oberlin and Antioch." Even after coeducation was instituted at Cornell, there were some awkward episodes. William C. Russell, the vice-president of Cornell, admitted in 1879: "When I heard of a lady student calling one young man into the room, shutting the door, kissing him, it produced distress which embittered months of existence."

Much of the opposition to coeducation in private universities came from alumni and students. A Vanderbilt student noted that "No man wants to come home at night and find his wife testing some new process for manufacturing oleomargarine, or in the observatory sweeping the heavens for a comet."

The solution to the pressure on the private Eastern universities to admit women was met by something that came to be called "joint instruction." In the late 1870s Arthur Gilman, a Harvard graduate, and his wife began giving instruction to women in the Cambridge community. They were joined by Harvard professors, and in 1882 the Society for the Collegiate Instruction of Women was chartered. Known as the Harvard Annex, it was recharted in 1892 as Radcliffe College. Elizabeth Agassiz, wife of the naturalist Louis Agassiz, was the first head of the new institution. Following the lead of Harvard and Radcliffe, Barnard College became a kind of adjunct of Columbia, as did Pembroke to Brown and Sophie Newcomb to Tulane.

The real story of higher education for women in the United States, at least quantitatively, is to be found in the history of the state universities, especially those in the Middle and Far West. In 1855 the University of Iowa accepted women. The University of Wisconsin followed suit in 1863. The board of visitors at the University of Wisconsin announced in 1872: "It is too late, amid the noontime splendors of the nineteenth century, to ignore the claims of women to higher education. . . . Whatever shall make her wiser and better, that she may learn; whatever knowledge she may be able to use, either in adding to her own happiness, or in promoting the happiness of others—that knowledge she may rightfully acquire." Wisconsin was followed by Missouri, Indiana, Michigan, and California. By 1898, 53 percent of the B.A. and Ph.D. degrees awarded by the University of Michigan went to women. In some universities women threatened to take over the institutions. At Northwestern the percentage of women was so high that an engineering program was instituted primarily in the hope of redressing the balance. Stanford in 1899 adopted a quota system to maintain a balance between men and women. By 1900, 71 percent of all American colleges were coeducational.

One consequence of coeducation for women was the tendency to herd them into the liberal-arts curriculum and to charge them with the responsibility for "culture." Another may have been the disposition of many males to look on cultural matters as feminine. As shrewd an observer as Henry Adams lamented the "feminization" of America.

There were two other discernible consequences of the founding of denominational women's colleges and the sensational growth in the numbers of women attending the large state universities of the West and Midwest. Many of the women who graduated from Mount Holyoke, Smith, Wellesley, and Vassar became celibates, married to careers. As I have noted, they were reformers, missionaries, and teachers. In the coeducational state universities, young men and women commonly found mates with whom they shared intellectual and/or career interests. They thus pioneered a new kind of marriage in which husband and wife, like Lester Ward and his first wife, Lizzie Voight, or Robert La Follette and his wife, Beth Case, both of whom had law degrees, enjoyed a degree of mutuality seldom observed in traditional marriages.

8
THE WAR BETWEEN SCIENCE AND RELIGION

"It is wonder—not mere curiosity, one of the lower virtues common also to cats, but wonder, a sense of enchantment, of respect for the mysteries, of love for the other—that is essential to the information and techniques and knowing that seeks insight and understanding."

—E. F. SCHUMACHER

As bitter as the "war between capital and labor," if less protracted, was *The War Between Science and Religion,* the title of a book by Andrew White, the president of Cornell. White argued, incidentally, that there need be no war, that each had its own place and was part of the truth of human existence.

The enlightened "religious" view was well expressed by Newman Smyth, a graduate of Bowdoin College and Andover Theological Seminary, who wrote in *Old Faiths in New Light* that Christians must begin "by accepting loyally the results of scientific research into the present constitution of things." As a general law, evolution was an arresting explanation of the development of the natural world. "Our objection to evolution," Smyth wrote, "is not that it may not be true, but that, if proved true, it is only a half-truth. . . . A philosophy worthy of the name must admit both sciences—the science of the natural and the science of the spiritual which transcends nature—or its conclusions will be only half-truths. . . . Nature is not a mere collection of specimens preserved for our dissection; and philosophy has a higher task to fulfill than to keep the doors of a world-museum. There is an 'inner life of things,' and a unity of the spirit in the creation."

University presidents, caught in a cross-fire between religiously

inclined parents and alumni and faculties increasingly determined
to exclude religion in any form from their bailiwicks, lost no opportunity to assure nervous parents that their universities were no
threat to the religious convictions of their sons and daughters.
They did their best to dispel the rumors that professors were an
ungodly lot and that skepticism and infidelity reigned on university
campuses. Their strategy was to denounce "sectarianism," the
often contentious divisions between various denominations and
"sects" (sects being religious groups anxious to be promoted to
denominations), while constantly affirming the institutions' dedication to "spiritual values."

When Andrew White declared in his inaugural address that "the
sectarian spirit has been the worst foe of enlarged university education," he was referring to the dogged rear-guard action of the
denominational colleges against the rise of the universities. It was
the contention of the embattled clergy and their lay supporters
that the emergence of the university signaled the elevation of the
"practical" and "material" over the "spiritual." Ezra Cornell himself
had announced that his university's aim would be "to make true
Christian men, without dwarfing or paring them down to fit the
narrow gauge of any sect," and the university's charter specified
that "persons of every religious denomination, or of no religious
denomination shall be equally eligible to all offices and appointments." Such statements fanned the flames of controversy. Prospective students were warned that they would become "raw
recruits for Satan" if they enrolled at Cornell (or similarly secular
institutions). President Noah Porter of Yale accused Cornell of
leading the forces of secularism.

When Johns Hopkins opened its doors, the notorious British
agnostic T. H. Huxley was invited to give an address. There was
no opening prayer or benediction. A Baltimore divine approved
the omission of the benediction on the grounds that "It was bad
enough to invite Huxley. It were better to have asked God to be
present. It would have been absurd to ask them both."

Anxious to negate such criticisms, Daniel Coit Gilman wrote:
"Among the characteristics of a university I name the defense of
ideality, the maintenance of spiritualism." The university should

recognize "every where the religious nature of man, considered individually, and the religious basis of the society into which Americans are born." In another address, Gilman contrasted: "Earth and man, nature and the supernatural, letters and science, the humanities and the realities, are the current terms of contrast between the two groups and there are no signs these distinctions will ever vanish."

Many faculty members of the old school, like Josiah Royce, joined in such assurances. Royce declared that the "American University" was "daily more ideal in its undertakings, more genuinely spiritual in its enthusiasm and in its scholarship, and really far less Philistine in its concerns than was the American College of former days." American society would not and should not abandon the field to the "practical and progressive" forces without an assurance that the aspects of human experience comprehended under the general rubric of religion would somehow be preserved. Sectarianism, it was clear, must go. The lifeless routines of formal religious observance and doctrinal rigidity devoid of enlivening passion must be replaced by a higher and nobler "spirituality," by attention to the great themes of human existence—love, loyalty, courage, fidelity, faith, hope, devotion to the public good, reverence for the accumulated experience of the race passed down through generations in the form of wisdom. Only so could the "material" and "practical" and "progressive" be prevented from becoming a new form of Philistinism. Royce was convinced that "science" would soon reveal itself as the ally and not the enemy of the disinterested "intellectual and moral life." The "University ideal" was already revealing itself as "an ideal higher, more theoretical, more scholarly, less 'popular' in the evil sense of the word, than its predecessor." "Strange, and yet inevitable, and most instructive, union of the spiritual and bodily concerns of men!" Royce exulted. "Classical scholarship" would not die. "The 'greatest minds of antiquity' will still speak to the world . . . ! 'Discipline' will in the end prosper. . . . Religion will arouse as much thought and devotion as ever." The new "Science curriculum," a still-undefined thing, would work in happy unity with the best and most enduring of the "traditional curriculum."

A fact that the defenders of the traditional curriculum commonly overlooked was that it had become a study of "mere words," devoid of life, vitality, and meaning. Advocates of the old order charged that the new scientific curriculum was concerned with "mere things" (as contrasted with "mere words"). The fact was, Royce declared, that "Classical study, if it was ever a study of *mere* words, must learn a lesson from the example of natural science, and become indeed a study of the things of the spirit." Wherever the "parallel course" of the old studies and the new had been instituted, they had proved to "the lovers of true literature and of human life the most inspiring of rivals, the friendliest of allies, although disguised as enemies. . . . [T]he exclusive opposition between 'words' and 'things' has no meaning," Royce concluded triumphantly. The truth was "at once Word *and* Thing, thought *and* object, insight *and* apprehension, law and content, form and matter." The traditional course for undergraduates must be "supplemented by higher courses, wherein the scholar as such should have a chance to have his say, to present his truth, to indicate the recent advance of his science. The real aim of the so-called materialists was not the substitution of "things" for "words" but "the training of the soul."

Despite the continuing erosion of religious belief among intellectuals and academics, Royce remained confident that some compromise could be reached between the scientists and the religionists. He wrote that the "academic study of Philosophy is preparing the way for a needed spiritual guidance in the religious crisis which is rapidly becoming serious," and he was encouraged by "the rapid progress in attracting students" to the Harvard philosophy department. It was philosophers who could best be relied on to interpret the old religious faith in a spirit compatible with the new scientific approach.

Such assurances had an increasingly hollow ring. It was, after all, the "father" of American sociology, Lester Ward, who had been one of the founders of the National Liberal Reform League. The manifesto of the league, started in 1870, made no bones about who the enemy was. The league had been established for "the dissemination of liberal sentiment; the opposition to all forms of superstition; the exposition of all fallacious moral and religious doctrines. . . ." The main objects of attack were to be "the leading doctrinal teachings of the so-called Catholic and Evangelical Protestant Churches," with the intention of promoting "the triumph of reason and science over faith and theology." Membership in the league was secret in order to prevent retribution from the devout. In its appeal for members, the league called on all Americans who shared its principles—"Liberals, Skeptics, Infidels, Secularists, Unitarians, Socialists, Positivists, Spiritualists, Deists, Theists, Pantheists, Atheists, Freethinkers, all who desire the mental emancipation of mankind from the trammels of superstition. . . ."

It was left to one, Clifford, whom William James called "that delicious *enfant terrible*," to pronounce the epitaph of religion. "Belief is desecrated when given to unproved and unquestioned statements for the solace and private pleasure of the believer," Clifford wrote. To believe on insufficient evidence was "sinful because it is stolen in defiance of one's duty to mankind. That duty is to guard ourselves from such beliefs as from a pestilence which may shortly master our own body and then spread to the rest of the town. . . . It is wrong always, everywhere, and for every one, to believe anything upon insufficient evidence." Clifford's likening belief on "insufficient evidence" to a plague or pestilence is worth noting. He does not overstate the case of the "scientific sceptic" who came to dominate the academic scene by the 1890s.

In the *Will to Believe,* James saw himself as battling the dogmatic intolerance of science for any belief based on Clifford's "insufficient evidence," which meant in effect any *"belief"*—certainly any *religious* belief in the conventional sense of the word "religious." Belief and faith, the will to believe, if they were not essentials of human life, were modes of thinking (and feeling) about the universe that must be allowed and, further, respected. To believe was to run a risk, to bet one's life on the outcome. "No one of us ought to issue vetoes to the other," James wrote, "nor should we bandy words of abuse. We ought, on the contrary, delicately and profoundly to respect one another's mental freedom; then only shall we bring about the intellectual republic; then only shall we have that spirit of inner tolerance without which all our outer tolerance is soulless and which is empiricism's glory; then only shall we live and let live, in speculative as well as in practical things."

The academic world, or the scientific temper that dominated, was deaf as an adder or a stone to James' plea for tolerance. Deviations from the faith of science would no more be tolerated than the deviations from the faith of orthodox Christians. Less, indeed, for science had grown up under the wing of the universal church.

It seemed to James that the scientist had nothing to fear from "the freest competition of the various faiths with one another . . . from the liveliest possible state of fermentation in the religious world of his time. . . . He should welcome . . . every species of religious agitation and discussion, so long as he is willing to allow that some religious hypothesis *may* be true." Many scientists, unwilling to make such a concession, "maintain that science has already ruled all possible religious hypotheses out of court. . . . With all such scientists, as well as with their allies outside of science, my quarrel openly lies. . . ."

James wrote in 1900: "The problem I have set for myself is a hard one: *first,* to defend (against all the prejudices of my 'class') 'experience' against 'philosophy' as being the real backbone of the world's religious life—I mean prayer, guidance, and all that sort of thing immediately and privately felt, as against high and noble views of our destiny and the world's meaning, and *second,* to make the hearer or the reader believe . . . that although all the special manifestations of religion may have been absurd (I mean its creeds and theories), yet the life of it as a whole is mankind's most important function." This was, in essence, James' theme in *The Varieties of Religious Experience.*

James described pragmatism as a turning "away from abstraction and insufficiency, from verbal solutions, from bad *a priori* reasons, from fixed principles, closed systems, and pretended absolutes and origins." The pragmatist "turns towards concreteness and adequacy, towards facts, towards action, towards power. . . . It means the open air and possibilities of nature, as against dogma, artifi-

ciality, and the pretence of finality in truth." As for religion, pragmatism was neutral on that issue, "so we may believe, on the proofs
that religious experience affords, that higher powers exist and are
at work to save the world on ideal lines similar to our own." James
was confident that pragmatism would prove to be "something quite
like the protestant reformation."

Men and women needed, in James' view, to be made "convinc-
ingly aware of the presence of a sphere of life larger and more
powerful than our usual consciousness, with which the latter is
nevertheless continued. The impressions and impulsions and emotions and excitements which we thence receive help us to live,
they find invincible assurance of a world beyond the sense, they
melt our hearts and communicate significance and value to everything and make us happy. . . . Religion in this way is absolutely
indestructible. . . . Something, not our immediate self, does act
on our life!"

In response to a questionnaire on his religious beliefs, James
wrote: " 'God', to me, is not the only spiritual reality to believe
in. Religion means primarily a universe of spiritual relations sur-
rounding the earthly practical one, not merely relations of 'value'
but agencies and their activities." James was convinced that " 'normal' or 'sane' consciousness is so small a part of actual experience.
We e'er be true, *it* is not true exclusively, as philistine scientific
opinion assumes." There was "a much wider universe of experiences" for the individual to choose from. When a friend evoked
the authority of "scientists," James replied rather tartly: "Of all
the insufficient authorities as to the total nature of reality give
me the scientists. . . . Their interests are most incomplete and
their professional conceit and bigotry immense. I know no nar-
rower sect or club, in spite of their excellent authority in the lines
of fact they have explored, and their splendid achievement there."

James' friend and former student John Jay Chapman echoed his
mentor: "There never lived a set of men more blinded by dogma,
blinded to the meaning of the past, to the trend of the future, by
the belief that they had found a new truth. Not one of them can
lift the stone and show what lies under Darwin's demonstration.
They run about with little pamphlets and proclaim a New Universe

like Frenchmen. They bundle up all beliefs into a great Dogma of Unbelief, and throw away the kernel of life with the shell. This was inevitable. A generation or two was well sacrificed, in this latest fusillade of the Dogma of Science—the old guard dogma that dies but never surrenders."

With the passing years, James' relations with his colleagues in the Harvard philosophy department grew distant. They objected to his "free and easy personal way of writing." His style made him, James wrote, "an object of loathing to many respectable minds." They abhorred anything that was not impersonal and "objective." James contrasted the primness of his colleagues with the "enthusiasm" and "literary swing" of a group of young Italians he met at a philosophical gathering in Florence. They had a spirit that was quite lacking in Cambridge, where, as he wrote his wife, "our damned academic technics and Ph.D.-machinery and university organization prevents [anything] from ever coming to birth." He grew impatient "with the awful abstract rigmarole in which our American philosophers obscure the truth. It will be fatal," he wrote to Dickinson Miller. ". . . It means utter relaxation of intellectual duty, and God will smite it. If there's anything he hates, it's that kind of oozy writing."

James was glad to retire. A professor at Harvard, he wrote to Theodore Flournoy, had come to have only two functions: "(1) To be learned and distribute bibliographical information; (2) to communicate truth. The 1st function is the essential one, officially considered. The 2nd is the only one I care for. Hitherto I have always felt like a humbug as a professor, for I am weak in the first requirement. Now I can live for the second with a good conscience." Retired, James was free to live "for truth pure and simple, instead of for truth accommodated to the most unheard-of requirements set by others. . . ."

In 1910 the journalist Edwin Slosson undertook to survey a dozen "Great American Universities." He reported that "the old warfare between science and classics" was "practically over." That the scientists had triumphed was true enough, but Slosson thought he discerned a widespread disillusionment with their triumph. There was a feeling that science had had "its chance" and had not "made good." It had been in the saddle, Slosson wrote, for almost a generation (he dated its rise from the late 1870s). The products of "scientific" training were "not so distinguished by their broad-mindedness, tolerance, practicality, truthfulness, logical power and freedom from superstition and like infirmities, as to demonstrate the intrinsic superiority of scientific training." Indeed, it was evident everywhere that "the evils resulting from poor teaching of the sciences are the same and quite as great as those produced by poor teaching of the classics." Nonetheless, it was clear that the National Liberal League and its allies had triumphed. The George Herrons and the William Jameses had been routed. Although most Americans remained doggedly religious, academic fundamentalism banished from the academy any form of belief for which there was "insufficient evidence" except the belief in the immutability and sufficiency of Science.

"Science after Darwin's time," Chapman wrote, "was seized with a fever of world conquest; its language must dominate. In correct circles it became bad form to use any word that was tinged with theology. New words were invented; modern psychology was developed. . . . The word 'God' was, of course, taboo, unfair, incorrect, a boorish survival." Religion was an illusion; "methods of accurate research had recorded a zero."

9
PH.D. AND TENURE

"When the habitual behavior of a man or an institution is false, the next step is complete demoralization. And hence to degeneracy, for it is not possible for anyone to submit to the falsification of his nature without losing his self-respect."

—José Ortega y Gasset

There seems little doubt from the perspective of the present day that the introduction of the Ph.D. as the so-called union card of the profession was, if not a disaster, an unfortunate and retrograde step. William James was dismayed at what he called "the Mandarin disease" of the Ph.D., a "Teutonic" invention, completely foreign to American ways. "To interfere with the free development of talent," he wrote, "to obstruct the natural display of supply and demand in the teaching profession, to foster academic snobbery by the prestige of certain privileged institutions, to transfer accredited value from essential manhood to an outward badge, to blight hopes and promote invidious sentiments, to divert the attention of aspiring youth from direct dealings with truth to the passing of examinations . . . ought surely to be regarded as a drawback. . . ." James exhorted colleges and universities to "give up their unspeakably silly ambition to spangle their lists of offices with these doctoral titles" and to "look more to substance than to vanity and sham. . . . Are we Americans," he asked, ". . . destined after all to hunger after similar [Germanic] vanities on an infinitely more contemptible scale? And is individuality with us also to count for nothing unless stamped and licensed and authenticated by some title-giving machine? Let us pray that our ancient national genius may long preserve vitality enough to guard us from a future so unmanly and so unbeautiful!"

It seems to me hard to improve on James' jeremiad on the Ph.D. We have become so accustomed to it, it is so ingrained in our ways of thinking about higher education, that we consider it part of the natural order of the universe. It is difficult to perceive its absurdity or fully understand the damage it has done to the intellectual and moral basis of higher education. To take only the most obvious example, the Ph.D. has shifted the responsibility for making a decision about the appointment of a junior faculty member from the institution doing the hiring (where, of course, the responsibility *should* lie) to the institution doing the certifying. It is rather like USDA-certified Grade A beef. Beef is inspected and graded on the well-grounded assumption that the consumer is not qualified to make such a judgment himself/herself. But does any hiring institution wish to make such a claim in regard to a future colleague?

As between two Ph.D. holders of equal academic ability, is anyone prepared to argue that the one stamped and certified by Harvard University is not going to be preferred, except in rare instances, to one certified by Western Illinois University? Or poor Slippery Rock, if it now grants Ph.D.'s? As the holder of a prized (and generally, I regret to say, overrated) Harvard Ph.D., I am acutely aware of the lead I had over equally qualified rivals for the better academic prizes; the more insecure an upscale university feels, the more disposed it is to opt for those prestigious degrees.

Further, the Ph.D. takes an unconscionable time to acquire in the fields that I know best. Five years is a minimum in history, for instance. Six or seven years is not infrequent, and ten or fifteen by no means unknown. I got mine in the relatively speedy time of five years, despite various well-planned impediments—e.g., a "mastery" of two foreign languages, typically French and German. The theory behind the language requirement was that German was "the language of scholarship." As for French, or Spanish or whatever, the rationale was vaguer. The fact was that, whether German was the language of scholarship or not, it no longer is, and it has little or no relevance, in any event, to the study of

American history. I have, for my sins, written twenty books and never felt the need to consult any work in the German language, which I have long since forgotten. Indeed, three or four years after I had displayed my "mastery" of German, I couldn't translate a page of German history text, and I would bet a bundle that the same would be true for the vast majority of my fellow "Americanists," as we are generically referred to. One might well ask why reason or humanity didn't prevail and allow such a meaningless (and time-consuming) requirement to be dropped. Well, primarily because it had no rational basis to begin with; it was simply a genuflection to the ideal of German scholarship, an incantation, a bit of ritual magic, an expression of the conviction that, if the history Ph.D. were to be taken seriously when placed beside Ph.D.'s in chemistry or physics, it had to take as long and be as arduous to achieve. How could history justify its claim to be a social *science* if all that was needed to qualify was a few days' conversation with a working historian, a half-dozen or so courses in the major and related fields, and a modest piece of research? I can only say that I learned more about how to go about historical research in an evening's conversation in Philadelphia with an eccentric amateur historian named Jack Powell than I learned in any combination of Harvard seminars or courses. But you can be sure that if it had been proposed to the Harvard history department that it take measures to adjust input to output—that is to say, to shorten the time required for the Ph.D. to some sensible time period or rational set of tasks—the cry would immediately have been raised that to do so would "cheapen the degree," the tacit admission being that the measure was time, not ability, or, as the irreverent sociologist Pitrim Sorokin put it, a Harvard Ph.D. required "only patience." I suspect one could write a fair-sized book on the psychological, intellectual, and, yes, moral implications of being forced to waste such an increment of time in order to satisfy formal requirements, and to do so in an environment presumably dedicated to the pursuit of truth (in the company of footnotes).

It was as a candidate for the Ph.D. at Harvard that I first encountered the Cult of Dullness. Since boyhood I had aspired to be a writer. I was not sure what kind of writer, but some kind.

So with my first graduate research paper I tried to write as well as I could. My professor, the urbane Crane Brinton, warned me gently that, although he himself did not object to a well-written paper (I don't see how it could have been *very* well written at best; it was on some obscure point of natural law), his colleagues might be put off. They might suspect that I was not really committed to dull writing (he didn't put it exactly that way) and thus not a suitable candidate for the Ph.D. I encountered the problem again when I sent my doctoral dissertation to a typist to have it typed up for presentation to my readers, who would approve or disapprove it. The typist called shortly to express her concern. It did not read like a Ph.D. Was I sure it would be acceptable? What was the problem? I asked. Well, she was enjoying reading it, and that made her uneasy on my account. She was concerned that it might not be accepted. It was not as dull as she felt it ought to be. (It might be said, parenthetically, that my dissertation was far from a distinguished piece of literature; since it was subsequently published, it is easy for a reader to confirm this judgment.) Based on my own experience and some reading of Ph.D. dissertations, I don't think it is going too far to say that what William James called "oozy writing" is required. I believe it is also the case that oozy writing encourages oozy thinking. I am reminded of Alfred North Whitehead's comment that style grows out of the "love of a subject in and for itself. . . . Style is the ultimate morality of mind." The Cult of Dullness not only survives; it flourishes. In the words of the art critic Harold Rosenberg, "No degree of dullness can safeguard a work against the determination of critics to find it fascinating."

The most basic requirement for the doctoral dissertation is that it has to be "original" research, in order to add to the body of knowledge in a particular field. There is, of course, nothing inherently wrong with originality. But there is, after all, only so much originality available at any one time, and what is put forward as "originality" should be tested against what has come, through time, to constitute "wisdom."

In practice, the shallowest and most jejune originality came to be preferred to the most time-tested wisdom. In science, "originality" had to stand the test of verification in the laboratories of other scientists, before it could claim to be a fact, but the non-sciences were subject to no such rigorous tests. "Original" propositions and hypotheses were simply buttressed by footnotes and bibliographies. These might, it is true, be reviewed by other researchers and rejected as insufficient or interpreted differently, but in essence they succeeded or failed to the degree that they were persuasive and fitted in with the intellectual atmosphere or the scholarly fads of the hour. Thus, when a "materialistic" or "scientific" approach to reality was in vogue, it did not take any special eloquence or mustering of "evidence" to "prove" to the satisfaction of most readers that, let us say, the American Revolution and the Civil War were the direct consequences of economic factors.

Not only is the Ph.D. dissertation constrained by the requirement that it be original (in the sense of dealing with material never dealt with before) and dull; it must also conform to the prejudices of the examiners. In other words, it must not be too original. Especially on the theoretical side, it must be compatible with the current "thinking" in the field. It must not be too advanced, and it must have no truck with notions now considered obsolete (although in fact these obsolete notions often return in time as the latest findings). It thus manages the not inconsiderable feat of being both stultifying and capricious. Two stories will illustrate the capriciousness of the system. In the June 1988 issue of *Encounter* magazine, Elie Kedourie, professor of politics at the University of London and one of the best-known scholars of the Middle East, tells of his failure to attain a D.Phil. at Oxford (the D.Phil. being the British equivalent of the Ph.D.). Kedourie submitted his dissertation on "England and the Middle East" to his examiners, the famous Sir Hamilton Gibb, dean of Near East studies at Oxford, and James Joll, another well-known scholar. When Kedourie met with his examiners, Gibb was in an obvious state of agitation. He informed Kedourie that the basic thesis of his dissertation was wrong. When Kedourie asked for specific instances based on missing or incorrect facts, Gibb waved his questions aside. The dissertation was unacceptable in its present form; he must change it in order to have it accepted. Kedourie refused. Gibb had not challenged his facts; he had quite arbitrarily ruled against Kedourie's conclusions based on facts he did not bother to challenge. As Kedourie explained to a university official: "To my detailed and patient reconstruction of events and policies . . . the examiners have opposed nebulous speculations . . . and have pretended by virtue only of their academic position, to force their opinions on me." Rather than submit, Kedourie withdrew his dissertation, later published as an important book, and abandoned his effort to win a D.Phil.

Since the British academic world is not as obsessed with the D.Phil. as the American academic world is with the Ph.D., and since Kedourie had a powerful advocate in Michael Oakeshott at the University of London, his academic career did not suffer. Had the same drama been played out in the United States, his career would undoubtedly have been over then and there. Much the same thing happened to the well-known defense analyst Roberta Wohlstetter, whose *Pearl Harbor: Warning and Decision* won a Bancroft Prize in 1962. When Wohlstetter was a graduate student in literature at Harvard, she wrote a dissertation in Renaissance literature that disturbed the prejudices of her thesis director. When he told her she would have to change her interpretation (much in the spirit in which Sir Hamilton Gibb told Kedourie he would have to change his conclusions about British Middle Eastern policy), Wohlstetter refused and withdrew from the Ph.D. program.

Such stories could be multiplied many times over. The point is that, in most instances, a graduate student must conform to the prejudices of his readers or abandon any hope of having a successful academic career.

I will spare the reader further recounting of the inanities (and horrors) of the Ph.D.—the oral "qualifying exam," the rejected dissertation, the lost dissertation, the delayed dissertation. It is all too grim for words. In any event, that the Ph.D. is an incubus on higher education can, I assume, hardly be doubted. To James' question as to whether we were destined to "hunger after . . . [Germanic] vanities" the answer is clearly in the affirmative. Americans love degrees with an unabating passion, and there is no sign that we are ready to follow a more humane or rational course.

When intelligent and decent people do foolish and cruel things, it seems safe to assume that they are the victims of institutions that encourage or demand such behavior. Such I believe to be the case with tenure. It is a major premise of this work that tenure and its partner in crime, the Ph.D., have inflicted what may turn out to be fatal wounds on higher education. The argument originally advanced for tenure was that professors needed to be protected in the expression of unpopular views by having an unusual degree—one might even say, an unprecedented degree—of security of employment. The fact is that, even after tenure had been accepted by all major universities, boards of trustees did not hesitate to fire professors who professed ideas that the trustees found objectionable. A number of instances have been mentioned. Professors of Marxist persuasion, for example, were weeded out, often with the help or at least concurrence of their colleagues whenever the "threat" of communism in the United States was considered sufficiently dire, which was, in fact, whenever the trustees said the threat was dire. This was invariably done on the grounds that the Marxist professors couldn't be "objective" because they had given their allegiance to a particular dogma or doctrine, and a "foreign" one at that. Thus they were violating the academy's "hypocritical oath," to be completely objective in all things. All the other professors were assumed to be objective as long as *they* said nothing offensive. As it turned out in one of the greatest of the American universities, the faculty members didn't even have to profess anything to be canned; they just had to refuse to sign an oath declaring their loyalty to the government of the United States and the state of California, a requirement that the regents felt no reasonable professor would scruple to sign.

The initial fight for tenure served a far more immediate and practical end. In the words of Laurence Veysey, author of *The Emergence of the American University:* "Demand for professorial tenure was in large measure a quest for security." Veysey quotes a candid Henry Seidel Canby: "Our strongest desire was to be made safe, to stay where we were on a living wage, to be secure while we worked. . . . We were dependent upon the college, which itself was always pressed for money, and could not be counted upon to be either judicious or just." In other words, the motives of the professors were no different from the motives of steel-workers or coal miners: they wished job security and proper procedures for protecting their right to due process. In actual fact, tenure seems to have been of more service in protecting professors accused of moral turpitude (or what the general public considered moral turpitude, which might be no more than getting a divorce) than in protecting professors' right to speak out on controversial issues. For one thing, by the time a faculty member had made his careful, laborious way up the "ladder," he or she had demonstrated a dutiful compliance with the standards of the institution. Indeed, if the basic purpose of tenure was to protect the faculty member in the expression of unpopular or unorthodox opinions, it would clearly be most valuable to a faculty member at the beginning of his career.

The fight for tenure was thus far less a fight for the right to express unpopular opinions than against an imperious and auto-cratic administration. Whatever its motivation, tenure turned out to exercise a decidedly negative influence on higher education. What faculty needed and deserved to have was review procedures that protected them from arbitrary actions by administrators or trustees. What they got was much more: a degree of security unequaled by any other profession and difficult to justify in abstract terms.

The campus of the University of California, Santa Cruz, has, like most University of California campuses, a number of faculty committees, among them a Committee on Educational Policy, on Privilege and Tenure, on Course Approval, on almost *ad infinitum*. In addition, they have innumerable *ad hoc* committees appointed to evaluate the scholarly progress of their colleagues, specifically their output or productivity in terms of research and publication. Since every faculty member must be evaluated every few years (advances in salary are usually in two-year increments—i.e., two years in first-step assistant professor, two years in step two, etc., on up to full professor), this debilitating process of constant review takes literally uncounted faculty hours, causes much grief, and often results in highly questionable or blatantly unfair decisions, leading, in that wonderfully revealing word, to "terminations," or, more happily, to tenure.

Since the assistant professor knows well that tenure depends almost exclusively on research/publication, you may imagine where his/her principal attention is directed. What is much more difficult to imagine is the strain that this barbarous system places on the psyches of the young men and women subjected to it. By the time they are considered ripe for tenure, they have spent some twelve to fifteen of the most important and formative years of their lives preparing for this moment (five or six, typically, in graduate school, six or seven in anticipation of tenure). What this does to their nerves, their families, their, as we like to say today, "self-esteem" should be evident. They live for seven years in a state of suspended animation, not knowing whether they are to be turned out in disgrace by their friends and colleagues or retained. The university, of course, comforts itself with the assurance that its decisions are entirely objective and unchallengeably fair.

These decisions, affecting people's lives in the most profound ways, are made by, one must assume, conscientious individuals, but they are nonetheless chancy in the extreme. Everyone who has spent any time in the academic world has a veritable anthology of horror stories revolving around the issue of tenure. Indeed, I have my own tale of tenure to tell. My academic advancement rested on precarious and (as it turned out) fortuitous circumstances. I had been invited to come to the UCLA department of history at the top step of the assistant professorship on the basis of the assurance of an editor of a university press that my Harvard dissertation, a rather pedestrian biography of James Wilson, one of the Founding Fathers, had, for all practical purposes, been accepted for publication. It was nice to have the modest amount of extra money that a second- or third-step (or whatever it was) assistant professor received, but the catch was that in two years I would be up for evaluation for promotion to associate professor, which brought with it TENURE. If, for any reason, the publication of my biography was delayed, or the press changed its editorial mind, I might find my stay at UCLA a brief one.

A year or so after my arrival in southern California, I received a letter from the editor of the press. One of their readers or referees, who had dallied so long over reading my manuscript that the press, having had two affirmative readings, had decided to go ahead with plans for publication, finally checked in with his criticism. His recommendation: the subject was not an appropriate one for a conventional biography, because relatively little was known of the subject's life. However, since he was unquestionably an important and original thinker, I should be asked to rewrite the manuscript as a critical study of James Wilson, political theorist. Since the TENURE decision was bearing down on me with alarming speed, I was frantic. I couldn't possibly drop a heavy teaching load, rewrite the manuscript from top to bottom, and then go through, once more, the long, uncertain review process. I said, in effect, This is it. Take it or leave it. No rewriting, no study of Wilson as a political theorist (that was, in fact, already in the biography). Fortunately for my career as an academic historian, the press decided to go ahead with publication. Even so, the book was not "off the press" in time to be considered by my TENURE committee; the members had to be (and were) satisfied to read the book in page proof. They considered it acceptable and I got TENURE. I have since written nineteen other books, including this one, and immodesty requires that I note that eight of them were Book-of-the-Month Club Main Selections (and one was an alternate), which is not, of course, to suggest that they are monuments of scholarship. My point is that, if the press had been sticky and my book had not been published or had been substantially delayed, I doubtless would not have received TENURE, in which case I would have had to go away in disgrace and would probably have ended up a faro dealer in Las Vegas or a secondhand-car salesman in Santa Monica.

I have a catalogue of similarly dramatic tales concerning others, many of them ending in major or minor tragedies. One of my favorite ones, because it suggests the capriciousness of the whole system of promotion, concerns a colleague of mine at UCLA whom

I shall call J.K. J.K. was too bright and satirical for his own promotion. He offended the tender sensibilities of his senior colleagues, something that it is disconcertingly easy to do in the
academic world. J.K. was "up for" promotion to full professor.
He had TENURE, but to have been halted at the top step of associate after years of service to the university would have been
the kind of humiliation that the university did not hesitate to visit
on those who "failed to remain productive" after acquiring
TENURE. J.K. had written a monograph on the Rhineland policies
of Marshal Foch (as I recall) and submitted it to the University
of California Press for publication—publication that would, presumably, assure his advancement to FULL PROFESSOR. The practice
was that the press depended on the recommendation of a "de-
partmental reading committee" dominated by—guess who?—senior colleagues of J.K., several of whom had no personal use for
J.K. However, supposedly putting their personal prejudices aside
and judging the monograph strictly on its own merits, they decided
that it was not up to the standards of the UCLA history department
and thus of the University of California Press. When word of this
decision was conveyed to J.K. with, it may be imagined, pious
regrets, he flew into such a rage that he was shortly hospitalized
with a spastic colon, a malady commonly associated with stress.

Fortunately, J.K. had had the prudence to take out a kind of
academic insurance policy. Without proclaiming the fact, he had
submitted his manuscript to the Harvard University Press in a
competition for the best work in the field of modern European
history for that year, the winner to be published with some fanfare
by the Harvard University Press. As in any good Grade-B movie,
truth and justice triumphed. J.K.'s monograph won the prestigious
prize as the best in the U.S. By the time of the announcement,
J.K. had been, as we have seen, turned down for his FULL PROFES-
SORSHIP, had recovered from his spastic colon, and was resigning
himself to spending the rest of his academic life on a shelf labeled
"Permanent Associate Professor by Virtue of Scholarly Inade-
quacies." When news of the prize-leading-to-publication reached
southern California, it caused some consternation. J.K. was promoted to FULL PROFESSOR *retroactively* as of the date he would

have been promoted had it been determined that his monograph was up to UCLA's standards. I have always valued the episode as the only known case where Harvard has effected the promotion of a UCLA professor while that professor was at UCLA.

That the most brilliant teaching will not save a young assistant professor if he/she fails to achieve the minimum standard of research/publication (many institutions like to point to an occasional exception, but the occasional exception has had to endure the humiliation of being just that, an exception, and he/she is never allowed to forget it) is well known. One form of humiliation in the University of California system is what is called "moral tenure." If a faculty member is retained for an eighth year, he or she is considered to have "moral tenure." Such rare survivors are generally stripped of their professorial title and taken off "the ladder." The ladder is the means by which junior professors climb up to the various benefits, including frequent "sabbaticals"—a sabbatical being, traditionally, every seventh year off for research uninterrupted by even the modest and constantly diminishing amount of teaching required when not on sabbatical. The sabbatical has been improved on in many institutions by an ingenious invention called a "semi-sabbatical." The semi-sabbatical comes at the end of three years. It is a half-year off, which, combined with the regular three months off in the summer, gives the professor three-quarters of a year off for research, a popular option with many faculty. Lately the university has employed another arrangement: an increasing dependence on "lecturers," heavily concentrated in the areas of language instruction and remedial English. They are denied the lofty title of professor, paid less, required to teach many more hours since they are not expected to publish books and articles; they are the peons of the academic world, second-class citizens in a supposedly democratic community of scholars.

Bad as the tenure system has been, there are indications that it is getting worse. Bowen and Schuster's study of tenure suggests that many faculty are highly, if privately, critical of the system. "At many campuses," Bowen and Schuster report, "that until recently had only infrequently denied tenure, the lives of countless assistant professors were filled with dread or resignation, as the result of a confluence of factors. First, vacancies were scarce; many departments—especially in the humanities—were already heavily tenured-in, and those departments that still had one or two professors were understandably ambivalent about becoming 100 percent tenured." One problem with departments that are "heavily tenured" is that student preferences are highly volatile. If student enrollments shift, for example, from English to psychology, and the English department is filled with tenured faculty members and a diminishing pool of students, bad feeling may arise between colleagues in literature and psychology. The authors point out that the declining percentage of junior faculty members in recent years who receive tenure has caused additional anxiety. "Coupled with low salaries and high living costs in urban areas, the probationary period for young faculty members was often a grueling and lonely ordeal." The researchers found that even tenured faculty, especially in the associate-professor rank, "felt threatened by the new emphasis on research. At the research universities, where promotion to full professor has long depended on a respectable promotions record," nothing much had changed. "But at those institutions where the criteria for promotion are shifting, where effective teaching or even mere longevity were no longer sufficient for promotion to full professor, mid-career faculty were feeling the pinch." Bowen and Schuster found that such campuses were "legion." Faculty insecurity was increased by the consciousness that there was a "new breed of well-trained young faculty fixated on scholarship and performing—albeit out of dire necessity—at levels heretofore rarely seen on campus." At many campuses that in the past had placed a strong emphasis on teaching, the pressures to publish had increased greatly. In consequence, the "non-tenured faculty on the tenure track were under great stress." This was evident from their own testimony "but also from the comments of many senior faculty and administrators who observed their plight." Under such pressures, many junior faculty members "had ceased to function as fully participating members of their campus communities . . . as they 'burrowed toward tenure.' "

One assistant professor of English told Bowen and Schuster, "I like the University. . . . I feel that I'm doing all the right things—

but it may not help. . . . I am a stone realist. I see my predicament as a function of larger social forces. I understand that I was born too late. If I had been born ten years earlier . . . I'd probably be an associate or full professor at a more prestigious institution."

A study conducted by Dwight R. Ladd in 1979 reported that three-fourths of the faculty surveyed agreed "that their interests lean toward teaching (as contrasted with research) and agree that *teaching effectiveness, not publications, should be the primary criterion for promotion of faculty"* (italics mine).

In recent years some of the most excruciating decisions on tenure have involved "minority" faculty, specifically women and blacks and, more recently, Hispanics. Universities have been under great pressure in the last decade or two to appoint minorities to "ladder" faculty positions. Some administrations, prodded by threats of withheld government funding, have imposed a quota system on departments—you must hire X number of women, blacks, minorities in general. All well and good, but female and especially black academics are in short supply. It is a seller's market. Not infrequently, representatives of minorities are hired whose qualifications (at least as the university specifies them) are uncertain. Even if they appear highly qualified, there is always an element of uncertainty, just as there is with white males: can the appointee turn out the required amount of what passes for research in time to meet the dreaded tenure deadline? Sometimes, of course, the answer is "no." Something close to panic ensues. Minorities are so scarce that the thought of discarding one is alarming. Moreover, the minority faculty member has a minority following who are often devoutly attached to him or her and who can be counted on to make a considerable fuss. Often the charge is the familiar one of racism or sexism. The faculty and administration usually feel that they have bent over backward to try to begin to rectify the racial and sexual imbalance in the faculty, an imbalance that is the result of generations of indifference, if not actual discrimination. Finally, there is the fact that minorities are often very vocal in charging "institutional racism," a rather comprehensive term that covers not only the racial imbalance in the faculty and in the student body but the perhaps more basic fact that the underlying concepts and principles in the various established academic disciplines outside the hard sciences are seen by minorities as white male distortions of much more complex realities, realities that include them and their cultures. It is small wonder, for example, that a Mexican American from a culture steeped in Hispanic Roman Catholicism finds the aggressively secular tone of the American university campus cold and uncongenial; the same for blacks and Arabs and Cambodians. In making a more or less respectable effort to include as many representatives of as many minorities as possible, the university, its curricular practices, and even the assumptions underlying its various disciplines often come under fire. This relatively recent development has added to the already considerable disarray of the academic noncommunity.

To me, the tenure ritual is comparable to ancient rites of human sacrifice. If a certain number of nontenured faculty are not terminated each year at University X, the general impression gets around that University X is not upholding proper academic standards, and University X suffers in the eyes of the academic world. Conversely, University Y is admired for its hard-nosed policy. Fortunately, one consequence of a growing disenchantment with the whole tenure process is the number of court cases brought by faculty members who think they have been treated unfairly. Twenty years ago such cases were virtually unheard of; now they are commonplace, and in a number of instances courts have ordered universities to reverse negative decisions on tenure or have granted litigants substantial sums of money on the grounds that they have been unjustly terminated.

10
HIGHER EDUCATION IN THE TWENTIETH CENTURY

"An education that does not give promises is not education.
Claiming to give facts, and facts only, is a declaration of
bankruptcy. Present day teaching is a series of farewell parties to
life."

—EUGEN ROSENSTOCK-HUESSY

The victory of William McKinley over William Jennings Bryan in
1900 was seen as a devastating setback for the forces of reform,
but the assassination of McKinley in September 1901, eight
months after he assumed office, and the succession of Theodore
Roosevelt to the presidency revived the flagging spirits of the
reformers and renewed the faith that something could be done to
curb the rapacity of Capital. As Lincoln Steffens, the muckraking
journalist, put it, "[W]e reformers went up in the air . . . took our
bearings, and flew straight to our first president, T.R." It was an
extraordinary moment: Progressives rallied behind the President;
young men and women inside and outside of the universities offered their services to the ebullient Teddy, who could hardly contain his joy over the good fortune that had befallen him.

Elected for a term in his own right in 1904, Roosevelt declined
to run for a second full term, confident that his handpicked successor, the amiable, porcine William Howard Taft, would carry
on the work of reform begun so spectacularly by Roosevelt. The
Progressives soon found themselves crowded out of the Taft inner
circle by Old Guard Republicans who made it clear that they
intended to reassert their domination of the party. An indignant
Roosevelt returned from safari in Africa to do battle with the

Republican troglodytes. At the Republican nominating convention in 1912, the forces of reaction met and defeated the forces of reform once more rallied under the flag of Progressivism.

Roosevelt was denied the nomination. "His offense in the eyes of the capitalistic class," Brooks Adams wrote, "was not what he had actually done for he had done nothing seriously to injure them. The crime they resented was the assertion of the principle of equality before the law, for equality before the law signified the end of privilege to operate beyond the range of the law."

Roosevelt decided to run as a third-party candidate of the National Progressive Party or, as it was more commonly called, the Bull Moose Party. William Allen White, the editor of the Emporia *Gazette,* was a delegate to the Bull Moose convention; the other delegates, he wrote, were "our own kind." Many were women: "women doctors, women lawyers, women teachers, college professors. . . ." With the Republican Party split, Roosevelt and Taft both went down to defeat. Woodrow Wilson, an ex-professor, was elected President of the United States. To the Progressives, recently riding high, all seemed lost. A dismayed Brooks Adams set about to rummage through history for examples of ruling or "capitalist" classes who, rather than accept a reasonable degree of reform, had clung to every article of privilege until open revolution brought them down. History indicated, if it did not prove, "that privileged classes seldom have the intelligence to protect themselves by adaption [to moderate reforms] when nature turns against them, and," Adams added, "up to the present moment, the old privileged class in the United States has shown little promise of being an exception to the rule." The bulwark of privilege had, in other societies, always been the courts. "So long as our courts retain their present functions no comprehensible administrative reform is possible." To support his thesis, Adams skipped from Uriah's grievances against Solomon for appropriating Uriah's wife to Charles II of England's use of the courts to support his arbitrary acts. Adams then went on to review the conflict between Hamilton and Jefferson over the nature of the Constitution. Indeed, the greater portion of Adams' book, which was titled *The Theory of Social Revolutions,* was concerned with the Supreme

Court's abuse of its powers in negating legislation designed to put the brakes on a runaway capitalism. Adams also gave much attention to the French Revolution and its aftermath. It was, in his view, an example of what might (or must) happen when an unjust and oppressive class was determined to resist social change. When, for example, a ruling class had appropriated an undue portion of the land, "a redistribution of property must occur, distressing, as previous redistributions have been, in proportion to the inflexibility of the sufferers." The "modern capitalist," Adams argued, "looks upon life as a financial combat of a very specialized kind. . . . He conceives sovereign powers to be for sale. He may, he thinks, buy them; and if he buys them he may use them as he pleases," confident that his "bought justice" will sustain him. "If he is restrained by legislation, that legislation is an oppression and an outrage, to be annulled or eluded by any means which will not lead to the penitentiary. . . . The capitalist . . . is of all citizens the most lawless."

If capitalism looked to the courts to protect its special privileges, it looked with equal confidence to the universities. "In the United States," Adams continued, "capital has long owned the leading universities by right of purchase, as it has owned the highways [the railroads], the currency, and the press, and capital has used the universities . . . to develop capitalistic ideas. . . . [C]apital has commercialized education."

What society needed most, Adams argued, was "the generalizing mind," a mind that, in generalizing, was apt to be critical of the *status quo* and capitalism's appropriation of the common wealth, the forests and mines, the oil wells and natural resources. Capitalism preferred the "specialized mind and that not of the highest quality." Science and technology were the handmaidens of capitalism. Under the stimulus of capital with its vast sums of money, "the scientific mind has now become an actual menace to order," Adams wrote, "because of the inferiority of the administrative intelligence." In other words, science dominated the administrations of the major universities and used them to its own ends. Adams professed to see "incipient signs of disintegration all about us." There was a "universal contempt for law," most evident "in the capitalistic class itself. . . . We see it even more distinctly in the chronic war between capital and labor . . . and perhaps most disquieting of all, we see it in the dissolution of the family which has, for untold ages, been the seat of discipline and the foundation of authority."

Brooks Adams ended *The Theory of Social Revolutions* with speculation about how "industrial capital" might extricate itself from the ruin that it was bringing upon the country. He assumed the capitalists would flee with what they could carry with them of their ill-gained fortunes when the revolution came.

Brooks Adams' somber reflections on the nation's future were common forebodings. William Allen White called his wife after the defeat of the Progressives in Chicago and wept bitterly over the telephone.

Before hope could revive with the emergence of Woodrow Wilson's own broad program of reform, World War I broke out in Europe. It was another staggering blow to the Progressive faith. Somehow the heralds of the new age had failed. Most of them could not bring themselves to consider the possibility that history might be impervious to the rule of enlightened minds. At just that moment when the course of history should have started to move in an ever-upward spiral propelled by trained and disciplined minds drawing on the discoveries of new social sciences, a disaster of almost inconceivable proportions burst upon the world. Many of the prophets of the new age could not at first credit reports of the conflagration sweeping Europe. The news shattered too many prized illusions. The whole vast structure of education, research, and scholarship was called into question. What had been the purpose, then, of this colossal effort of will, this unprecedented melding of science and money, fountains and cascades of money, buildings, laboratories, professional schools, technological innovations on a scale never before imagined? Half the world seemed bent on its own destruction to no understandable rational end. No one could comprehend or explain the cause, or causes, of the most terrible cataclysm in history.

Like the rest of the nation, the academic world was sharply divided over the question of America's involvement in the European war. When Wilson, running at least in part on the slogan "He kept us out of war," brought the United States in not long after his re-election, the divisions grew far deeper.

The American Association of University Professors issued guidelines for faculty members: "If a speaker should declare that all participation in war is immoral, or should praise the example of the Russian troops who deserted their posts and betrayed their allies, or should assert that the payment of war taxes is contrary to sound ethical principles—such a speaker may be presumed to know that the *natural tendency* of his words is to stir up hostility to the law and induce such of his hearers as are influenced by him to refuse to perform certain of the obligations of citizenship." Under this formula a number of faculty members were fired. Nicholas Murray Butler, the president of Columbia, sacked Henry Wadsworth Longfellow Dana (one would have thought his combination of distinguished New England names alone would have saved him) and the psychologist James Cattell, a graduate of—where else—Johns Hopkins. John Dewey issued a strong protest, and the historian Charles Beard resigned from Columbia. A young philosophy professor at the University of Wisconsin, Carl Haessler, opposed the war and the draft and was convicted and sent to prison. Haessler was only one of a number of American academics who suffered for their convictions.

If the repressive measures of Wilson's administration alienated many academics, all was forgiven when he issued his famous Fourteen Points, calling, among other things, for the self-determination of people long under the thumb of authoritarian and alien regimes. The horrors of the war, if they could not be wiped away, would at least be expiated by establishing a universal system of justice which would begin by redrawing the map of Europe so that all peoples who had suffered under the rule of powerful neighbors (or, as we would say today, "dominant ethnic groups") would be freed from such servitude, their freedom guaranteed by a "league of nations" dedicated to preserving peace.

To presume to resolve ancient European rivalries, many sealed by centuries of conflict, at one fell stroke may have been astonishingly naïve, but it was also indubitably American and thoroughly in the spirit of the first generation of Johns Hopkins students who believed that scholarship should be used to ameliorate the ills of the nation and, indeed, the world.

Woodrow Wilson, who was probably a closet socialist and who had helped to create the reforming zeal of the Hopkins era, hit on the idea of assembling a team of scholars, geographers, historians, and assorted academic experts to assist him in remaking the world. He would take them with him when he went to encounter his European allies. Thus mind would be enlisted in behalf of humanity on a scale exceeding the wildest dreams of the scholar reformers. Where they had directed their attention to reforming the municipal governments of Cincinnati and Philadelphia, the whole world would now be their research library and their classroom. The idea of transferring a line, determined by patient researches in the archives of European history, from a map to the terrain between, say, Yugoslavia (a new invention in itself) and Italy in such a fashion as to put finally to rest all passions and all bitterness was an intoxicating prospect. Florence Harriman, a pillar of the Democratic Party, wrote in her diary in March 1919: "It seems to me that God has given the world a new Pentacost to make a new Crusade. The old crusade was made to save an old tomb, the new is to bring the benison of God on every baby's cradle. A better chance for education, for housing; and for every female child an opportunity such as has never been dreamt of before. . . . [L]et us be grateful every day that we have been given the chance to take part in this great world movement towards brotherhood and peace."

The assembly of scholars was called, modestly, the "Inquiry." Walter Lippmann was its secretary, and Isaiah Bowman was the head of the section on territorial claims. Bowman had done graduate work at Harvard and taught geography at Yale before becoming head of the American Geographical Society in 1915. At forty-one he was one of the older members of the Inquiry. Lippmann wrote to Newton D. Baker that what he was looking for was "genius—sheer, startling genius, and nothing else will do." Baker, Wilson's Secretary of War, was a graduate of Johns Hopkins. Like Frederic Howe, he had been an aide to Tom Johnson in the reform of Cleveland's municipal politics and served as mayor of that city. Another important member of the Inquiry was Sidney Edward Mezes, a graduate of the University of California with a Ph.D. from Harvard. Mezes was president of the College of the City of New York. Charles Homer Haskins was a graduate of Johns Hopkins, and dean of graduate studies at Harvard. "Basic maps," Mezes wrote, "were constructed for the whole of Europe and the Near East. . . . In volume this was one of the largest undertakings of The Inquiry . . . aiding as it did, toward an understanding of the most contentious regions the Conference had to consider." Frederic Howe was a member of the Inquiry as an expert on the Near East.

It was generally conceded by peace-commission members from other nations that the Americans were the most knowledgeable and best prepared on the various details that had to be considered. But it soon became clear that the combination of ancient fears and animosities and modern greed would be more powerful determinants than scholarly judgments. As the Versailles Treaty process wore on, the members of the American delegation, peace commissioners and members of the Inquiry alike, grew more and more disillusioned. Trained intelligence, scientific knowledge, and patient scholarship seemed, in the last analysis, to weigh little in the scales of history.

Bernard Berenson found Walter Lippmann at his desk in the offices of the Committee on Public Information. "I came to ask you," Berenson later wrote to Lippmann, "whether you were aware that we Americans are being betrayed, that no attention was being paid to our aims in the war, and that a most disastrous peace treaty was being forged." Lippmann's eyes, Berenson later recalled, filled with tears.

Lincoln Steffens predicted that another war would break out before many years had passed. Jan Smuts, the great South African leader, wrote that the world was being "thrust into ruin. . . . And so instead of making peace we make war, and are going to reduce Europe to ruin. . . . What a ghastly tragedy this is!"

The treaty process ended in disaster. Perhaps never before or since in human history was so much hope (and intelligence) invested in a task that came to such an unhappy conclusion. The relevance of the Inquiry to the major themes of this work is, I trust, obvious. The vision of the original Hopkinsites (and that vision was of course not limited by any means to Hopkins, although Hopkins was its inspiration and exemplar) had languished. Its acolytes had, for the most part, failed to effect the social and political changes that they had hoped for. The Inquiry seemed for a moment to revive the dream. It was followed by crushing disillusionment and by a period (the twenties) of hedonistic self-indulgence.

It seems safe to assume that this course of events contributed significantly to the disposition of professors, already evident, to withdraw ever further into their "scientific" researches. A natural consequence was that the researches became more and more for their own sake, for the sake of research itself, and less with the intention of improving the world.

The morale of the academic community was not improved by acrimonious disputes that broke out among historians over the responsibility for the war. Each faction claimed to be more scientific than the other; the simple nastiness of the debate was unnerving. Finally, a kind of consensus emerged: it was the fault of the international munitions makers, men like Du Pont in the United States and Krupp in Germany. They had brought war on in order to make profits selling munitions to all parties involved. That hypothesis seemed to satisfy almost everyone except, of course, the Du Ponts, Morgans, et al., but one might be forgiven for questioning how "scientific" it was.

In the field of education generally, the ideas of John Dewey, disseminated through the highly influential Columbia Teachers College, came into their own. The notion of a practical education for "citizenship" achieved an almost universal acceptance. Even revolutionary China proved susceptible to Dewey's influence. General Sun Yat-sen invited Dewey to create a modern curriculum for Chinese schoolchildren. McGuffey's great readers were replaced by textbooks on civics. The old morality of good and evil gave way to the new morality of adjustment. One-room schoolhouses (150,000 in 1930) were replaced by "consolidated" schools which offered a much wider, if somewhat shallower, range of subjects.

The twenties saw a sharp drop in the number of professors fired for unorthodoxy. It was, after all, a time not of conflicting ideologies or sharply drawn political lines (although many intellectuals and some academics drifted into the Communist or Socialist parties), it was a generally unbuttoned time of jazz, hip flasks, raccoon coats, rolled stockings, the Charleston, rumble seats, sorority and frat life. The students went one way and the professors another. Of the gap between professors and students, the reporter Edwin Slosson wrote: "The less personal attention [the students] get from their professors the better some of them like it." To the faculty the students seemed frivolous and anti-intellectual. To the students the faculty seemed remote and uninterested. A student journal entitled *The New Student* voiced a common lament in 1927: "Where we used to dream of new faith and new communities developing out of the colleges and flowering through a thankful country, now the main hope is that students will be less bored by lecturing. . . ."

Richard Sewall, professor of literature at Yale, recalled his own undergraduate years as a time when "students wanted life." Not finding it in the classroom, they went "all-out for vitality and excitement wherever they could find it. . . . This was the era of The Lost Generation, of Joe College and Betty Co-ed, of the coonskin coat and the Chrysler roadster, of bootleg gin, and Red Grange. The faculties looked on (as I remember) in a sort of dazed tolerance, not knowing quite what to do about it."

Although the business of higher education went on much as usual during the 1920s, deep dissatisfactions lay below the surface and were manifest by a number of new "experimental" colleges founded during that period. In Bennington, Vermont, a women's college was started with the aim of freeing students from academic routines and encouraging creativity. Strong emphasis was placed on independent study, and the arts were featured. Sarah Lawrence in New York City was another women's college committed to undergraduate instruction, to small classes and close contact between teachers and students.

One of the most prominent educational reformers was Robert Hutchins, the youthful president of the University of Chicago who started a "college" within the university. Hutchins blamed most of the ills of American higher education on Americans' "love of money." It was the love of money that led to the large numbers of students crowding university campuses. It was the necessity of dealing with large numbers that had produced "the American system of educational measurement. Under this system the intellectual progress of the young," Hutchins wrote, "is determined by the time they have been in attendance, the number of hours they have sat in classes, and the proportion of what they have been told that they can repeat on examinations given by the teachers who told it to them. . . . Undoubtedly, fine associations, fine buildings, green grass, good food, and exercise are excellent things for anybody," Hutchins wrote. "You will note that they are exactly what is advertised by every resort hotel. The only reason why they are also advertised by every college and university is that we have no coherent educational program to announce."

Quite appropriately, the embodiment of Hutchins' educational principles, Saint John's College in Annapolis, Maryland, had no department of history. It had (and has), indeed, no departments at all, which was certainly a notable improvement over the typical institution of higher education. Students and faculty meet in informal seminar settings to discuss great thoughts as presented in "the great books" from Plato to modern times.

Abraham Flexner, whose famed study of medical education in the United States laid the basis for the modern medical school, turned his attention to American universities. As he described it, they were "composed of three parts: they are secondary schools and colleges for boys and girls; graduate and professional schools for advanced students; 'service' stations for the general public. The three sorts are not distinct; the college is confused with the 'service' station and perhaps the graduate school; the graduate school is partly a college, partly a vocational school, and partly an institution of university grade. . . ." Flexner's criticisms were similar to those of Edwin Slosson a decade or so earlier. The classes were too large, the teaching often perfunctory, and the system of "credits and units" common to most universities and colleges "an abominable system, destructive of disinterested and protracted intellectual effort. . . . The hopelessness of America," Flexner added, lay "in the inability and unwillingness of those occupying seats of intelligence to distinguish between genuine culture and superficial veneer." Flexner scoffed at such dissertation topics as "Trends in Hosiery Advertising."

It should be noted that the neglect of undergraduate students did not pass unnoticed, especially in the older Ivy League universities. Woodrow Wilson had established the so-called preceptorial method at Princeton. Every student had a preceptor, a faculty member assigned to guide his studies, to be a friend and counselor. Wilson saw it as "a means, not so much of instruction, as of intellectual development" through a kind of "intellectual contagion." He wished to combine the "intellectual and spiritual life." Although Wilson himself was often ill at ease in personal relations, he was an inspiring teacher, more through the force of his intellect than through close personal relations with his students.

A. Lawrence Lowell, the successor to Eliot as president of Harvard, was an enthusiastic recruit to Wilson's ideas. The preceptorial system at Princeton was matched by the Harvard "tutorial" and the construction of luxurious "houses" (instead of dormitories). The houses were conceived of as a series of small colleges, each with a "master" on the model of the colleges of Cambridge and Oxford, with common rooms and handsome oak-paneled dining halls. The students had suites, typically bedroom, living room, and bath. At Harvard the architecture was predominantly Georgian. The delicious meals were served by uniformed motherly Irish women (in order not to stimulate the libidos of the undergraduates). To a relatively uncivilized Dartmouth "Indian" it seemed, I well recall, positively sybaritic. After the war, as a graduate student and "tutor" at Winthrop House, I found life much more austere. In establishing the houses, the hope had been that faculty and students would find common ground there. The fact was that the job of tutor was soon foisted off on graduate students like myself and the houses largely failed in their objective of encouraging the social and intellectual mixing of faculty and students. The pull or, if you will, inertia of the research-and-graduate scheme of things proved irreversible. Although the houses provided a delightfully upper-class atmosphere for undergraduate students and undoubtedly relieved the disposition to morbidity and even suicide that had earlier been met by recruiting bishops and Boston social ladies, they failed in their primary purpose.

Yale, not to be outdone, built "colleges," again clearly with "Camford" in mind. Yale favored neo-Gothic architecture (as did Princeton). If the "great traditions of the past" could not be captured in the curriculum, they could be reproduced in the architecture. The Gothic campuses of Yale and Princeton had, to the Western visitor, a touch of the absurd, as though one had stumbled onto a Hollywood stage set. One expected to see knights on horseback and medieval ladies with their retinues. The architecture did not change or seriously challenge the dominance of science; it simply pointed up the incongruity of the whole enterprise. The buildings became archaic monuments to the tycoons who put up the dough. There was something engagingly incongruous (or perhaps unwittingly appropriate) about a Gothic tower erected in honor of a railroad tycoon or a mining baron.

The Harvard philosophy department in the 1920s was largely committed to some variety of logical positivism, "scientific" philosophy that brushed aside the old metaphysical questions in favor of propositions that could be proved by scientific methods. But there was one last brave gesture in Cambridge. Henry Osborn Taylor had been a student of Henry Adams, and Adams had infected him with his own passion for history. Taylor had subsequently studied Roman law at the University of Leipzig and after a brief and successful career as a lawyer had devoted himself to scholarship, writing two notable works, *The Classical Heritage of the Middle Ages* and *The Mediaeval Mind.* Now an old man, Taylor conspired with Lawrence Henderson, a revered professor of chemistry, to prevail on Harvard to appoint Alfred North Whitehead, recently retired from a long and distinguished career at Cambridge, England, to a chair in philosophy at Harvard. Whitehead arrived in 1925 at the age of sixty-four, and for the next nine years made his magnificent presence felt, to the chagrin of his philosophy colleagues, who viewed him as a relic of an outmoded era. Ignoring advice to give students no more than ten minutes' time lest they interfere with his scholarly work, Whitehead and his wife opened their home to students and created a lively salon. Single-handedly Whitehead fanned into flame the ashes of the fire that William James had so long tended. It brought back memories of earlier and better days and was doubtlessly a considerable satisfaction to Taylor.

The indifference or inattention of university faculties to social and political issues was evident to any observer. Frazier Hunt recalled his own undergraduate days with some bitterness. It was the "intolerance and complete isolation of our colleges and universities that deserved most criticism," he wrote. The professors had to conform. "Men with the slightest touch of divine discontent were unwanted. They were unsafe. The constant threat of excommunication by conservative trustees, legislatures and powerful graduates dampened and extinguished any brave spark of true questioning."

As though to reinforce Hunt's indictment, the universities showed little inclination to respond to the onset of the Great Depression. If one were to judge from the typical university curriculum, there was little, if any, recognition that the nation was entering the greatest crisis since the Civil War. On the university campuses it was business as usual. The institutions of higher learning suffered economically along with the rest of the country. Fewer students could afford to go to college. Faculties were forced to accept drastic cuts in salary; many were dismissed and few were hired. Without jobs there seemed to be little purpose in going to college. A popular song went:

> *I sing in praise of college,*
> *Of M.A.'s and Ph.D.'s,*
> *But in pursuit of knowledge*
> *We are starving by degrees.*

Little groups of student radicals appeared on some campuses. The Young Communist League recruited a handful of members here and there, and the American Student Union, a "front" for the league and the party, built up a substantial membership.

By far the most significant aspect of the Depression for the academic world was the recruitment by the New Deal of hundreds of academics. As governor of New York, Franklin Roosevelt had drawn on the advice of Columbia economics professors and political scientists. Rexford Guy Tugwell was an expert on agricultural matters, Raymond Moley and Adolph Berle were economists, Felix Frankfurter was an adviser on legal (and other) matters, William O. Douglas left the Yale Law School to join the administration. Roosevelt's advisers would have intellectual jam sessions that lasted for hours in lively and often heated exchanges while Roosevelt, for the most part, simply listened. Roosevelt had been an Assistant Secretary of the Navy under Wilson and considered himself a disciple of the Virginian. He was undoubtedly influenced, in assembling his Brain Trust, as it came to be called, by Wilson's recruiting of scholars for the Inquiry. Roosevelt had been a member of Wilson's entourage, and he observed the work of the Inquiry at first hand. So it might be said that an interrupted but traceable line ran from the Johns Hopkins of Frederic Howe and Josiah Royce to Franklin Roosevelt and his recruitment of scholars to advise him—not, of course, to mention those who were lured from university campuses to take jobs in his administration. Again it was a demonstration of the prospective advantages of an alliance between scholars and practical politicians.

From the end of the New Deal to the present day there have been no episodes comparable to the labors of the Inquiry or the contributions of the Brain Trust. Individual academics often act as advisers or consultants to government officials and administrators, but there have been no academics in government with influence comparable to that of a Moley, a Tugwell, or a Berle (unless, of course, it was Berle himself). Ironically, the closest we have come in recent years, John F. Kennedy aside, would be Ronald Reagan, who has undertaken to load up the federal bureaucracy with right-wing ideologues, many of them academics.

———

The most conspicuous feature of the immediately post–World War II years in academe was the "Red Hunt" carried out on many university campuses by the Dies Committee, aided and abetted by Senator McCarthy, whose line was communists in government, while the Dies Committee pursued radicals on college campuses and in the labor movement and the entertainment world. A period of extraordinary growth, stimulated by the GI Bill of Rights, took place after World War II as established campuses grew rapidly and new campuses by the dozen were built. In addition, a number of experimental colleges were started, testifying to a continuing conviction that something was seriously wrong with higher education.

Some of the experimental ventures were promising, but such vast sums of money and such expenditures of energy were required to accommodate the flood of students that there was little time or energy left for trying to do things more intelligently and humanely. Moreover, with the spell of science still unbroken, there was probably not much that could have been done. The controls were all in the hands of the academic fundamentalists.

As the powers of university presidents and chancellors declined with the passing of what Thorstein Veblen called the Captains of Erudition, academic departments became small baronies. John Lichtman, assistant professor of philosophy at the Berkeley campus of the University of California, was highly critical of the typical academic department, "where men competing for recognition establish small empires under a mutual security agreement that insures each the safety of his own domain. This safety is further enhanced against the forays of others by increasingly narrowing the limits of one's investigation until the subject is so esoteric that each individual can rightly claim to be the only living authority in the field."

There can be no question that the rise of departments contributed directly to the fragmentation of learning that distinguishes the modern university, and the American university most conspicuously. A "strong" chairman was someone who could negotiate more faculty positions for his department than "weak" chairmen in rival departments. Faculty positions, called FTEs (Full Time

Equivalents) in the University of California system, were the life-blood of departments. The more FTEs (it might be calculated, for instance, that a department needed—usually desperately?—two and a half FTEs; translated, that meant two full-time instructors and one half-time) a department could extract from the administration, the more powerful it became in relation to departments with fewer FTEs. One of the most reliable ways to accumulate FTEs was for a department to offer large courses required of all students or of all majors. Since FTEs were usually calculated on the basis of the number of students enrolled in courses taught in a particular department, the more students, the more FTEs. A premium was thus placed on large courses taught by a single instructor with a small army of poorly paid teaching assistants. In the FTE calculus, five hundred students in a required course in American history could provide a claim for several more FTEs. These FTEs would not, of course, teach in American history; they might well be in Chinese history of the Ming Dynasty or medieval English history and teach courses with a handful of curious undergraduates. Their primary responsibility would be to a comparably small number of graduate students. The department also kept a jealous eye on its members to be sure they did not stray from their assigned fields. I remember well a poor wretch hired as a kind of backup man for me in colonial American history who, doubtless hoping to crawl out from under my shadow, asked to be permitted to teach a course in the Jacksonian period, a vast span of some fifteen years, thereby provoking the reproach of a senior colleague who allowed that he had never been sure of the poor wretch's total commitment to colonial American history; his worst suspicions had now been confirmed. The poor wretch did not survive. He was terminated.

The evils of departments are too extensive to catalogue here. It is sufficient to say that they are the conservative if not reactionary core of the existing system, and one dares to say it will never be reformed until they are dismantled, or at least greatly curtailed. The loyalty of the average professor is not to his students or to the institution that employs him but to his department and, even more deeply, to his "field," for it is his field, or the scholars in his field, who ultimately validate him as a scholar and, indeed, a worthy person. Again, in the words of Lichtman: "The immediate result [of the power of the department] is that the University is more and more populated by scholar-researchers who more closely resemble idiot-savants than men of wisdom; students find it more and more difficult to gain some comprehensive vision of themselves as world-historical beings." It was the department, in the person of the chairman, who stood at the shoulder of the young instructor, cautioning him not to get too involved in teaching lest he fail to publish and thus perish.

The university withdrew from an intractable world. It prized erudition and despised the "popular." What the uninitiated could understand was not worth understanding. Plainness and simplicity, directness and intelligibility were placed under the ban, along with any remnants of the older concerns, at first quite evident in the new learning, for the larger questions of existence—the meaning of life and death, the nature of love, the grounds of hope and faith, all those elements of human nature that William James, Josiah Royce, and other evangels of the "moral" or "spiritual" life had fought so hard to preserve in the face of the hostility of science. The fact was that science was the only clear benefactor of the collapse of faith that followed the almost incomprehensible disasters of the new century. Freed of any lingering constraints from the "religious" or "spiritual" side, freed, moreover, from responsibility to any "outside constituency," to any locus except that of their disciplines, science presided over an increasingly barren inheritance.

11
GENERAL EDUCATION / WESTERN CIVILIZATION

> "Compared with the medieval university, the contemporary university has developed the mere seed of professional instruction into an enormous activity; it has added the function of research; and it has abandoned almost entirely the teaching or transmission of culture."
>
> —JOSÉ ORTEGA Y GASSET

In 1885 David Starr Jordan, then president of Indiana University, developed the notion of requiring or encouraging a "major" for students. The idea was for the student to emphasize a particular subject or discipline rather than simply taking either the "old" classical curriculum or the newly fashionable "elective," the latter being, in essence, whatever a student's interests or whims or the latest academic fashion might dictate. From the beginning of the "new" studies, an anxiety about throwing the baby out with the bathwater was evident in virtually all discussions about what constituted a proper education. When Yale embarked, in 1901, on a plan of "course concentration" (in effect, a major), it required "distribution" as well. The idea of "distribution" was that students, while being required to focus or concentrate their efforts in a particular academic area or "field," should have at least a smattering of knowledge about other fields. Thus an English major or "concentrator" should have a nodding acquaintance with the *arrivistes,* the social sciences, and, most important of all, the sciences. In 1905 Cornell designated four areas of knowledge in which students were expected to take course work. In most institutions such courses were already part of the curriculum; students had to choose one from among many "course offerings" in a particular field. For example, a political economy major might be able to satisfy his/her distribution requirement in English with a highly specialized course in, say, the Georgian poets, or medieval chansons, the idea being that what was important was not so much the specialized content of such courses but the "methodology" of the scholars in that field. Science presented a particular problem. Few students could satisfy the distribution requirement in science by taking an advanced course in calculus or physics. It thus became the common practice to offer simplified science courses for non-scientists. Many such courses were little more than formalities. Their principal function was to satisfy a rather dim notion of what "a general education" should be. They were therefore, doubtless with notable exceptions, more useful for appeasing the conscience of faculty than for giving nonmajors a real insight into "how science works."

The most popular alternative to "distribution" was a required course in "Civilization" or, as at Columbia in 1919, "Contemporary Civilization." In the words of James B. Crooks, professor of history at the University of North Florida: "Educators saw the difficulties in attempting to identify specific . . . courses [that], taken together, would constitute a 'general education,' " but they also felt the need for some unity or coherence among the proliferation of student choices. "Increasing numbers of academics," Crooks writes, "believed that all students should have some similar background for understanding their humanistic tradition, contemporary social issues, and the recent explosion of scientific knowledge." At least they felt that way every twenty years or so. The history of general education is thus a dizzy roller-coaster ride of ups and downs, of periods of busy reform followed by rapid decline and then a new surge of activity—conferences, studies, reports, fresh spasms of good intentions. In 1914 Alexander Meiklejohn, then president of Amherst College, initiated a freshman course entitled "Social and Economic Institutions." The next notable general-education fever came after World War II with the famous Harvard *Report on General Education in a Free Society.*

James Conant, the last of Harvard's "great" presidents and himself a scientist, declared that the West's "liberal and humane tradition" was "basic to civilization." The committee that prepared the report sought "a unifying purpose and idea" which must be conveyed to all students as part of any true education. This amounted to the "intellectual forces that have shaped the Western mind."

President Truman also appointed a commission to study higher education in the United States. Its conclusions were similar to those of the more famous Harvard "Report." It reaffirmed the need for "General Education" and called for a "core of unity" and "a body of common experiences and common knowledge . . . some communication of values, ideas and attitudes . . . as a cohesive force . . . the transmission of a common cultural heritage toward a common citizenship. . . ." The *Journal of General Education* was established to promote the cause. The argument between a specialized "scientific" education and one that stresses "the accumulated wisdom of the past" is the now familiar argument between Jefferson and Adams which has gone on, in one form or another, since the beginning of the republic. Although Jefferson and "science" have clearly carried the day, some residual guilt remains about completely abandoning the past.

Recently attention has been drawn to the issue of general education versus specialized education by the pronouncements of former Secretary of Education William Bennett and by Allan Bloom's *The Closing of the American Mind*. Both Bennett and Bloom have campaigned for required courses in Western Civilization. They have been rebutted by students and faculty arguing that courses in Western Civilization present students with an exclusively white, basically upper-class view of man's common cultural heritage. This argument seems to be related to the so-called opening-the-canon movement. The "canon" is, generally speaking, that body of works, from Plato to Freud and Marx, judged to be "great" or "classic," some in political thought, many in literature. These are works that, it is argued, no educated person should be without a knowledge of.

The arguments for "opening the canon" are various. Some clearly have a Marxist bias—i.e., that the canon has been determined on class lines. Some feminists and minorities attack the canon as sexist (too many males) or racist (not enough works from nonwhite cultures).

One consequence of Bloom's "closing of the American mind" and the counter-move to "open the canon" has been a number of conferences on the subject. Princeton and Cornell, among others, have hosted conferences. Professors, incidentally, seem to love conferences. I must say that to me they seem a dreadful penance, where the proportion of intellectual gold to dross is usually infinitesimal. But if professors are to bore their students, they might, I suppose, just as well bore each other. David Gaines, a professor of literature at Southwestern University in Georgetown, Texas, gives an entertaining account in the *American Way* magazine of a recent conference at Duke University on Bloom, Bennett, et al., described by one participant as "a mega-conference on canon reformation." At Duke, the canon-openers were in a clear majority. They were sympathetic to the student "Know-Nothings" who have no interest in books by "dead white guys."

I have considerable sympathy with the Know-Nothings in that I can see no reason, given the world as it is today, not to include a considerable non–Western Civilization element in any required general-education program. Otherwise, it does seem to me that the message is: Your culture is not as important as our culture. And it gives this message to "live white guys and gals" as well as to the "ethnics" or the "minorities" or whatever we are going to call those who are not white guys.

The point on which I am quite unyielding is that a historical perspective is far more essential to a healthy life than, let us say, a high-fiber diet or the Bhagwan or the Reverend Moon or any other modern-age palliative.

As for opening the canon—by all means, open it. Do anything that can be done to shake up the academic fundamentalists. For years, for example, Harriet Beecher Stowe (and *Uncle Tom's Cabin*) was dismissed by professors of American literature as second- or third-rate, not to be mentioned in the same breath with, say, Henry James or Mark Twain. There is certainly room for the opinion that *Uncle Tom's Cabin* is a far more brilliant achievement than all but one or two novels by Henry James. I recall the late Kenneth

Rexroth bemoaning the fact in the 1970s that at no campus of the far-flung University of California was there a course on our greatest poet, Walt Whitman (I trust this has been remedied). I have my own canon to offer in American history. I think, for example, that it is an open scandal that few of the American-history majors that I have had occasion to talk with have read such American classics as *Uncle Tom's Cabin,* Frederick Douglass' autobiography, William James' *Varieties of Religious Experience,* any of the remarkable writings of Jane Addams, Henry George's *Progress and Poverty,* John Bach McMaster's *History of the United States* (not to mention the works of Parkman, Prescott, Motley, and Bancroft), Henry Adams' *History of the United States During the Administrations of Jefferson and Madison*), any of George Templeton Strong's remarkable diary (one of the greatest diaries ever written), Lincoln Steffens' autobiography, W. E. B. Du Bois's *The Souls of Black Folk* (unless they were black or had wandered into a course on black history), or a dozen other great works that are, in my view, indispensable for any serious student of American history. So, by all means, open up the canon in American history. Throw out all the recent up-to-date, flabby little monographs (now required reading in most history courses) and replace them with the Right Historical Stuff, the heart and soul of our history, the thoughts and emotions, the passions and dreams of real people.

But back to Western Civilization. The Western Civilization programs have grown out of the uneasy awareness that the average college graduate's knowledge that the human race has a long, fascinating past is dim, and that without some knowledge of that past a man or woman cannot be fully human; he or she cannot be truly a person or at home in the world. Many societies do not give formal history training to their members, but virtually all such societies have history incorporated in their cultures in a way that makes it omnipresent for every man, woman, and child. From tribal myths that account for the origin and "history" of the tribes to such ancient cultures as those of China, Japan, and India, the past is a living presence.

Since our society is singularly lacking in such "cultural" representations of our past and cannot anticipate creating them—in large part because of the briefness of our past as a nation and the extraordinary variety of our multiform "pasts," pasts made up of the historical experience of every race and nation that has come to the United States before and since our birth as a republic—it is essential that we *learn* our past. It cannot be absorbed by the kind of cultural osmosis common to traditional societies. It must therefore be grasped intellectually. It must be studied and learned.

The great Existential philosopher Soloviev makes the point in the form of a folk tale. A young knight, lost in the woods, encounters an old crone. He asks the way out of the forest (the present). She agrees to guide him if he will carry her across a nearby stream. He willingly agrees, but as he crosses the stream with her on his back, she grows heavier and heavier, until he can hardly move. As he passes midstream, she grows lighter, and finally, when he reaches the far bank, he discovers that she has turned into a beautiful woman. The old crone, Soloviev tells us, is Clio, the muse of history. We must take her up and bear the burden of history if we are to find our way out of the trackless forest of the present.

That history is a burden cannot be doubted, nor dare we fail to take it up. The modern spirit is represented by the young hero of James Joyce's *Ulysses*: "History, Stephen said, is a nightmare from which I am trying to awake." Henry Ford's more down-to-earth comment was: "History is the bunk." Both are cries of the Secular Democratic Consciousness, the last echoes (one hopes) of the Enlightenment, which viewed history as a worthless tissue of superstition and error.

All the serious thinkers I know of speak as with a single voice on the critical importance of knowledge of the past, our collective memory. The individual without memory is unable to function in society. The condition is much the same with nations. In the familiar words of George Santayana, the nation that does not remember its past must repeat it. The only reasonably reputable contemporary I have come across who endorses the idea that knowledge of the achievements of the race is irrelevant is that spokesman for the counter-culture Theodore Roszak. He wrote: "It does no good at all to quote [Aristotle, Dante, and Thomas

Aquinas] to celebrate their insight, to adulate their wisdom. Of course they are wise and fine and noble, but they stand on the other side of the abyss."

I would like to suggest some obvious reasons for the failures of the recurrent efforts to find a secure and enduring place for Western or, better, World Civilization courses in the university. First and foremost, the universities' collective heart is not in the enterprise. To teach such a course in lectures in a style that will captivate and hold the attention of restless and inattentive young people with a thousand more pressing things on their minds requires great gifts of intellect and personality—such qualities as passion, conviction, wide knowledge, and genuine cultivation, as well as a gift for explicating and integrating complex and unfamiliar ideas and generalizing major themes. These qualities are, needless to say, in short supply in the university. The great majority of the faculty are neither interested in nor capable of organizing and teaching such a course. In addition to needing a brilliant and learned (and mature) lecturer, it, by common consent, requires numerous small sections in which the "great works" that are required reading for the course can be discussed in some detail, the inevitable confusions cleared up, and questions answered. Who does this essential part of the "core" program? Why, teaching assistants, of course. Young men and women at the beginning of their careers, most of them the products of highly specialized "pre-graduate" programs who, however bright and committed to teaching, simply do not have the background and experience to handle such difficult (and in a real sense alien) material effectively. Nonetheless, whatever good is gotten out of such "core" programs by students is usually due to the dedicated efforts of those at the bottom of the academic pile. What message do you think students get from perfunctory lectures (often by specialists drawn from different disciplines—the classics professor's lectures on the Greeks, the professor of medieval history on the Middle Ages, etc.) and sections taught by the low men and women on the totem pole? They get the message that this is a chore imposed on them for their own good by a professoriate that is unwilling to make a serious and sustained commitment to it. Take this. It is Western

Civilization. It is good for you, even if the taste is bitter. You can't claim to be an educated person unless you know the following. But do you, Professor? Do you really and genuinely know these things that you say are good for us? Are you truly committed? Do you read Virgil and Dante? Or did you once? Do you love the Renaissance artists, poets, and philosophers? Do you read John Calvin's *Institutes of the Christian Religion* and recall the theses Martin Luther nailed to the church door in Wittenberg?

The hearts of the professors are undeniably elsewhere, in their studies and laboratories, in their "disciplines." Not only are they not equipped to teach what they expect students to learn, but they are patronizing to those of their colleagues who make a genuine effort to perform this almost impossible mission. And sometimes deny them tenure because, in undertaking the heroic task of trying to make vivid and relevant two thousand years or more of history, they scant the research/publication requirement.

Weighed in the scales against specialized, "scientific" studies, where the academic payoffs lie, the promotions, the call to better jobs at more prestigious institutions, Western civilization in all its curricular forms and permutations is no more than a feather. Who, one may legitimately ask, is diddling whom? The historian Frederick Rudolph, in a book commissioned by the Carnegie Foundation for the Advancement of Teaching and published in 1977, expressed the opinion that general education was "hopelessly engaged in the artificial respiration of a lifeless ideal," and a second Carnegie Foundation study the same year found it "so poorly defined and so diluted with options that it has no recognizable substance of its own."

Ortega y Gasset was equally critical of general education. Too often the proponents of general education "conceive of it as something largely ornamental," something that distinguishes the "educated" and "cultivated" man or woman from the mass of people. In the Middle Ages, often referred to as the time when the universities assumed the responsibility for the preservation and dissemination of learning, "culture" was not "an ornament of the mind or training of the character. It was, on the contrary, the system of ideas, concerning the world and humanity which the man of that time possessed." It was essential knowledge, and it was made up not of "classics" but of "convictions which became the effective [guides] of his existence." The simple fact is, you can't teach Western Civilization if no one really believes in it. It is then, in Ortega y Gasset's word, mere "ornamentation." It does not touch the soul, it does not guide one's steps through life. It is simply something that rests passively in the mind, so far as it survives at all. The Classical Christian Consciousness was the fruit of two thousand years of a fascinating and intricate process. At its center was, first, a set of deeply held convictions about man and society and man's relation to the gods held by the Greeks. This culture may be said to have virtually invented abstract thought. It was followed by the "driving force of Western Civilization," the medieval Church, the Renaissance, and, most important of all for an understanding of the modern world, the Protestant Reformation. To put the matter as succinctly as possible: when you agitate for Western Civ programs, you are asking the Secular Democratic Consciousness to teach the Classical Christian Consciousness, and that is, obviously, a losing proposition.

Furthermore, what we might call the Western Civ syndrome, at least in the form in which Robert Hutchins, Mortimer Adler, and Allan Bloom have espoused it, is a form of "presentism," since it takes the line that there are great ideas and great books that are equally relevant at all times. These are, in essence, works that address the Big Questions. As such, they certainly provide welcome access to the existential questions of the meaning of life, the nature of civic virtue, the love of truth, and the devotion to justice, but they are basically ahistorical in that they are inclined to ignore the historical context of ideas. Since most ideas (and philosophies) are the product of the particular circumstances of specific times, the teaching of Western Civilization in and of itself is no guarantee that students will get a genuine sense of history. Certainly it is helpful to impart the knowledge that there are enduring values and persistent human problems that men and women have struggled with since the beginning of recorded time, but that is clearly only half the story.

There is a final, and for me quite conclusive, argument against teaching "Western Civilization." A defender of the university-as-it-might-be will perhaps say something like this: "Despite the fact that the values that were formed by and that formed what we call Western Civilization have lost their efficacy for modern man and woman, isn't it nonetheless important to learn how that happened?" I'm afraid my answer would still be no. I am only interested in living ideas, not in dead ideas. Now, I personally happen to believe that most of the ideas of Western civilization are vitally important ideas that can and should be part of the lives of men and women today, as they were centuries ago, so I can still teach Western Civilization with a good conscience. But the fact is that I do not want to teach Western Civilization, in part because Western Civilization is part of World Civilization; it is the most direct and immediate precursor of Modern European Civilization. At the time it was, like all other cultures that I am familiar with, a "racist" civilization that placed itself over and against the other major cultures and subcultures of the world and insisted that it was superior to them in virtually every measurable way. That, as I say, is the way the great world cultures have typically behaved toward other, "lesser" races. But we are now at a new stage in world history. The Bible tells us that God made "of one blood all nations of men." We are now in view of that ancient dream of a common human society. Thus our problem is one of *inclusion*. Intellectual, moral, social, religious, racial, etc. The students who resist the reimposition of the old familiar Western Civilization course that has failed so often and for such readily identifiable reasons are, in my opinion, correct. "Western Civilization" as a required academic subject not only trails its defeats behind it; its basic impulse is retrograde and, I suspect, racist in its inner core. It presents us with the unhappy spectacle of young men and women who have felt excluded by an indifference to or a patronizing attitude toward the cultures that nurtured them, arrayed against the most reactionary elements of the intellectual establishment, who, for all their arguments, are saying (or not saying, but acting in a way that says in essence) that our culture is a better, deeper, richer culture than yours, and that you must learn it whether you wish to or not; whether it is a culture that few contemporary Americans believe in or are even aware of, it is better than "yours." Eugen Rosenstock-Huessy has described very vividly the ascent of man through tribal culture to the "great empires" of Babylon, Assyria, Egypt, to the Greeks, and thence to Western Christendom (I suspect that if our "Western Civilization" advocates were to be more candid—and more accurate—and offered their course as "Western Christendom," they would find far fewer supporters). But the point is that all academic efforts to give a comprehensive view of the history of mankind must from this point on eschew the merely Western and take in the whole range of human history. Well before there was anything that could be identified as Western Civilization, hundreds of different cultures and peoples had poured their riches into a common store. Each new phase of history requires that our past history be rewritten to incorporate the new experience. We have to "get right" with the past in order to have a future. This is well illustrated at the moment by the rewriting of Russian history to include the enormities of Stalin and the errors of Marxist-Leninism in order that the Russians may have a real future. On a different scale, we must "enlarge our past" in order to make room for the future. So it is not surprising that many students, and not just minority students, see the present campaign for Western Civilization as a required part of the curriculum as a step backward and one with unfortunate, if doubtless unconscious, racial overtones. What makes the whole issue an especially obnoxious one is that it evades the real issue, which is the rigid and dogmatic scientism that characterizes the university and that excludes even a discussion of the classic values of Western civilization from the established academic disciplines. The champions of scientism, the enemies of any genuine intellectual openness in consideration of the aims of life, are, of course, delighted to have the enemy—Western Civilization—packaged for undergraduate consumption, as long as the question of its real power and relevance can be confined to freshmen sections taught by teaching assistants.

The place to discuss the real nature of the psyche/soul is not in a World Civilization section but in a psychology course. The place to discuss the role of religion in American history is not in a course on religion but in a history course. The same for the Reformation.

The same for the religious foundations of the New Deal, let us say, to pick a tough one. No, it must be said emphatically to the universities: Leave Western civilization with a large or a small "c" alone. Stop pretending to do something that your institutional organization robs of any real significance. To profess to teach World Civilization in the stronghold of "scientific research" and soul-warping specialization is to display that most unattractive of vices—hypocrisy. You don't have the human resources to do a decent job (a fact now proved over almost a century). It can never be done properly, and thus shouldn't be done at all until the university has a change of heart and becomes, in fact as well as in name, a universe-ity, a genuine universe of learning.

The guilt of the universities in failing to open up to their students "the culture which must sustain them cannot," Ortega y Gasset notes, "be compensated for by the prodigious and brilliant services which they have undeniably rendered to science. . . . A crime perpetrated against the fundamental conditions of human life cannot be atoned for through science. . . . Hence it is imperative to set up once more, in the university, the teaching of the culture, the system of vital ideas, which the age has attained. This is the basic function of the university. This is what the university must be, above all else.. . . The vague desire for a vague culture . . . will lead us nowhere."

12
THE REVOLT
OF THE YOUTH

"Unfortunate is the youth who does not know the pleasure of the spirit and is not exalted in the joy of knowing and the joy of beauty, the enthusiasm for ideas, and quickening experience in the first love, delight and luxury of wisdom and poetry."

—JACQUES MARITAIN

In 1962 Paul Goodman, itinerant teacher and prolific writer, published a book entitled *Community of Scholars*. Goodman described in scathing terms the fragmentation of the academic world into jealous dukedoms. Of American colleges he wrote: "One could not name ten that strongly stand for anything peculiar to themselves, peculiarly wise, radical, experimental, or even peculiarly dangerous, stupid, or licentious. It is astounding that there should be so many self-governing communities, yet so much conformity to the national norm. . . . Most of our colleges being what they are, I fear that many of our best youth would get a better, though very imperfect education if they followed their impulse and quit; and certainly many teachers ought to be more manly even if they risk their jobs." American colleges and universities, Goodman felt, were lacking in any real sense of purpose. "Rather, they are great, and greatly expanding, images of Education, no different from the other role-playing organizations of the modern world. Fortified in their departments and tenure . . . the senior scholars are not much disturbed by either the student or by one another or by the administration. And society is satisfied by the symbolic proof that a lot of education is going on, fat syllabi, hundreds of thousands of diplomas, bales of published research. . . . The administrators

152

engage in a tooth-and-nail competition to aggrandize their institutions. . . . [T]hey behave like department stores opening new departments and sometimes branches, and increasing efficiency by standardizing the merchandise and the sales force." Goodman's remedy was "to take teaching-and-learning on its own terms, for the students and teachers to associate in the traditional way and according to their existing interest, but entirely dispensing with the external control, administration, bureaucratic machinery, and other excrescences that have swamped our community of scholars."

Goodman's book became the text for the revolt of the youth, an inspiration to tens of thousands of bright and dissatisfied students at universities around the country. A year later a very different book appeared. In 1963 Clark Kerr, president of the University of California, published a series of lectures he had delivered at Harvard under the title *The Uses of the University*. Kerr discussed the various functions of the modern university and its widely varied clientele: "the 'collegiate' of fraternities and sororities and the athletes and activities majors; the 'academic' or the serious students; the 'vocational' or the students seeking training for specific jobs; and the 'nonconformist' or the political activists, the aggressive intellectuals, and the bohemians. These subcultures are not mutually exclusive, and some of the fascinating pageantry of the multiversity is found in their interaction one on another."

Kerr acknowledged that what he called the "multiversity" was "a confusing place for the student. He has problems of establishing his identity and sense of security within it." The fact that student and professor had far more freedom than ever before was, Kerr pointed out, a mixed blessing. With a wider range of choice often came a sense of alienation from a central concept of education or learning. The student suffered especially from lack of genuine contact with the faculty. If there were gains, they were primarily on the faculty side. Abraham Flexner had called the "American professoriate . . . a proletariat." That condition had changed dramatically. Professors were not only much better paid, they had generous health and retirement benefits and "some were at the center of national and world events. Research opportunities" had been "enormously increased. . . . [The professor] need not leave the Groves for the Acropolis [to prosper financially] unless he wishes. . . . He may . . . become . . . essentially a professional man with his home office and basic retainer on the campus of the multiversity but with his clients scattered from coast to coast." Inconsistent as the multiversity might be in its various roles, "it has," Kerr wrote, "*few peers in the preservation and examination of the eternal truths* [italics mine]; no living peers in the search for new knowledge; and no peers in all history among institutions of higher learning in serving so many segments of an advancing civilization. . . . Though it has not a single soul to call its own, its members pay their devotions to truth."

It was, of course, precisely the last claims that were so soon to be disputed by student activists. The university had long barred from its precincts the "examination of the eternal truths." They were considered not appropriate subjects for consideration. They did not lend themselves to the methods of modern research. It was difficult if not impossible to treat them "objectively," or "scientifically," so, as we have had ample occasion to note, they were simply excluded from academic discourse, from research, from the classroom and the lecture hall.

To angry students, the university, far from having a number of "souls," seemed to have no "soul" at all and to have far more concern with piling up vast indigestible or incomprehensible masses of fact and theory than with "eternal truths." If the university was devoted to truth, that devotion was nowhere evident to students, who could seldom even talk to their professors and often completed four years of undergraduate study without having one teacher who knew them by name. It must be said that Kerr, to his credit, was troubled enough by the unwillingness of large campuses like Berkeley to offer undergraduate students anything like a proper education to prevail on the regents of the university to open a campus in 1965 in Santa Cruz on the collegiate model of Cambridge and Oxford. There the emphasis was to be on the teaching of undergraduate students in colleges of which the students would be "members" and the faculty "fellows." The faculty would, of course, be expected to carry on the classic and essential role of research and publication in order to "push back the frontiers of knowledge."

Kerr's background was in economics and labor negotiations, and he put the teeth of more conventional academics on edge by talking about the university as the leader of the "knowledge industry." He seemed to applaud the fact that universities were tied closely to the Department of Defense and its various subsidiaries. The complaint of students, soon to surface, that it was not the business of a university to run enterprises engaged in making atomic bombs more and more deadly, was referred to only in passing. "The total system"—the university, the private research foundations, the government laboratories—was "extraordinarily flexible, decentralized, competitive—productive." "Knowledge costs a great deal to produce," Kerr wrote. "Thus it only pays to produce knowledge if through production it can be put into use better and faster." "Knowledge has expanded and expanded," Kerr added, "from theology and philosophy and law and medicine and accounting to the whole range of humanities, the social sciences and the sciences and the professions." More knowledge had resulted from and led to "more and more research on a larger and larger scale. Research has led to service for government and industry and agriculture. . . . [A]ll of this is natural. None of it can be reversed. . . . The campus consistent with society has served as a good introduction to society—to bigness, to specialization, to diffusion of interests."

The fact was that Kerr's entire vocabulary was an offense to the idealistic students who were soon besieging his office. They were the words of capitalism—"product," "productive," "cost effective," "put to use," "better and faster," etc. It *was* a new language. Aside from the required nod to "eternal truths" (which seemed a painful anachronism in the context of Kerr's book), the terminology was that of the age of technology, communication, and production. In view of the enormous sums that the universities required—federal and state, public and private—it was necessary to stress their "productivity." The "well-rounded individual," "the trained intellect," the "cultivated man," all these standard items of most discussions of education, had fallen—mercifully, I suspect—by the wayside.

Despite his upbeat tone, Kerr was clearly aware that something was amiss: "the undergraduates are restless," he declared. "Recent changes in the American university have done them little good. . . . There is an incipient revolt." Kerr was also aware that all was not well with the faculty, who seemed to be the principal beneficiaries of the changes. "Knowledge is now in so many bits and pieces and administration so distant that faculty members are increasingly figures in a 'lonely crowd' intellectually and institutionally," he wrote.

The revolt of the youth started modestly enough in the fall of 1964 when students, manning a table at Sather Gate on the Berkeley campus of the University of California, were told by a campus officer that they could not distribute their materials at that location. The startling response was an eruption of angry dissent. Demonstrations, sit-ins, confrontations with university officers and the campus police became daily events. The upheaval at Berkeley was the opening gun in a war that was to last intermittently for the next eight years. Three identifiable elements lay behind what came to be called the "student rebellion."

First there was the fact that, at least on the Berkeley campus, the situation of undergraduate students had grown progressively more disheartening over the preceding decade. Neil Smelser, the Berkeley sociologist, noted that in the eleven years from 1953 to 1964 the student body had grown by 80 percent while the faculty increased by only 18 percent. "In the meantime," Smelser notes, "nonfaculty research personnel . . . increased from 565 to 1,430." In consequence, undergraduate students "found themselves being serviced more by junior faculty, temporary faculty, and semifaculty." "Students," Smelser added, "might well have perceived that they were being invited to an élite institution only to be educated mainly by its second-class teachers, in a large, impersonal setting."

Marshall Meyer, in his review of student politics at Harvard in the Vietnam years, admitted that there had been "Much talk of needed educational reforms" and complaints "that the size and impersonality of the university, coupled with an often absent and overly professionalized faculty," had "cut students adrift from adult control." Meyer dismissed the charges on the grounds that "no research evidence" supported the charge.

Another element was the civil-rights movement in the South, a movement that had drawn young white liberals south to join forces with Southern blacks in their fight against segregation. Many of these students returned to their campuses fired with a zeal for social justice. Todd Gitlin, then a student leader, wrote: "SNCC moved us, seized our imaginations. From 1960 on, SDS felt wired to these staggeringly brave, overalled, work-shirted college students. . . . SNCC had suffered, SNCC was *there,* bodies on the line, moral authority incarnate."

Finally, there was the Vietnam War. A minor aspect of the student revolt initially, the war became a more central element with each passing year.

The most important aspect of the student rebellion for this work is the critique that it produced of the university. The editors of the *University Crisis Reader* point out in the introduction to their book that early in the Vietnam protest movement, the protesters "began to develop a theory about the universities that viewed their liberal ideology as a camouflage for society's corporate and military structure." The charge of corporate influence or control was, of course, not new. It was at least as old as the rise of the university itself. It was the military connection that was new. It was the argument of the radical students that the university was not merely the tool of the corporate-military world (or, as President Eisenhower called it, the military-industrial complex), but "one of its main pillars."

Clark Kerr's *The Uses of the University* was frequently quoted by dissident students. Kerr had written: "The University and segments of industry are becoming more and more alike. As the University becomes tied to the work of the world, the professor— at least in the natural and some of the social sciences—takes on the character of an entrepreneur. . . . The two worlds are merging physically. . . . [The university] is a mechanism held together by administrative rules and powered by money."

Student critics of the university during the Vietnam era also delighted in quoting the unfortunate president of Michigan State, John Hannah, who in 1961 declared in what can best be excused as an excess of patriotic zeal: "Our colleges and our universities must be regarded as bastions of our defense, as essential to preservation of our country and our way of life as supersonic bombers, nuclear-powered submarines and intercontinental ballistic missiles."

A Brandeis student's complaint was echoed by numerous other students: "We wondered that our classes, with few exceptions, seemed irrelevant to our lives. No wonder they're so boring. Boredom is the necessary condition of any education which teaches us to manipulate the facts and suppress their meaning."

The SDS leaders of a strike at Columbia issued in September 1968 what was soon called "The Columbia Statement." It had been composed in what was called the "Math Commune." Ardently Marxist in tone, it was an all-out attack on "the system of capital" with its imperialistic tendencies. "The men who ran the monstrous corporations, whose interests were allied with war and empire were the same men who ran the Universities." Two Columbia professors had helped set up fortified camps in Vietnam (called "concentration camps" in the statement). What the students were engaged in was not a protest but "an insurrection" against an oppressive "capitalist" administration and weak-kneed liberal professors, some of whom admitted privately to the students that they sympathized with their aims but dared not publicly support them. "[B]efore we established the communes," the insurrectionists wrote, "our education was systematically oriented towards isolating the individual, inducing him to follow the lonely track of material interest—getting a better grade from a superior, getting a degree, impressing the Dean for a letter of recommendation, taking on a useless subject for a lifetime in order to avoid the draft for two years. . . . In America," the statement continued, "with a military budget of $80 billion, the war machine owns American Universities." (Brooks Adams had written in 1912 that capital owned the universities "by right of purchase"). The students concentrated their fire on the universities' claim of "neutrality." They quoted David Truman, the president of Columbia, as saying that for the university to sever relations with the Department of Defense would be to display "partiality."

The exhilarating experience of the insurrectionists was, in their words, that "they [briefly] . . . smelled, tasted, and touched a society which needed each of us totally, a society in which we were not fragmented, to which each of us was vital, a society in which our minds and our bodies equally were required of us, a society in which we were whole." There is still today something very poignant about the statement. The students were convinced that a "period of continuous revolution had come upon us, and men all over the world [had begun] to envision the new society. World history had somehow formed the ineffable motivations of the Columbia insurrection." The words echoed a thousand similar pronouncements of the Secular Democratic Consciousness since the American Revolution. At Concord, Massachusetts, on July 4, 1798, the Reverend Samuel Thacher had declared in almost equally rhapsodic words: "All hail, coming revolutions! . . . We have witnessed towers of lawless power toppled in a day . . . the consequent emancipation of a race. . . ." Much the same dream had stirred the hearts of Frederic Howe and his fellow graduate students at Johns Hopkins.

To the charge that in their resort to violence they were attacking the very foundations of civilized academic discourse, where controversial issues were supposed to be debated in an atmosphere of calm rationality, the students replied, not unreasonably, that the university was an accomplice in the violence that the United States government was inflicting on a native population thousands of miles away. "We cannot separate," the students wrote, "the modern forms of violence—the Green Berets, CIA, nerve gasses, mace, chemical inventions, world strategies, and psychological techniques—from the cerebral character of modern Imperialism. The most heinous crimes of our century are not the crimes of passion; they are the crimes of intellect. . . . The most rational, orderly, disciplined minds of our time are working long hours in our most efficient laboratories, at the task of eliminating us."

To the charge that they were bent on destroying the university, the delegates to the New University Conference, held in February

1969, replied: "if one means by University a body that applies its labor and intelligence to the collective good, which affirms life and liberty, then we do not destroy the University; we intend to build it. . . . We believe that a University should have nothing to do with human subjugation, except the overthrowing of it. A University's labor, research and knowledge should release the creative capacities of our society and advance the liberation of oppressed peoples of the world." Instead, the university was preoccupied by "positivist philosophy, behaviorist psychology—these anti-humanities of the schools. . . . Behaviorist psychology amoralizes the social sciences. . . . A positivist philosophy blames the intellect that might otherwise dare to speak of general developments and which would grasp the similitudes that interlock entire civilizations." The students blamed what appeared to the statement's authors to be the reluctance of "liberal professors" to support the student "insurrection" on the fact that their morale had been destroyed by the wave of McCarthyism, when professors were expelled from universities for holding heretical views "while fellow teachers sat by and watched."

"Many professors," the declaration continued, "pursue all sides of a question as an end in itself. They find a certain refuge in the difficulty of defining good and evil. The result is a clogging of their moral sense, their capacity for collective justice." Dante might have been thinking of the modern professor when he reserved "The hottest places in hell . . . for those who, in a time of moral crisis, maintain their own neutrality." "A University could not, even if it wanted, choose to be really value-free. It can choose good values; it can choose bad values; or it can remain ignorant of the values on which it acts. The notion of value-free inquiry, of social research without reference to social ends, is the bugaboo of escapist science. . . . It is a typical fallacy of American teaching, that to remain silent on crucial issues is to be objective. . . ." The real debate was not between activists and intellectuals but "between those people who demand that the intellect be applied to humanity . . . and those academics who refuse to use their resources for the common good." I must say I do not see how the matter can be more directly or succinctly stated. Or how it can be refuted. Virtually every philosopher or writer on higher education in modern times has affirmed this theme; there is no such thing as "value-free" thought or research; those who act sincerely on such a premise deceive the world and, more dangerous, themselves.

Even the governor of California discovered a sympathy for student grievances. In a speech to the Commonwealth Club, doubtless written by a disenchanted former Berkeley student, Ronald Reagan offered his interpretation of the student uprising. There was, he declared, "a revolutionary movement involving a tiny minority of faculty and students. . . ." They had played skillfully on "the disappointment and resentment of an entire college generation that finds itself being fed into a knowledge factory with no regard for their individual aspirations or their dreams." The solution that Reagan clearly favored was to use all the powers of the law to suppress the "revolutionary movement" but to "establish contact with these frustrated young people and join in finding answers before they fall to the mob by default. . . . Their legitimate grievances must be understood and solutions must be forthcoming. 'Publish or perish' as a university policy must be secondary to teaching. Research, a vital and essential part of the process, must not be the standard by which the university rates itself. Its function is to teach and its record must be established on the quality of graduates it offers to the world—not on the collection of scholarly names in its catalogue." The students, Reagan declared, were being short-changed. "Instead of being challenged and stimulated by the distinguished scholars whose names adorned the university catalogue, students found themselves herded into classes taught by teaching assistants hardly older than themselves. The feeling comes that they are nameless, faceless numbers on an assembly line—green cap at one end and cap, gown and automated diploma at the other. They want someone to know they are there—they aren't even missed and recorded as absent when they aren't there."

A relative handful of faculty members checked in with the students. A Nobel Laureate, George Wald, spoke out at MIT about the complicity of the universities in the Vietnam War. "Something has gone sour, in teaching and in learning," Wald told his predominantly student audience. "It's almost as though there were a widespread feeling that education has become irrelevant."

Another student advocate, Jacob Bronowski, a senior fellow for the Salk Institute for Biological Studies, offered an interesting analysis of the "student revolt" in a talk he entitled "A Search for the Meaning of the Generation Gap." Bronowski reminded his readers that "in general . . . protest is the age-old instrument for human progress." The striking thing about the protest of young people was that it was *"not doctrinal."* It was directed at specific grievances, and although its rhetoric was often revolutionary, its aims were comparatively modest. "A whole generation of liberals and humanists, to which I belong," Bronowski wrote, "is bewildered at the discovery that the young include us in their charge of hypocrisy. We made liberalism respectable by our labor, and turned it into an intellectual faith; and now we are distressed to find that our heroic memories of the hungry thirties and the Spanish Civil War are dismissed as out-of-date mythology." Bronowski believed that the liberals, specifically the liberal academics, who had flourished in worldly things, had "somehow forgotten to find new foundations for the old truths." It was those "old truths" that rebellious youth was searching for.

Richard Sewall, professor of literature at Yale, dared to hope that the campus upheavals that marked that era, most dramatically the Free Speech Movement on the campus of the University of California, Berkeley, indicated "a coming of age on the part of students, a putting away of the trivia inherited from the past . . . a real desire to enter into and share the true spirit of the University community, which is and always has been . . . the meeting of mind with mind through personal encounter and through books."

Peter Clecak, a professor of English at the Irvine campus of the University of California, wrote: "Most humanists probably agree that the disparity between the aims and achievements of liberal education has become nearly intolerable." Many students complained of "a lack of 'identity' and an absence of 'community,'" noted Clecak. Others found "the institution or the 'system' confusing, impersonal and depersonalizing," and expressed "contempt for those of us who fail to develop—or even to seek—a style adequate to what we profess and adequate to the students' need for admirable and imitable adults. In short, they find the faculty morally corrupt, emotionally stunted and intellectually sterile—irrelevant (that battered term) to their lives."

Such charges were serious ones but ones that most faculty members refused to take seriously. Although they might well concede the impersonal nature of their institutions, they would reject the idea that they, in their own lives, should make any effort to be, or that students had any right to expect them to be, "role models."

Amid the charges and counter-charges generated by the "student revolt" (for which, incidentally, no one that I know has produced a convincing explanation; certainly the Dr. Spock explanation—that young men and women raised by permissive parents following the tenets of Dr. Spock were simply acting out hostility toward authority—won't wash), very few of the responses of the "academic establishment," of professors and administrators, attempted to rebut the most serious charges of the students, which were essentially (but in no particular order of importance): the alliance between the universities and the federal government for research in weapons and/or materials for destruction and warfare; non–war-related research having to do with methods of civil control; techniques of political persuasion to be used on leaders of friendly as well as not so friendly nations; the neglect of teaching in favor of research; the lack of interest by most faculty in students, and the general inaccessibility of professors; the absence of any coherent notion of what an education should be; and "institutional racism" in the form of the conspicuous absence of black and minority students and faculty on university campuses. If the students overused "imperialism," faculty members overused such phrases as "civilized discourse" and "reasoned debate." When the dust had settled, nothing had changed substantially. All the charges that the students made in the 1964–69 era are equally valid today.

In 1973 David Riesman and Verne Stadtman edited a volume called *Academic Transformation,* published under the auspices of the Carnegie Commission on Higher Education. Sixteen professors (and one journalist) wrote essays on the student upheavals in various colleges and universities ranging from Old Westbury to the University of California, Berkeley. The essays have the virtue of immediacy. The most recent protests and demonstrations were hardly over when the authors sat down to report the events and their significance. Oddly enough, David Riesman, reviewing the articles in a lengthy conclusion, expressed his misgivings that the call by students for more teaching (as opposed to research) might result in less freedom for the faculty and a new ethic of "teach or perish" in place of "publish or perish" (the latter injunction one that Riesman implicitly supported). The emphasis on teaching, which Riesman termed "the teach-in style," seemed to him to be spreading. On the other hand, some faculty members might be encouraged "not to bother with trivial enough publishable research when they can find institutional support for a conscientious concern for teaching and advising." But Riesman's principal fear was that "the student and faculty Left" might join "the Philistine Right in [an] attack on the privileges of the research-oriented professor. . . ." Riesman's other major concern seemed to be the growth (or, more accurately, the threat) of faculty unions, which he feared might be tempted to intervene in decisions about tenure.

It is odd to hear Riesman, whose interest in innovative higher education was well established, speak patronizingly about "senior faculty who have become converts to the new vogue of caring about students." It seems to me that Riesman, in effect, confirms the students' charges that the professoriate, for whatever reasons, was far more concerned with its precious researches than with educating them. As it turned out, Riesman needn't have feared. The pressure to publish and the neglect of teaching reasserted themselves ferociously. The flood of second- and third-rate research rose ever higher. Professors taught less and less.

The relationship between psychoactive drugs and the student rebellion, and the evolution of the entire counterculture, is an intricate and important one. Many of the student activists, and many of the broader student population, took these drugs, which had a profound effect on their consciousness. Three young men who were in graduate school in history in the 1960s have told me that taking LSD was the experience that turned them against further graduate study and careers as university professors. For one graduate student in history at Stanford, an LSD experience was like a revelation. He had been staying with his brother in Los Angeles, and his brother persuaded him to take LSD. Suddenly he saw the world around him with startling clarity and vividness—the grass, the trees, the sky—and he saw also, in the same moment, the shallowness and futility of the university; he never went back to graduate school.

Frank Barron, an associate of Timothy Leary in the early psychedelic-drug experiments at Harvard, tells of a priest friend who took LSD and emerged from the experience stripped of what was left of his religious beliefs and announced: "It means that everything is up for grabs." The known, the familiar, the ordinary constraints, the structures of normal social life were in an instant suspended. There was a sense of penetrating all falsities and subterfuges, all masks and pretensions, and coming clear to the heart of life. What was often left was a void that some novitiates would find it difficult to fill. One would not want to say that the radical student critique of the universities was derived directly and exclusively from the psychedelic experience, but the analogies are striking. The university was deconstructed by its student critics, its faults, its silent complicities laid bare. Its response, like the response of all beleaguered bureaucracies, was defensive, reactionary, protective of its "values."

There were, of course, two forms of revolt against higher education. One was an aggressive attack on the university by students in residence. The other was withdrawal. In 1964, when I was correcting the proofs of a book about the role of the small town in American history, the Free Speech Movement erupted on the Berkeley campus of the University of California. I was struck by the fact that the leader of the movement, Mario Savio, cited as a major student complaint the fact that there was no genuine contact between faculty and students. The uprising, Savio declared, had created "a community of love" among the protesters for the first time in the modern history of the university. I was so struck by the phrase that I wrote a long footnote at the end of the book in which I speculated that the absence of community had created in American society generally, and in the universities specifically, a sense of "alienation," a word popular at the time. "In recent years," I wrote, "we have seen the development of several types of 'pseudo-communities' [the term was later to be "intentional communities"], groups of individuals who share some critical problem of social adjustment of personal malaise." I mentioned Synanon, a drug-rehabilitation program that had started in Santa Monica, California, a few years earlier. I noted that Synanon had attracted many middle-class individuals who had no drug problem but were drawn to "the warmth and intimacy of its communal living. . . . [I]t may be," I added, "that in a mass society, the creation of pseudo-communities of various kinds is the best hope for protecting the individual against the demoralizing effects of alienation."

By 1967 the counterculture was in full tide, with the gathering of young people into communes one of its main developments. First, thousands and then tens of thousands of young men and women abandoned middle-class, suburban homes, university campuses, and post-graduate studies and formed communes, cooperative living groups, many of them agricultural, others content to be urban communes. All had had individual ethical codes. Some were political in tone and intent; many were religious. Eastern religions were especially in vogue. Since the communards were rebelling against middle-class American life, and Protestant Christianity was identified in the minds of the young with middle-class culture, it was less in evidence than, say, Zen or Tantric Buddhism or Sufism. Where there were Christian communes, they tended to be of the fundamentalist variety. Yet, much as they varied, certain elements were common to most communes. Casual sex and drug use were among the less appealing aspects of the commune movement (at least to older and more conservative Americans). A large number subscribed to the principles of anarchism, but there were other common denominators. There was great emphasis on openness, on sharing one's own feelings and emotions with others. A confessional impulse was common; the "encounter group," in which one laid bare one's innermost feelings and confessed one's sins of selfishness or pride against others, against the community, flourished. Much attention focused on food, which was overwhelmingly "organic," and on the environment, on peace, on spiritual experiences. Astrology and various forms of the occult were popular. Music and dance were central. The most favored word was "spiritual." What has become known as the New Age philosophy evolved from that movement, developed a whole theory of history, with a vague, Emersonian Over-Soul kind of religion, and a vocabulary of its own. I have in front of me a New Age publication. In it is an article entitled "What Is the New Age." "The 'New' Age," the author tells us, "is the Aquarian Age and it's all about 'spirit and flow.' The 'old' age was the Piscean Age. It taught us about 'structure and form.'

"The New Age started in 1976. Between then and 1987 both the 'new' way and the 'old' way worked. . . . Historically, we stand in the formative years of an age that will continue for about 2400 years." After a review of some of the characteristics of the Piscean Age, the author tells us that "A predominant choice made during the Piscean Age was that God was outside rather than inside each of us. From this came the structure of an outer authority-oriented religion." This fact meant that there had to be "mediators between the worshippers and God. . . . This approach carried over to our governments and gave rise to concepts of patriotism, nationalism, racism and sexism. Earlier expression took the forms of feudalism, monarchy and serfdom. . . . Aquarius on the other hand says, 'I know.' And what Aquarius knows is the oneness of all life. The oneness of life is the All, the One, the Infinite spirit that is within *and* outside each of us, as well as the rocks and trees and animals and computers. Aquarius unites the polarities and introduces equality. Since we are equal, I don't need you to rule me; I can rule myself. Since God isn't only outside me, I can speak to Him/Her myself through meditation and prayer."

There is, of course, much more: The relation of Aquarians to nature; the renewal of the earth; the earth as a kind of living organism, "Gaia." There is "One Infinite Spirit, the All that Is,

God, is truth. 'Everything that is, or was or will be, already is.' Each age is a unique rhythm or movement that expresses ageless eternal truth.''

It is a safe bet that the writer of these lines is the graduate of one of our "great universities." What she has written is a kind of manifesto against those universities. The Age of Aquarius stands for "ageless eternal truths" and against all forms of authority, for a restoration of the natural world and against the mere description of it or the relentless exploitation of it. It is not so much against science as it is against a scientific view of the world. Bizarre as it is in some ways, it is also profoundly touching. It is the kind of declaration that puts academic teeth on edge and confirms professors' worst suspicions of the anti-intellectualism of the young. Seen another way, it is a judgment (and a very conscious one) on the academic world and on certain forms of modern consciousness. It is a statement of everything that the academic world rigorously excludes, sentiments quite literally "beyond the pale." From the academic point of view, it is the return of the irrational; for the young people who adhere to such descriptions of reality, it is an effort to recapture the spiritual dimension of life, and as such I believe it has to be taken seriously, however eccentric it may seem. The issue is whether we are prepared to reconcile ourselves to a society that exists on two levels of consciousness: one doggedly scientific, materialistic, positivistic, the other rather moonily detached from the practical world of atomic bombs and computers. The obduracy of "scientism" has produced the "counterculture" of the Age of Aquarius.

The same impulse that made communal living attractive to individuals in the mid-sixties eventually led into large and in some instances frighteningly powerful groups, full-blown cults invariably led by a single charismatic "teacher." Among the best known are the Hare Krishnas, formed in 1966 by A. C. Bhaktivedanta Prabhupada, an Indian swami from Calcutta. He began giving classes on the *Bhagavad-Gita* in a Second Avenue storefront in New York City. His disciples were directed to give up meat, coffee, cigarettes, alcohol, and drugs, as well as casual sex. They were required to wear Hindu robes, shave their heads, mark their foreheads with red clay, and chant the sacred mantra 1,728 times a day. In the words of Anne Fadiman, the swami appealed to young men and women "who craved spiritual discipline but dismissed Jesus and Moses as stodgy totems of the parental establishment." Krishna, on the other hand, "had played the flute, gone barefoot, worn flowers and danced with milkmaids."

Then there was the Maharishi, who, with his followers, formed the Student International Meditation Society, which by 1968 claimed twelve thousand members.

One of the most successful cults is that of the Korea-based Reverend Moon, an alleged incarnation of Jesus Christ. With thousands of adoring and obedient followers drawn from the ranks of upper-middle-class youths, the cream of the crop of young people, he built a financial and real-estate empire.

Synanon itself became a vast undertaking with thousands of members, multi-million-dollar budgets, and a fleet of planes and buses.

Jonestown was, of course, the site of the most tragic of all the cults. Like the others, it drew many educated, middle-class young men and women as well as hundreds of poor blacks and lower-middle-class adherents. John E. Smith, a Yale professor, did not hesitate to connect the tragedy of the People's Temple at Jonestown to the fact that in the universities the " 'rational' and 'meaningful' have been so narrowly defined that religious, ethical, and metaphysical beliefs have been excluded from the domain of reason and cast on the junk heap of the meaningless and emotional, where no critical evaluation is possible."

Of all modern cults, that of the Bhagwan Shree Rajneesh in Oregon may well be the most bizarre. After presiding over a puram or Buddhist religious commune in Poona, India, the Bhagwan transferred his operation to a ranch in Oregon. There, as a brochure informed the curious, the Bhagwan (God) and his disciples would "live together in a non-possessive way, neither possessing things nor possessing persons; people living together, creating together, celebrating together and still allowing each one his own space; people creating a certain climate of meditativeness, of love, of living in that climate." Hard to argue with any of that. It was, indeed, the classic utopian dream; it was the aim of the earliest Christian communities and the hope of succeeding generations. Uncounted numbers of men and women have gathered together to live by similar principles throughout history. What was truly bizarre about the Bhagwan's commune was the strain that it might be thought to have imposed on the credulity of the highly—one is tempted to say, extravagantly—educated men and women who flocked to it. What the skeptic saw was a dissipated, self-indulgent Indian guru who encouraged every wild excess from physical violence of the most brutal and degrading kind to ingeniously aberrant sex; who was arbitrary and tyrannical almost beyond belief; who collected jeweled watches and Rolls-Royces on a hitherto unimagined scale. All this was acquiesced in, supported, and praised by his infatuated followers, the great majority of them people with college degrees and many with advanced degrees. Ph.D.'s were a dime a dozen in the puram, and the largest professional group represented were psychologists. Many of the Rajneeshees had given all their worldly goods to the Bhagwan. When the journalist Frances FitzGerald visited the puram, she was astonished at the professional backgrounds of the Rajneeshees. The commune's city planner, Swami Deva Wadud, had been a professional city planner in San Mateo, California, and boasted an M.A. from the Harvard Graduate School of Design. His assistant was an Australian with a Ph.D. in linguistic philosophy. Another disciple had a degree from Harvard in "visual and environmental studies." The "president" of the commune had been a systems analyst for IBM and Univac and studied computer sciences at the University of London. The list seemed endless. The chief publicist had a Ph.D. from Yale.

A study by University of Oregon psychologists indicated that the average age of the disciples was slightly over thirty. Eighty percent were from middle- or upper-middle-class backgrounds; "their fathers were, overwhelmingly, professionals or businessmen." Seventy-five percent had attended college, two-thirds had bachelor's degrees, and 12 percent had Ph.D.'s. Half had Protestant backgrounds, a quarter were Jewish, and a quarter Roman Catholic. FitzGerald, not surprisingly, puzzled over the "question of what these people were doing in the wilds of Oregon with a silent guru [the Bhagwan had resolved, after the manner of many prominent Indian gurus, to keep silent] and his Rolls Royces. The guru was only visible to his devoted followers once a day when he rolled past the faithful in one of his Rolls Royces while they lined the main street of the puram, clasped their hands and bowed, ecstatic to be in such proximity to the Master."

This was not, of course, an episode limited to the Americans. The French consul at Poona told FitzGerald that an estimated 250,000 Frenchmen were living in India in the mid-seventies, seeking enlightenment from a wide variety of gurus. At the height of the movement, there were dozens of Rajneesh purams scattered about Europe and Australia, a large number in West Germany and a substantial number in England. Common to all was the fact that they attracted a disproportionate number of highly educated and successful men and women. These were not the marginal types often drawn to cult movements. They were the best products of our educational system, idealistic and visionary, the human material out of which generations of leaders in social reform have been drawn in America. They were, moreover, "trained intelligences," in Robert Hutchins' phrase. They were not the typical "shallow" graduate of American colleges and universities whose interests are directed largely at the sports and the social aspects of collegiate life and whose concern with academic or intellectual matters is usually cursory. Whatever our judgment of the quality of undergraduate instruction may be, doctors, lawyers, architects, engineers have had to demonstrate a substantial degree of "trained intelligence" to earn their degrees and practice their professions.

When I asked a psychologist friend if he had given any thought as to why a third of the followers of the crazy old Bhagwan were psychologists and a number of them had Ph.D.'s in psychology, his answer was an arresting one. It was his hunch that they were men and women who had passed through the barrier of "deconstruction" purely intellectually or with the aid of drugs and seen the world as essentially devoid of meaning. All that was left as a shield against the void was the formation of communities of like-minded spirits, bound together by "love and harmony," sharing the knowledge that everything considered "real" by the straight world was false and absurd. In that context the Bhagwan's Rolls-Royces and diamond watches were symbols whose principal purpose was to mock the values of greedy yuppies and vulpine capitalists. The point of the Rolls-Royces was to demonstrate the absurdity of a materialistic world.

It seems to me that the cults of our day demonstrate dramatically that as basic as the need for food and sex is the need to believe in something or somebody, a need expressed throughout history, most typically, by religion. In *Out of Revolution*, Eugen Rosenstock-Huessy has written: "When a nation, or an individual, declines the experiences that present themselves to passionate hearts only, they are automatically turned out from the realm of history. The heart of man either falls in love with somebody or something, or it falls ill. It can never go unoccupied." Because our society offered young men and women nothing they could believe in, nothing that could comfort their souls or direct their energies into fruitful channels, they fell ill, and their illness, in its most extreme form, was the Bhagwan Rajneesh and his devilish manipulations of those who came to him yearning for redemption, for, as he put it so irresistibly, "living together, creating together, celebrating together . . . people creating a certain climate of meditativeness, of love, of living in that climate." No wonder they came, those yearning, desperate souls of whom it could only be said with certitude that they were profoundly dissatisfied with their own lives and were determined to love and believe in someone as unlikely as a mad old Indian who claimed to be a god. Now, the agency of our society with which the young men and women who flocked to the banner of the Bhagwan (and thousands of other soothsayers, seers, and fallen prophets) had been most closely identified since their childhood is the educational system, and it might be expected to have had its greatest influence in the last years. It was in college and graduate school that the system's power over those in its keeping would be most clearly and positively expressed.

In reading Frances FitzGerald's account of the Rajneesh puram, I was struck by the fact that for someone of my generation an analogy with the mood of the 1920s and '30s is almost inescapable.

In the post–World War I era, alcohol, drugs, sexual experimentation, "nervous breakdowns," suicides, and feelings of futility and alienation were commonplace, but the Great Depression brought a strange kind of revival. Many educated, middle- and upper-class young Americans became members of the Communist Party or fellow-traveling Marxists of one stripe or another. They "fell in love" with Marx or Stalin, or Trotsky, because communism seemed to offer a way out of the jungle of materialistic capitalism. The most notable difference between the earlier era and the recent one (which, of course, we are still in) was that, for the young idealists of the thirties, science, order, rationality, and materialism, the major components of the Secular Democratic Consciousness, were still potent (Marx called his doctrines "scientific socialism"). Socialism in some form or other promised that the rational mind could direct the course of history in such a manner as to produce the ideal social order, a world without inequality, discrimination, or oppression, a "classless society" guided by wise and enlightened "workers." The increasingly evident failure of socialist societies around the world has destroyed at long last the intellectual (or educated) class's faith in the triumph of reason in its most recent manifestation, Marxism. The members of that class are left once more without the consolations of faith. The dream of a utopian socialist order which they loved with a blind, unreasoning, but generous love is no longer dreamable (except, apparently, by university professors). The question now was: What were they to love next, when the old love had lost its power? The academic world offered no hint. It went on as it had done for a generation or more, in the same dreary, well-worn ruts. The students, with their great collective toothache, cried out in pain and bewilderment. When their cries could no longer be ignored, they were scolded for breaking the rules of civilized academic discourse and then, figuratively speaking, they were killed. That was *The Lesson.* So they turned away. They took up with the devil, in the deceptive form of an old Indian wise man. They turned their backs on all the remarkable intellectual, aesthetic, and spiritual resources of their own tradition to clutch the teachings of the East. This time they fell in love with love. If reason, science, and rationality had failed, the new God must be within. The individual, it was thought, was a virtually untapped spring of creative potential. He or she was capable of a kind of indiscriminate love which would heal all wounds that history had inflicted. The philosophers of the Enlightenment had insisted not only that individuals were rational, reasonable creatures but that they were inherently *good*. All that was left of the notion of rational man, redeemed by science, was the idea of the essential goodness of humanity. The key to this goodness, it now came to be believed, was love, openness, self-realization in a loving community. Anything that smacked of reason or rationality was rejected out of hand. It was reason and her handmaiden science that had, after all, brought the world to the deplorable state it was at present in, with the threat of nuclear annihilation hanging over the species.

If religion and all the ideas associated with it were excluded from the academic world, they would be sought out, "picked up on," elsewhere, in Indian ashrams, Goan or Nepalese communes, or Christian fundamentalist bands. It seems never to have occurred to professors that they might have some responsibility for the weird spiritual hegiras of their former students. The students were blamed but not the teachers.

Erik Erikson, writing in *Daedalus* in 1967, speculated about the roots of the youth rebellion, then still in its initial phase. "Although many young people entertain a greater variety of sensual and sexual experience than their parents did, I see in their pleasure-seeking relatively little relaxed joy and often compulsive and addictive search for *relevant* experience," Erikson wrote. "And here we should admit that our generation and our heritage made 'all' experience relative by opening it to ruthless inquiry and by assuming that one could pursue radical enlightenment without changing radically, or, indeed, changing the coming generations radically. The young have no choice but to experiment with what is left of the 'enlightened,' 'analyzed,' and standardized world that we have bequeathed to them. Yet their search is not for all-permissibility, but for new logical and ethical boundaries." When the boundaries had been explored, Erikson predicted, the new "hedonistic" perversity would lose much of its appeal. To Erikson it was evident that it was his generation that had "desacralized" life by "naïve scientism, thoughtless skepticism, dilettante political opposition, and irresponsible technical expansion." The theme of "resacralization," or, in plainer terms, the search for the sacred in the wilds of the Haight-Ashbury, is brilliantly adumbrated by William Craddock in his novel *Be Not Content*.

It is doubtless too simple to attribute the social, cultural, psychological, religious (pick your own term) breakdown of our society solely to the educational system; the problem of which cults are evidence is obviously more complicated. But the realm of "higher learning" is clearly where the collapse of values and the loss of direction in the larger society bore most heavily on the young men and women who searched, by the hundreds of thousands and eventually by the millions, for "alternative life-styles" or a "counter-culture." The things they searched for were the very things that had been excluded from their educational experience. In addition to the avoidance of all the Big Questions, to the absence of any glimmer of spiritual life, to any grace or joy, or opportunity to celebrate, and any genuine human contact between "teachers"—who, indeed, sought to escape so far as they could from teaching at all—and the taught, there was the matter of what drew these unusually talented (and successful, as our society measures success) young people to their gurus. We can best judge what was missing from their educational experience by taking note of what they hoped to find in the communes to which they fled.

It may fairly be asked: is it reasonable to argue that a proper education would have immunized our young men and women against the Bhagwan and the rest?

The sociologist Peter Berger, writing in 1969, "shied away" from Jungian explanations of formal religion as an expression of "alleged religious 'needs' that are frustrated by modern culture and seek an outlet in some other way." It seems to me that such cults as Synanon and the Rajneesh Puram come close to demonstrating the "need" theory. But Berger makes an interesting point. He argues that the aberrant behavior that we have noted is the result of boredom. "Intellectuals are notoriously haunted by boredom," he wrote before the dramatic rise of the cults, "if only because they mainly talk to each other. There is no telling what outlandish religiosity, even one dripping with savage super-naturalism, may yet arise in these groups. . . ."

Do not the two forms of protest, the active and the passive, instruct us in the ills, not simply of our society in general but, more specifically, of those in the realm of higher education? The campus activists of the sixties made their critiques of the universities as educational institutions. Their hope was to reform the universities and thereby make them agencies of a more generous and humane world. They gave evidence of wishing to work "within the system" to reform it. The communards and cultists, some of whom had been numbered among the activists, made their own kind of critique by simply rejecting every aspect of the rational, scientific world of academe. Theirs was the politics of denial.

13
PUBLISH OR PERISH

"[T]he growth of scholarly writing and publication, which ought to be a welcome thing, can turn into a cancerous growth that destroys the symbiosis of which it is a part. . . . We are faced . . . with an urgent need to hold down the volume of printed matter to the point where it can be handled in a human way by libraries and scholars."

—AUGUST FRUGÉ

Since teaching is shunned in the name of research, it is essential for us to consider the subject of "academic research." On those relatively rare occasions when the research syndrome is attacked specifically, the critic's fire has usually been directed at the imbalance between teaching and research, seldom at the content of the research itself. The disposition has been to concede that research *per se* has a significance that is more or less beyond question. It is devoted to pushing back those famous old frontiers. Thus it has escaped critical scrutiny. For one thing, such an examination requires the kind of "value judgment" that professors prefer to avoid. Moreover, professors who are in the best position to evaluate the real value of the research to the larger society have a vested interest in the system. If they have tenure, they are hardly disposed to criticize a system that, at the cost of considerable stress and strain on their part, has rewarded them with lifetime security of employment.

Perhaps the most cynical view of the whole tenure process is taken by graduate students and young instructors who have felt the harshness and absurdity of the system most keenly. But they have hardly been in a position to criticize it publicly, because they have, as we say, bought into it when they directed their time and

energy toward an academic career. It should also be noted that the system itself is of a nature to attract the less independent and original young men and women. It requires, from those who wish to enter, a degree of conformity hardly to be found in other professions. Those individuals whose primary interest is in teaching students are well advised to find another line of work. The system is, like all such systems, self-selecting. We are inevitably reminded of John Jay Chapman's observation at the turn of the century that young faculty members with enthusiasm were weeded out at Harvard on the unstated (and doubtless more or less unconscious) grounds that they could not be entirely objective. "Such," Chapman added, "is the power of natural law." The "natural law" that Chapman observed in operation at Harvard spread, like a plague, to major universities across the country. Fortunately, since enthusiasm is hard to stamp out, some enthusiastic teachers have slipped through to give their students the benefit of their enthusiasms.

The first fact to be established is that there is no direct relationship between research and teaching. The notion that research enhances teaching, although thoroughly discredited by experience *and* by research, is one that lingers on and is often trotted out by the ill-informed as a justification for the publish-or-perish policy. A typical expression of this notion is that by Professor William Hutchinson of American University who wrote in a summer 1966 edition of *The American Scholar:* "The fact is that no very vital instruction of any kind can be carried on without scholarly books and the studies and monographs that undergird them." Needless to say, there is a vast amount of firsthand evidence to refute that claim and very little evidence to support it. Two recent research projects directly contradict it. Martin Finkelstein, in a study made in 1984, declared that he had been unable to find any grounds for the proposition that "good research is both a necessary and sufficient condition for good teaching." The facts were quite otherwise. He reached the conclusion that "research involvement detracts from good teaching. . . ." Hugh Brown and Lewis Mayhew in *American Higher Education* reached a similar conclusion. The fact is, they wrote, that, "whenever studies of teaching effective-

ness are made as judged by students, no relationship is found between judged teaching effectiveness and research productivity." How, indeed, could it be otherwise? In the modern university, the most distinguished scholars or researchers commonly do the least teaching. This has been a general complaint virtually since the rise of the university. Most of a professor's research is too specialized or too esoteric or too poorly written up to be of any interest to his/her undergraduate students.

One of the problems lies with the definition of "research." It has been made into such a comprehensive term that it now includes the most routine and pedestrian labors as well as the most brilliant original work. It is, of course, a major contention of this book that the routine and pedestrian far outweigh the brilliant and original; that routine and pedestrian research is not merely a very expensive nullity but a moral and spiritual drag on the institutions in which it takes place and a serious distortion of the nature of both the intellectual and the scholarly life. The economic cost is also scandalously high, if only because the less teaching a teacher does, the lower the general quality of teaching, the more huge classes, teaching assistants, etc., the higher the cost of the teaching that is done. If a professor teaches, say, one course in a session, a quarter, or a term, instead of three, his/her "cost effectiveness" is one-third of what it would be if he/she taught three. In other words, a high price is paid by the system for the time spent in research. Everyone who has attended a college or a university has known famous or, one step down, "distinguished" scholars who were the bores of the world as teachers. In their laboratories or studies they might be able to communicate to their students the inner spirit as well as the "methodology" of their researches, but as far as conveying anything but the most routine information to large groups of passive listeners, they were washouts.

It is my contention that the best research and the only research that should be expected of university professors is wide and informed reading in their fields and in related fields. The best teachers are almost invariably the most widely informed, those with the greatest range of interests and the most cultivated minds. That is real research, and that, and that alone, enhances teaching.

Research defined as purposeful intellectual activity is certainly a legitimate requirement for a university teacher. Research necessarily resulting in publication is quite another matter, and it is to this wholly unrealistic and generally destructive requirement that we must turn our attention. Under the publish-or-perish standard, the university is perishing. Research *and* publication are not necessarily related. The argument that the results of research should be published are twofold: first, that the results of a scholar's research should be made generally available to other scholars to increase the fund of knowledge in a particular field; second, and closely related, that the scrutiny of other scholars in the field is necessary to verify and improve the quality of knowledge. In regard to the vast majority of so-called research turned out by university professors, these two propositions are as fallacious as the argument that published research is essential for good teaching.

One way to get a "fix" on the publication issue is to take a hard look at the institution that makes the whole process possible—the university press. The Johns Hopkins Press began in 1878, just two years after the opening of the university. The first task of the press was to publish the *American Journal of Mathematics,* and the first manager of the press was Nicholas Murray, the uncle of the famous Nicholas Murray Butler, president-to-be of Columbia University. The *American Chemical Journal* followed a year later. It was 1887 before the press produced its first book. The notion soon took hold that a university press was needed in order to publish the researches of faculty and students. It was evident that commercial or "trade" publishers were loath to publish most scholarly books, because of the modest sales, sales primarily to other scholars and students "in the field."

After the somewhat reluctant institution of the Ph.D. degree at Hopkins, it became the custom and then the rule to publish dissertations. That policy helped to establish a standard for both students and faculty. The number of monographs produced by an institution numbering initially a few dozen students and faculty was small, and the quality on the whole high. Many of the books published by the Johns Hopkins Press in its early years are still "standard works" in their respective fields.

William Rainey Harper established the University of Chicago Press a year after the university opened, "as an organic part of the institution." The press published thirteen books written or edited by Harper himself under its imprint (the press might well have been thought of as "an organic part" of Harper). From its early years the press published the *Journal of Political Economy, The Journal of Geology* and the *Journal of Near Eastern Studies.* In 1899 it published John Dewey's highly influential *School and Society.*

In 1893 the University of California started a press, with the purpose of printing scholarly monographs by members of the Berkeley faculty, primarily in the sciences, for exchange with other universities in the United States and abroad. Eventually its monographs covered more than forty academic disciplines.

The Columbia University Press, founded in the same year, established a working relationship with the publishing house of Macmillan and through Macmillan published thirty-seven books in the first decade of its existence.

By 1948 there were thirty-five presses that were members of the Association of American University Presses. Twenty years later the number had risen to sixty, with an additional twenty to thirty university presses publishing on a more modest scale—fewer than five books a year. The annual title output had increased even more rapidly, from 727 titles in 1948 to more than twenty-three hundred in 1966, an increase of 319 percent. The increase in titles was reflected in the increase in sales from $4.17 million in the earlier year to $22 million in 1966. The twenty-three hundred titles represented more than 8 percent of the twenty-seven thousand nonfiction titles published in the United States in the latter year. Large subsidies were, of course, required for most of the titles published. The director of the Yale University Press, Chester Kerr, wrote: "We publish the smallest editions at the greatest cost, and on these we place the highest prices, and then we try to market them to people who can least afford them. This is madness." But it was a madness that was to prevail and grow. More presses came into existence and more titles poured from them.

Under the optimistic heading "The mounting need for scholarly publishing," Gene Hawes, in *To Advance Knowledge: A Handbook on American University Press Publishing* (1966), hailed the rapid expansion of university presses. Their growth represented, in Hawes' words, "a whole new order of respect for the powers of expert knowledge, in which the United States and most other nations see a fundamental means of reaching previously inconceivable levels of good health, material abundance, personal freedom, and cultural richness for entire populations. This, too, is new in history as a realistic prospect," Hawes added. Peace, prosperity, and progress through university presses! Hawes calculated that more than $36 billion in "goods and services produced in the country each year is due to new knowledge." As "publishers of expert knowledge, they [university presses] help to advance the future well-being of mankind in ways that seem clearer today than at any time in the past."

The historian Earl Schenk Miers told a group of scholarly publishers in 1966 that the work of their presses "is of desperate importance to me, to my children, and to their children." Much of this desperately important work was made possible by a grant of $2,725,000 from the Ford Foundation distributed to thirty-five university presses. The grant served to underwrite the publication of 644 books by the presses that received funds. In 1962 the program was extended for three years, with a harvest of 546 books.

The euphoria expressed by Gene Hawes in *To Advance Knowledge* was completely dissipated ten years later when university presses found themselves faced by a crisis. The number of volumes published each year had increased astronomically, and many presses, subsidized though they were, trembled on the verge of bankruptcy, caught in a rising tide of "must-publish" books and spiraling printing costs. August Frugé, director of the University of California Press, described the situation of university presses in these words: "New book sales were down; some presses closed their doors. Journals, particularly in the humanities and social sciences, were proliferating at a time when subscriptions were declining. Library budgets were falling behind the need; serial subscriptions were taking up funds previously used for monographs. There were too many books and articles of marginal quality, and publication was too difficult for young scholars. . . . The search for publication, on which may depend . . . promotion . . . is often a desperate one." In Frugé's words, the University of California Press found itself "slipping from one untenable position to another. The best scholars would have nothing to do with some of the new series [of monographs]. We found ourselves taking in second-level books disguised as monographs, thus running a second-rate publishing program alongside a first-rate one." Often the weakest books were "the obligation, or semi-obligation, books that the press finds difficult to refuse and accepts without enthusiasm." It brought to mind "August Frugé's Second Law of Progress. 'The better the technology, the less efficient the human use of it.' "

Faced with a crisis, press directors and librarians called for help, and the American Council of Learned Societies galloped to the rescue. Describing the situation as one of "spreading chaos," the ACLS assembled an impressive list of university-press and library heavyweights to whom it gave the title the "National Enquiry." Interestingly enough, the Enquiry soon discovered that it had best concentrate its attention on publication (or communication, if you will) in the fields of the humanities and social sciences. The scientific fields were quite unmanageable and must be allowed to go their own way, the assumption being that they constituted an arcane world of their own, beyond control or evaluation.

The fruit of the survey, entitled *Scholarly Communication: The Report of the National Enquiry,* noted that, as readers, scholars had little complaint about the availability of scholarly material (how could they, when the presses were turning out far more than they could even pretend to read?). But as "authors" it was quite another matter. Indifferent to the flood of largely unreadable (and unread) monographs rising about them, they called heroically for more. "Pressures to publish for professional advancement are strongly felt" and generally accepted, the report tells us; "however, the view is widespread that quantity matters more than quality, a situation that many scholars resent. Refereeing is often viewed as too slow, and younger scholars express doubts about the fairness of that system. The delay from journal acceptance to publication [in some cases as much as three or four years!] is seen as a problem, particularly when career advancement is at stake."

When faculty members were asked by the staff of the Enquiry how "the system" might be improved, they listed greater efficiency, speedier publication, and *less pressure to publish* (italics, needless to say, mine). Directors of presses complained that, although their impulse was, like that of any publisher, to seek out the very best manuscripts for publication, they had become, in the words of a press director, "certification tools, inundated with essays written primarily to provide credentials." The closest the *Report* could bring itself to an outright criticism of the publish-or-perish syndrome was to state: "Editors would prefer to see either less emphasis on publication as a criterion for advancement or, if this change is not made, they think they merit more support from the university community for providing a certification function that properly should be performed by the faculty."

Bowen and Schuster in their study found some authors willing to pay as much as $30,000 to insure publication of their monographs. Considering that their professional careers rest on publication, it is no wonder that they are willing to pay such a sum.

The Enquiry *Report* agreed "that scholars should be judged on the quality of completed research rather than on its publication, since publishability of a manuscript often depends on . . . matters that are irrelevant to the quality of scholarship. . . . If publication were no longer essential to career advancement, the pressure to publish would be reduced—which, in turn, would lessen the incentive to start new journals and publish more monographs. . . . So long as publication is a criterion for advancement, there will be pressures to increase outlets for publication."

August Frugé's minority report took the line that publishing in the traditional sense should be reserved for a relatively few outstanding works. Publishing "cannot possibly keep up with the growth in numbers. Printing can. But if printing is allowed to do so, in the guise of publishing, then the future is chaos and confusion. The numbers will overwhelm us," he wrote. "Is publication necessary . . . ?" Frugé asked. "For the most significant works, yes. For the others, surely no."

Under the pressures we have described, substantial changes in publishing practices had already been made even before the Board of National Enquiry began its deliberations. In addition to conventional publishing, with its various stages of editorial review, manuscript revision, publication, and promotion, practices referred to as "fractional publishing" had been adopted by many presses. Fractional publishing cut down dramatically on the cost of getting a book printed and given modest circulation. Typically, the author is expected to present a "press-ready" manuscript, ideally one that has been printed on a computer printer and is ready to be photographed for printing in book form. Such works, with an anticipated readership of a few hundred, included the greater portion of the highly specialized scholarly monographs turned out by university professors. The development of fractional printing was a tacit admission of overload. To the critical observer, it gave the game away. Any pretense that the mass of monographs published by professors engaged in research had any but the most limited utility (something approaching zero in many cases) was abandoned. Professors, of course, did not particularly like to be relegated to fractional status, but a book was a book, and it did not carry on its cover the words "fractional printing." The general public is not even aware of the existence of fractional publishing.

In the words of August Frugé: "Fractional publishing . . . will be used for works that will not repay the full [editorial] treatment or that cannot attract a commercial or university press. There is no way out of this; it is built into the circumstances and will take place regardless of anyone's attentions. A quick and easy technology allows a less discriminate choice; what is allowed comes to pass if there is no counter force."

However, even fractional printing would not take care of that rising monographic tide. An ingenious variant was invented by desperate university presses. It was called, rather ominously, OD, for "On Demand" publication. On Demand printing was just what it said it was. A monograph, assumed to have a sale too small to cover the costs of publication (the sales required to recover costs in conventional publication are generally estimated at from two to three thousand), is recorded on film, and after an agreed-upon minimum number have been printed and distributed, the film is stored away in the event that additional copies are "demanded." When a request for the work in question comes to a press, it simply prints up a copy.

University Microfilm International, or UMI, as it is commonly called, has two modes of On Demand publishing. In Frugé's words, the Imprint Series is intended for use "in cooperation with university and society presses that select, edit, and compose the works and place their imprint on them. . . ." The Sponsor Series relies on direct contact with the author, who prepares his/her own "camera-ready copy" and secures the sponsorship of a scholarly agency. The "books" in both series are sent to the Library of Congress for cataloguing and listed in bibliographies. Little promotion is done, since "most titles are expected to sell fewer than one hundred copies."

Frugé writes: "To the extent that universities are universities, they *must* judge faculty members on the quality and value of completed research." Yet, he adds, "it is unfortunate that the judgment of research, especially in the humanities and social sciences, has been tied to the book market. It would be good to break that connection, or loosen it, and still retain the essential value of peer judgment. Acceptance of a manuscript for preservation in microform storage may be considered a lesser form of recognition but it is still recognition. . . . Every author will, of course, prefer full publication, but if microform storage and retrieval is accepted within the university, then the author will find himself in good— or at least numerous—company. . . . The rule is not merely publish-or-perish; it is do-good-research-or-perish. Getting publishing out of the tenure game will not harm peer review. . . ."

Frugé himself has "three measuring sticks or guidelines" for choosing works that ought to have "full publication." They are: "1/ significance of topic; 2/ usefulness; 3/ quality of mind. The last of these, as Paul said of charity, is the greatest of the three." "By mind," he adds, "I include what have been called spirit, wit, understanding." Frugé is the first to admit that such criteria would narrow the range of works published by university presses marvelously, and it is clear he yearns for such an outcome, but it is equally clear that his years of laboring in the academic vineyards had not encouraged him to expect such a transformation.

When it became clear, in the 1960s, that not enough monographs could be published (or printed) or produced in some form of book that would secure promotion for the authors, an alternative form of publication had to be devised. The scholarly journal had been around for almost a century and, pedestrian as most of them were, had performed on the whole a useful function. Articles in journals, like books, constituted publication, and hence provided a basis for promotion to tenure, the principal difference being that it generally took three or four articles to equal a book and in most fields there was less prestige in a handful of articles than in a book, which stood up on library shelves more conspicuously. On the other hand, the journals shared the problems of the university presses, which, incidentally, publish most of the journals. That is to say, most prestigious journals had backlogs of *accepted* articles that often ran two or three years behind actual publication. Same problem. The desperate assistant professor up for tenure. The solution proved disarmingly simple. More journals.

As August Frugé pointed out for the aspiring academic, books are "more risky." "There are more uncertainties and delays in getting a book accepted for publication and herded through the press. One consequence was that young scholars turned increasingly to article writing as they [began] the struggle for intellectual growth and the search for advancement." Moreover, as each academic discipline began to fragment into "subfields" (like, for instance, "semiotics" or the study of "signs and symbols"), the subfield felt it must have its own journal. University "institutes" and "centers" also felt they needed journals to advertise their existence and enhance their image. The consequence: the "number of journals in language and literature rose from 54 to 215 in ten years." Journals in American and English literature increased from thirty-nine to 114 in the same period; in philosophy, from thirty-

Killing the Spirit

nine to ninety-one. It turned out that the quickest and easiest way to get published was to start your own journal and publish the articles of like-minded friends and colleagues. With the new technology of processors and computers and desktop printers, the start-up costs of journals was minimal: $500. If libraries could be prevailed upon to subscribe to the journals, which the major research libraries were inclined to do almost automatically and virtually certain to do on the request of a faculty member, that would account for two or three hundred subscriptions. A few hundred more scattered about would bring the circulation up to four or five hundred, enough to justify the continued existence of a journal, especially if it received departmental or institutional sponsorship. And since, even in the academic world, it is, generally speaking, easier to say yes than no (the principal exception perhaps being in regard to tenure), many journals got (and have) departmental or institutional sponsorship, which guarantees a modest level of support; the costs of the journal are typically absorbed in departmental or divisional budgets. This form of publication on the cheap helped to relieve the book publication logjam and facilitate the promotion of tens of thousands of professors who otherwise might have languished in the never-never land of the nontenured; who might, at best, have slipped off the "ladder" and become permanent members of the academic underclass— lecturers.

One of the stratagems employed by professors desperately seeking tenure is to keep submitting rejected articles to different journals so that they can write on their résumés "under consideration by the journal of such-and-such." Not much, but better than nothing; it may serve at least to postpone the day of reckoning, since every department chairman and review committee is uncomfortably aware of instances where manuscripts and articles turned down by any number of presses and/or journals have eventually been published to considerable acclaim. It is small wonder the Enquiry declared: "Specialized scholarly journals have proliferated beyond anyone's ability to read and absorb. . . . Libraries, the great preservers of knowledge, are foundered by sheer bulk and the rapid rise in cost. . . . A new Babel will soon be upon us." The comparison of the situation in the scholarly world with the Tower of Babel is an apt one. The Tower of Babel was characterized by a "confusion of tongues": people could not understand each other, for they all spoke different languages. Could we have a better analogy to the academic world today, with specialization piled on specialization and no one in one field able to speak intelligibly with his colleagues in other fields?

The *Report* of the Enquiry noted flatly that the increase in the number of journals was directly related to "the rise in academic unemployment and competition for advancement." In other words, it had nothing to do with the *need* for more research/publication. Even with the remarkable proliferation of journals, 56 percent of the scholars contacted by staff of the Enquiry revealed that they had in hand manuscripts that had been rejected. Rejection is indeed common, and of course adds to the time and the uncertainty attendant on publication and, in consequence, on promotion. Obviously, the untenured assistant professor is most vulnerable. If his/her publication date fails to coincide with his/her evaluation for tenure, the candidate will be out in the cold.

On a personal note, the first article I submitted to a scholarly journal in my field, the venerable *William and Mary Quarterly,* went to several referees for their opinions. One replied very favorably; the other was not heard from. The decision was made by the editor to publish the article, and I was so informed. A few weeks later the report of the other (or another) referee came in. This anonymous reader called down the wrath of heaven on my essay. It was baseless, "sophomoric," a disgrace to the profession; its publication would set back research in the field (of colonial American history) "20 years" (for some reason the twenty years stuck in my mind; that seemed quite a setback to be caused by the initial article of an unknown assistant professor).

The editor, obviously alarmed and disconcerted, decided nonetheless to publish the essay, but he relieved his anxiety a bit, I suspect, by sending a copy of the letter along to me, saying I might want to make some revisions in the light of the referee's belated criticism. Since the basic criticism might be summed up as "Decontaminate and burn this manuscript," I was at something of a loss to know how to respond. The article was published as written; colonial American scholarship survived; the piece was subsequently included in an anthology of articles on the causes of the American Revolution and incorporated in a book of mine on the writing of history. Had the dilatory referee been prompter in his denunciation, the editor might well have rejected my article, and had my promotion to tenure depended on it— Well, there you are.

My fourth book came near to suffering a worse fate. It was on the role of the small town in American history. Writing it was a bit risky, since my field was, as I have noted, early-American history (essentially the colonial period and the Revolution) and I was not supposed to stray out of it under pain of being written off as an academic dilettante. In any event, I sent the manuscript off to a press known for interest in Western and small-town history. Weeks passed without word, without even acknowledgment of receipt of the manuscript. Finally, after several months, I sent a wire to the director of the press. What had happened to my manuscript? I got a wire in reply. Very good reports from two referees; they expected to publish it. Or words to that effect. Then, a few weeks later, an embarrassed and apologetic letter. All bets were off. A senior faculty member of great power in the university had pronounced an anathema on the work. Presumably it would set back Western studies twenty years.

The manuscript then started on a round of university presses— Chicago, Princeton, Yale, as I recall. This circulation through university presses was, not surprisingly, a slow (and demoralizing) process. Finally, I started on regular trade publishers—Macmillan, Doubleday, Random House, Knopf. Knopf, the most prestigious of all, for my money, accepted the manuscript. The editor at Knopf wondered if he hadn't glanced at it when he was an editor at Macmillan. I ignored the query. Knopf published the book—handsomely, as usual. It was "well reviewed," as they say, went into paperback, and was eventually recognized as a worthy work. A historian even wrote a book based on it (and a work or works of Daniel Boorstin) and proclaimed it a new brand of history, although it is nowhere recorded that anyone took his claim very seriously. That is to say, regretfully, that there is no Smith School of historians. I tell this personal tale because it makes a valid point, which is that a perfectly respectable book can travel a long, rocky path before publication and, indeed, may not get published at all. At least as far as the academic world is concerned, if there is anything in a manuscript deviating from the prevailing orthodoxies, the chances of treading on a referee's toes are considerable. Just the man who is *the* expert in the field is apt to be the one most hardened in his prejudices and the one most likely to do you in.

To my mind, one of the most negative aspects of the pressure to publish is that it discourages any bold or original work on the part of junior faculty. When so much rests on not simply doing the research but, more important, getting it published, the risks of doing something unorthodox, something that might offend strongly held prejudices in a particular field, are great. On the other hand, the temptation to do something glitzy and striking is also great. If the glitzy monograph can get past what may be a conservative publications-review committee, it may make a splash and lead to attractive job offers at other institutions. So fine calculations must be made. And all in an atmosphere of pressure and anxiety.

In the course of "researching" this chapter, I was astonished to learn that one-third of all manuscripts published by university presses in 1973 had been submitted to at least four or five presses previously. A number of authors had given up after submitting their manuscripts to "a median number of eleven publishers," and manuscripts "temporarily shelved"—that is to say, manuscripts whose authors had abandoned the effort, at least for the moment—numbered 33 percent. All of which seems rather staggering. "Depressing" might be the better term. Those rejected and "temporarily shelved" manuscripts may be assumed to add up to tens of thousands of, in effect, wasted hours, days, months, literally years, time that could have been far more profitably and pleasantly employed in teaching students. I find it a bit chilling to learn that, despite, in many instances, the most dogged industry, the results are often simply unpublishable under any rubric. Perhaps it is fairer to say that much research does not get published simply because the process of review is highly fallible. Since everyone connected with university-press publishing seems to be in agreement that many published works are mediocre by any reasonable standard and can only be justified for publication at all on the ground that they are "filling the gaps," it seems reasonable to assume that there is a very uncertain line between what gets published and what doesn't. Obviously, in some instances it is simply a matter of persistence. An author who gives up after five rejections has an unpublished manuscript on his/her hands (usually the fruit of years of "research"). The only difference professionally between him/her and a "published author" may be that the successful author tried six more presses before he/she finally got published. It all sounds disconcertingly like roulette. But the point that I wish to emphasize is that the real victims are the students that the professor might have been teaching and the taxpayers (and tuition payers) who are supporting the system that forces professors to behave in such an irrational (and costly) manner.

Make no mistake about it, the public, in the form of parents and taxpayers, bears the very considerable cost of so-called research scholarship, especially in the humanities and social sciences. In my equation, every dollar that can be charged, directly or indirectly, to research represents an equivalent charge on the cost of instruction. Obviously, in many cases, in the sciences at least, it is a charge justified by the returns, however indirect, to society at large. In many other cases, it is equally clear that it is not (and remember that even in the sciences a vast amount of "busywork" goes on to no very exalted end). If we could find a more rational and humane way to make decisions about the retention and promotion of faculty than by extracting publications from them, we could begin to solve a host of problems plaguing higher education.

When I began to teach, a "full load" was six courses a year; it is commonly five now, and there is a movement under way to reduce it to four. Seven courses a year would seem to me to be a reasonable number, a number that, with summers, leaves, sabbaticals, etc., would allow all the research activity a professor felt compelled to do (not because he had to do it to win promotion but because he desired to do it).

Since scientists are not all that different from the rest of us, there is no reason not to believe that they, too, are puffing up research, inflating publications, doing "busywork" whose aim is not to advance science as much as it is to advance scientists. They are under the same relentless pressures to publish. This assumption is given credence by periodic scandals in which it turns out that claims that cannot be replicated have been made by reputable scientists for their researches. There is even a slang phrase, "cooking the evidence"—i.e., falsifying the results of an experiment. Since science is a far more precise activity than, say, literary criticism, the chances of being unmasked are proportionally greater. A mediocre monograph in modern European history simply sinks out of sight after having secured a promotion for its author and is listed in his bibliography, but the flawed experiment often returns to haunt the experimenter and can fatally damage his career.

The New York Times of February 14, 1989, informs us that a committee of the Institute of Medicine reports that "careless and sometimes even fraudulent medical research" has become much too common. The committee attributes the problem to "Financing pressures and an overemphasis on publication of research in scientific journals. . . ." Among the institutions where careless or fraudulent practices have come to light recently are the Massachusetts General Hospital, Yale University, Cornell University, Harvard Medical School, and Boston University. Such incidents, the committee report notes, "raised new questions about the ability of the academic institutions to conduct objective investigations of misconduct by their own faculty members. . . ."

Less reprehensible than cooking the evidence is the conduct of research for the sake of research, the carrying out in lavishly equipped laboratories of generously funded research done primarily to justify the existence of the laboratory and its support team of graduate students and research assistants, done, often, because it is in a "hot" field where applications for funding are almost automatically approved. I have heard a distinguished scientist estimate such research to make up from 75 to 80 percent of all the scientific research that goes on in major American universities. I know one professor of biology who, in the midst of a project, felt such pangs of conscience that he closed down the experiment and returned the unexpended funds to the grantor. Such scrupulousness is rare, and it has its price. The next time the professor applies for a grant, his application may be more critically reviewed. It is obviously safer to do what you have contracted to do and keep your mouth shut. Neither the granting agency nor the parent university is apt to be pleased by such unwelcome integrity. It calls into question the soundness of the whole enterprise. The inevitable thought is: suppose every scientist shut down all experimental work that was not of the highest order of importance? The answer, quite clearly, is that the whole top-heavy system would come tumbling down.

As though the situation were not bad enough at the major universities, the publish-or-perish disease threatens to spread like a plague to institutions hitherto relatively immune. In 1969 E. Alden Dunham, in a book entitled *Colleges of the Forgotten Americans,* surveyed 279 state colleges, most of them desperately anxious to become "first-rate research universities." In Dunham's view, there are only twenty to fifty "first-rate research universities" in the country, turning out 90 percent of the Ph.D.'s, and very few, if any, of the ambitious 279 could hope to achieve that (to me) dubious status. The so-called Forgotten Americans were simply students who attended some 279 state colleges and teachers' colleges (many state colleges had been teachers' colleges).

The University of Northern Iowa was one such institution. Dunham saw signs there of efforts to "bring in the kind of faculty who are wedded to their discipline, research, graduate students, doctoral work and university status." In order to accomplish such results, colleges like Northern Iowa hired ABDs (all but dissertations) from "elite" universities. Of course, such candidates were under special pressures to complete their dissertations and get their degrees. If and when they did, however, they often went on to more prestigious institutions. In Dunham's words: "Money is made available to hire professors of English . . . to take care of freshman and sophomores, whose numbers are increasing. The professors of English being hired can't wait to gain position and rank so they may concentrate on what they have been hired for— research at the graduate level." Such faculty "want to turn this essentially teaching institution [Northern Iowa] into a carbon copy of the research institution which they just left as graduate students."

So what we have are state colleges (and, trailing behind them, teachers' colleges) striving desperately to upgrade themselves into legitimate (or illegitimate) universities instead of being content to teach students well. Seeing their colleagues in the better-known and more prestigious universities enjoying all kinds of cushy perquisites—teaching loads light as a feather, semi-sabbaticals, frequent additional leaves with grants, etc.—the state-college faculties would be less than human if they did not aspire to the same status, especially since they have little respect, in the main, for their better-paid and more fortunate colleagues. Conversely, the professors at the so-called elite institutions fear the upward thrust of institutions they consider hopelessly inferior. Since all state-supported institutions of higher learning draw from essentially the same pot, state tax revenues, if the colleges are able, by turning themselves into universities, to claim a larger share of that by no means bottomless pot, there will be less for the old-line "original" state universities. And more competition for federal grants to do defense-related research. Not, of course, to mention the private foundations that are already under fire for distributing their largesse undemocratically to the elite institutions while generally ignoring the lower academic classes.

The original universities can do little to stem the rising academic tide that threatens their perks except to demonstrate their higher status, which they typically do by upping the monograph ante. More published research deserves more tax-dollar support, they argue to often skeptical legislators. One way they can demonstrate their higher standards and greater rigor is by "terminating"—i.e., failing to give tenure to more assistant professors. That is why I call these dreadful terminations ritual murders. They are, in essence, the price old-time university faculties are glad (or at least willing) to pay to preserve their turf. A terminated professor, however able, is not apt to be picked up by an upscale state college or university, because to do so is to appear to acknowledge tacitly that the former-state-college-now-university has lower standards than the old-time university, by accepting the university's rejects. So this cruel and irrational system goes on, the principal sufferers, besides those terminated, being the students and the taxpayers.

The California Master Plan for Higher Education barred even the best state colleges from giving the doctorate and calling themselves universities. That privilege was reserved for the campuses of the University of California. But it proved impossible to hold the line. The state colleges had too many allies in the California legislature. They won the right to call themselves universities, but it proved a hollow victory: they are still denied the right to grant Ph.D.'s.

Ortega y Gasset pointed to the dilemma of the modern university in having "professional instruction which is for all, and research which is for a very few." But the modern university insists on maintaining the pretense that "research is for all"—at least for all professors who wish to have tenure. The result is this strange incremental activity of producing highly specialized monographs that no one even pretends are of first-rate quality.

Robert Hutchins wrote that research "in the sense of gathering data for the sake of gathering them has . . . no place in a university." Virtually all discussions of teaching versus research reveal a conscious ambivalence or (apparently) subconscious contradictions. In their study of university faculties, Bowen and Schuster pay the usual lip service to research. They list penicillin, hybrid seed corn, and the Pill as notable examples of "basic research conducted in universities." "Humanistic scholarship," on the other hand, is described as "the discovery and rediscovery of past human experience . . . and the transmission of this knowledge from generation to generation. These activities are of inestimable value because they enable each generation to understand itself and its problems in the perspective of human experience." But this, of course, is exactly what scholars in the humanities and social sciences are *not* doing. Instead, they are transmitting the latest information in their own highly specialized fields, information in the main of very little interest or relevance to their students and none to the outside world.

Why, it may be asked, am I so feverish about the inferior quality of most of the research being done in the modern university? If it contributes little or nothing to our insatiable desire to understand ourselves and our past, it is a harmless enough activity; it breaks no bones and tears no flesh, unless, of course, it is in a "defense" field, making more deadly bombs and inventing more ingenious ways to kill people. For the most part, research in the social sciences and particularly in history does not directly endanger lives and may even, here and there, do some good, since most of it is motivated by a rather benign liberal ethos, and thus "discovers" things that support social progress.

My answer would be that, aside from the enormous amount of time such research takes away from teaching, it falsifies human experience and the true nature of research. If bad research (not technically "bad" or methodologically bad but unimportant and largely irrelevant research) does not drive out good, it constantly threatens to bury the good in a vast pile of mediocrity. It encourages the notion, moreover, that routine, pedestrian work has some useful function in God's plan for the universe. Research is not a right and certainly should not be a requirement. It is only tolerable if it is the passionate pursuit of a problem or vision that obsesses the researcher and will not let him/her rest. It could be argued that all reasonable impediments should be placed in his/her path to test his/her resolve. Certainly nothing should be done to encourage research for the sake of research/publication. Is not the atmosphere hopelessly polluted when professors are forced to do research in order to validate themselves, in order to make a living, in order to avoid being humiliated (and terminated)? What kind of research can possibly come out of such a system? The whole nature of intellectual activity is hopelessly distorted, the nature of knowing, the roots of life. If, in that place that our society has designated as the holy of holies, our magnificent cathedrals of learning, we cannot be true to ourselves and our students, what hope is there for our immortal souls? In Karl Jaspers' words, we have allowed ourselves to be persuaded "erroneously" of "the intrinsic value of any factual discovery whatsoever, of each and every correct application of method, extension of knowledge, and scientific occupation." The result: chaos. "There was the uncounted mass of arbitrary factual finding, the diffusion of the sciences into a vast unrelated aggregate, the complacency of specialists ignorant of and blind to the larger implications; the triumph of the 'production line' approach to learning, forever losing itself in the endless waste of mere factual correctness." Jaspers is speaking here apparently of the "hard" sciences, but the same things may be said with equal confidence of the other academic disciplines.

If it is true that research, in the best sense of that much-abused word, cannot really be suppressed, it is certainly reasonable to do all that is possible to discourage anything but the best. That obviously presents us with a major dilemma. Since the university, as we know it, is organized around the motif of research, since appointments, promotions, institutional prestige, government funds, private donations, and heaven only knows what all depend on its rank as a "research institution," it may seem the merest folly to propose the deflation of research to some humane and rational level and the corresponding elevation of teaching. But folly or no, facts is facts, as they say, and routine, time-serving, aimless, mediocre research must be identified as such and gently but firmly suppressed. Since, by general agreement, only a relatively few of the tens of thousands (or is it hundreds of thousands?) of professors in various academic fields are capable of first-rate research, and since, as we have noted time and again, these can't be stopped, we must find useful labors, like teaching, for all the FTEs retired from research.

14
TEACHING

"A university is . . . an Alma Mater, knowing her children one by one, not a factory, or a mint, or a treadmill."

—JOHN HENRY NEWMAN

Now that I have demonstrated conclusively that the vast majority of what passes for research/publication in the major universities of America is mediocre, expensive, and unnecessary, does not push back the frontiers of knowledge in any appreciable degree, and serves only to get professors promotions, it may be appropriate to give some consideration to teaching. It can be said unequivocally that good teaching is far more complex, difficult, and demanding than mediocre research, which may explain why professors try so hard to avoid it.

If we are to discuss teaching, it may be well to start by giving some attention to the aims of education. Ortega y Gasset reminds us that we must base our teaching, "its methods and institutions upon the plain, humble principle that the child or the youth who is to be the learner cannot learn all we should like him to know—the principle of economy in education." The consequence, in Ortega's view, is that the university "must be the projection of the student to the scale of an institution." We must acknowledge first that the student is "a being of limited learning capacity—and second, what he needs to know in order to live his life." The university must focus "once more on the student . . . and not the professor, as it was in the heyday of its greatness." All discussion of reform must begin "with the ordinary student," not the genius, not the prospective scientist or professor of abnormal psychology but the citizen of the republic who must earn a living in addition to living a humane life.

To teach students to think clearly is obviously highly desirable, but as Sir Richard Livingstone reminds us, "to teach people to see and feel is more important still." The heart is a more reliable organ than the brain. It is this fact that Alfred North Whitehead had in mind when he wrote: "Moral education is impossible without the habitual vision of greatness." The best educators in the best ages have always kept this in mind. Plato wrote that, when a Greek boy "has learned his letters and is beginning to understand what is written, [his teachers] put into his hands the works of great poets, and he reads them sitting on his bench at school; and they contain many admonitions and stories and praise of famous men of old, which he is required to learn by heart, in order that he may imitate or emulate them . . ."

Plato's words call to mind an experience toward the end of my academic career. I was chairman of an eccentric graduate program at the University of California, Santa Cruz, called "The History of Consciousness." Although the title was irresistible and attracted students from all over the country like a magnet, it proved extremely difficult to define it and to decide what combination of courses or studies might be considered properly to constitute a rational program. With faculty and students meeting to try to find some common intellectual ground, a colleague suggested that the students try to define the program by considering what kinds of individuals they would like to be as a consequence of having been in the program, working their way backward, so to speak, from later careers to graduate studies. One of the few things the graduate students seemed to agree on was that a decade or two later they did not wish to be in any significant way like their teachers. Their teachers represented just those aspects of higher education that seemed to these exceptionally bright young men and women least to be admired and emulated. I considered that odd session the death rattle of American higher education. Such a response was hardly imaginable to me. I felt that my own life—not just my professional life and scholarly prejudices, but the entire fabric of my existence—was derived from and inspired by my teachers. My greatest desire was to emulate them.

Certainly it is true that a teacher teaching in today's world has special problems to confront. In Sir Walter Moberly's words, "students feel themselves to be living in a different world from their teachers, a world which is far grimmer and less secure economically, politically and morally." This was doubtless an element in the response of the students in "HistCon," as it was called. "What the world most needs and most lacks today," Sir Richard Livingstone wrote in 1948, "is a clear and worthy view of life. . . . What do we do to give the undergraduate such a view. I think we must reply, 'Little or nothing.' " The situation is no better in 1989.

A "worthy view of life" is made up, in essence, of ideas. Ortega y Gasset notes that we "cannot live on the human level without ideas. Upon them depends what we do. . . . [W]e *are* our ideas." The sociologist Louis Wirth makes the same point: "A society is possible in the last analysis because the individuals in it carry around in their heads some sort of picture of that society." Without such a picture, society begins to unravel. It seems to me an alarming, even terrifying fact that our ideas determine our actions and that our collective ideas define our society, for better or for worse. The ideas of fascists and racists determine behavior just as surely as the ideas of saints. To think wisely and well is to live wisely and well. So we can never be indifferent or casual about what young men and women are taught, or, equally, not taught. To not teach something is to relegate it to the junk pile of discarded and irrelevant ideas.

Robert Hutchins, one of the most influential educators of our time, discusses and dismisses what he calls "the great-man theory of education." It holds, briefly, that for an undergraduate simply to sit in the presence of a famous scholar is "an education in itself." Such a notion seems to Hutchins "a vacuous reply to the charge that we have no intelligent program for higher learning." Hutchins' own prescription seems to me hardly more helpful. His ideal university is organized to "train the mind," or "refine the intelligence." Hutchins is, of course, not alone in maintaining that it is the educator's primary responsibility to "train the intelligence" of the student. He is also confident that he knows how to do this. The student is to be trained at Hutchins' college to think clearly and rationally, and this is to be accomplished by having students read and discuss the great works of literature, philosophy, and science. I think such a curriculum highly desirable in itself, but I am not persuaded that the result is something that can be defined as "trained intelligence." Indeed, I not only do not know how to produce a "trained intelligence"; I do not even know *what it is*. I have not observed in myself or my students over a reasonably long life some particular and identifiable quality that can be isolated from a whole congeries of other qualities and clearly identified as a "trained intelligence." Nor have I observed it in my colleagues, some of whom are very learned men and women in the best sense of the word. A trained intelligence suggests to me an intelligence in track shorts doing wind sprints or running twenty miles a day.

Another frequently cited goal is to produce a "well-rounded person." As far as the "well-rounded person" is concerned, I keep seeing in my mind's eye an object as round and flat as a pancake. Of course, we know what the intent is. We would like an individual at home in the world, a young man or woman with broad intellectual and aesthetic interests and professional competence in a particular field. But the latter is much less important than the former. To be "at home" is, it seems to me, a splendid notion. It implies a relationship to the universe, to nature, or, as we prefer to say today, to the environment or one's ecosystem, a commitment to civic duty, a striving for civic virtue. Without civic virtue in the citizenry there can, for a fact, be no civilization. Civilization is not a "natural product" or process; it is not something that simply happens. It is the consequence of the efforts of innumerable individuals, famous and obscure, who sacrifice some degree of personal gratification, forgo certain pleasures, assume certain tasks, and, perhaps above all, accept their responsibilities.

A true person is a person whose aesthetic sensibilities are developed so far as they are capable of development, which means an attachment to those aspects of human experience we denominate the arts: music, poetry, literature, crafts, painting, sculpture.

Any individuals insensitive to this range of human experience are, to a degree, emotionally impoverished. Life in all its variety and richness cannot touch them. They are, in consequence, not entirely at home. Their inner life is diminished.

The arts are too often today presented to us as something we can put on like a mink coat, an appendage of middle-class with-it-ness, subject to the most transient fads and disheartening fanaticisms. No more "art-appreciation" courses. The words put one's teeth on edge. Better to call them "art-survival" courses. The arts are essential to a true life because they put us in touch with the greatest spirits of all times. They constantly cheer us up by reminding us of the inexhaustible richness of the human imagination as it plays upon the raw material of the world's sights and sounds. It (art) or they (the arts) remind us every day of how we may be lifted in spirit by the music of the spheres, the glories of the natural world.

Finally, the true person has some vision of higher things, of a realm beyond the immediate existence, beyond the material world. He or she may not be able to define very precisely what these larger, transcendent elements are, those we sometimes refer to as spiritual or "religious." They touch the deepest levels of our consciousness and solace us, inspire us, reconcile us to our humanity. They are the wellsprings of life. The most familiar and most mysterious is love—"agape," as the Greeks called it. Love is, of course, what holds the world together. It is the mortar in our perilously fragile lives. It cannot be bidden, bought, sold, earned; it is indistinguishable from grace. None of us are worthy of it, and yet all of us must have it to live. It can't be taught. We can have any number of courses on sex education (sex has little to do with love, although love of course may include sex, rather as an afterthought), but who can imagine a university course on love? (UCSC has one.) Love has to be demonstrated or experienced. Teachers who love their students are of course by that very fact teaching their students the nature of love, although the course may in fact be chemistry or computer science. That is why universities and colleges grow cold and sterile in their innermost being. If a professor doesn't know his students, he obviously can't love them. He may be fair and decent to them in the abstract, but they, tender young souls that they are, need above all to be loved and cared for. And, in a curious way, the professor, although he seldom realizes it, needs them as much as they need him. So long as he refuses to take them to heart, they are simply an inconvenience, a burden, a part of his "teaching load."

Will it surprise the reader to have it said that a true education, one designed to produce a true person, must include instruction in courage? Can we make our students courageous, assuming, of course, that it is agreed that courage is a highly desirable human quality and that no society can long maintain itself in a healthy state whose members are in any general sense lacking in courage? We surely cannot inject courage into our students as a doctor injects a vaccine into a patient. But we can talk about the role that courage plays in every aspect of life and thereby encourage courage. We can make clear that the most important discoveries in science, the most important revelations in the arts, in virtually every field of human endeavor, have had a major component of courage. Great things are not accomplished by cowards but always by individuals bold enough—or perhaps, in some circumstances— mad enough to fly in the face of the most firmly held and respected conventions of their society. Rosenstock-Huessy reminds us that there must always be individuals willing to draw down upon themselves public calumny and sometimes far worse by speaking out too soon, before the general public is willing to listen, in order that others, coming later, may speak "in time." And this is not even to consider the desperate physical courage of martyrs and patriots willing to sacrifice their lives for their principles. Courage is, of course, as important for a physicist as for a leader of the people in politically dangerous times, although not so likely to be fatal in its consequences. The Hungarian dissident George Konrad notes: "Since writing is a dangerous enterprise, and one pays a price for doing it, whoever writes what he thinks is an adventurer and must take into account every possibility, like a prisoner planning a jail break."

More important than talking about the role of courage in all human affairs, important as that is, is the demonstration of courage.

Granted, the university is not the ideal ground for demonstrating courage; it is nonetheless required there even if in modest amounts and no student can observe it (except perhaps in the lives of his fellow students) unless the student comes to know his/her teachers and observes in them courage (or the absence of it). So there is yet another argument for the necessity (as opposed to the desirability) of personal contact between teacher and student.

An unforgettable story demonstrating the role of courage in the advancement of science was told by the Nobel Prize–winning physicist Harold Urey. Following a lyric (and thoroughly unscientific) lecture by Urey about the moon, a student asked him what he considered the most important quality for a scientist. After a moment's reflection, Urey replied to his rather startled listeners: "Courage." He then went on to explain how a physicist in the early part of this century had come upon the formula of heavy water (the discovery of which won Urey his Nobel Prize). The experiment ran so counter to existing principles in the field that the scientist, afraid of drawing on himself the ridicule of his fellows, put his proof in a drawer and tried to forget about it. Had he had the courage, Urey pointed out, to risk the scorn of his colleagues, he would have made an important name for himself in the annals of modern science (and Urey might not have won the Nobel Prize).

There is another aspect of the true person that should be developed or encouraged by higher education (and by lower, too, for that matter). This is a proper respect and concern for the physical body. No one has improved on the Greek ideal of a sound mind in a sound body. Since the Cartesian mind-body split typified by the notorious *Cogito ergo sum,* "I think therefore I am," Western man has suffered from the notion that thinking is the most basic and essential human activity and that the mind rules the body. One result has been a disposition on the part of intellectuals in Europe and America to neglect the body. On the educational level, this has resulted in the unhappy division between the "jocks" and the "grinds."

Charles Francis Adams, Jr., was convinced that he suffered from the fact that his father scorned the physical side of life. As a boy he had never been taught to sail or ride a bicycle or encouraged to engage in any strenuous sport. At Harvard the story had been much the same. The students were treated as though they hardly had bodies at all. Adams learned to ride a bicycle after he was sixty years old, and when he did so he realized "how irreparable has been my loss in not acquiring other muscular aptitudes while doing so was possible." Indeed, when Adams, after studying law, enlisted in a cavalry troop of the Union Army at the outbreak of the Civil War, he was ecstatic at the invigorating effect of military life. "My enjoyment," he wrote his mother, "springs from the open air sense of freedom and strength. It is a lawless sort of feeling, making me feel as if I depended only on nature and myself for enjoyment."

Adams wrote his father a few months later: "I was never better in my life. The exposure has been pretty severe and the change of life great; but I am always well in the open air and jolly among a crowd of fellows." To his brother, Henry, who worried that Charles Francis' mind was lying fallow, he wrote: "Perhaps, but after all the body has other functions than to carry around the head, and a few years quiet will hardly injure a mind warped, as I sometimes suspect mine was, in time past, by the too constant and close inspection of print." At the age of twenty-seven he discovered "that I never knew myself. . . . I am growing and developing here daily, but in such strange directions."

Obviously, we cannot have wars in order to develop hardihood and manliness in our young men (and womanliness in our young women). We must have what William James called "a moral equivalent." Recognition of the unbalanced one-sidedness of American education generally, led, several decades ago, to the development of the Outward Bound program. Instituted primarily for youth of high-school age, it had the philosophy that young Americans needed to test themselves in "the wild," in arduous and demanding encounters with nature where skill and courage were required. Outward Bound is an effort to create a moral equivalent to those aspects of military life that Charles Francis Adams found so invigorating, that transformed him, by his own testimony, from a

Boston bookworm, an intellectual, all brain and little body, into a "Bohemian."

Many institutions of higher learning have, or have had until recently, compulsory athletics for all members of the student body, but such physical activities as exist are overshadowed by the hysteria generated by "big-time" sports, and at best they are poorly integrated with the academic curriculum, the prevailing attitude being that physical activities are peripheral, of minor importance, fringe benefits for those students who wish to avail themselves of sports activities. Physical education, which once enjoyed a respected position, especially in the great state universities and in women's colleges, has moved to the margins of the academic world, tolerated but afforded little respect by the professoriate. But to be at home in the world is also to be at home in one's body, and that means, in turn, that on some sensible level the interplay between mind and body must be acknowledged and cultivated.

I thought myself somewhat alone in my enthusiasm for the physical side of things until I read these words by the respected professor of literature Roger Shattuck: "We spend a good deal of time in universities and colleges developing and defining interdisciplinary programs. . . . I have never in my life heard of a single such program that includes training of the body. Yet we have all read Plato, and possibly St. Ignatius and Stanislavsky and Artaud and some Zen or yoga." Shattuck was reminded of this striking deficiency by a film sequence he had seen. "In the slanting light of dawn a few mature men stood under the trees and went slowly and attentively through the traditional movements of T'ai Chi Ch'uan. Calisthenics we would call it. But this ritual was beautiful and partook visibly of an intellectual concentration and a spiritual presence. . . . Has such training and performance been banned forever from our education?" Shattuck asked. "Between required physical education and the huge spectaculars staged for the public at large there seems to be a physical desert."

It is dance that for Shattuck represents the ideal development of the body. "A college of arts and sciences that establishes a department of dance in its midst will be doing more to extend the meaning of education than can be done through any other single innovation I can think of. . . . It is depressing to think that we are educating a nation of cripples."

Another aspect of the experience of the race that should be honored and cultivated is that which deals with festivals and celebrations. Josef Pieper, a German theologian, wrote an instructive essay entitled *In Tune with the World: A Theory of Festivity*. His opening sentence points out: "Certain things can be adequately discussed only if at the same time we speak of the whole of the world and of life. If we are not ready to do that, we give up all claim to saying anything significant. Death and love are such subjects. Festivity, too, must be included in that category." Pieper's section headings are suggestive: "The subject of festivity involves the whole of existence. . . . The festival: 'something different for a change' . . . The trick of finding people who really are able to rejoice . . . Day of rejoicing. Receiving what is loved . . . The origin of festivals: praise of God in public worship . . . The fruit of festivity is pure gift." Pieper laments the decline of festivals. The modern holiday, often spent on crowded highways in search of transitory pleasures, is the antithesis of the true festival.

Most festivals are, of course, religious in origin, but festivals are closely related to work and especially to agriculture, to the bringing in of harvests, the pressing of grapes, the planting of crops. Festivals have, or should have, a close relationship to the arts, particularly to music, to song and dance. Festivals should be marked by joy and a kind of self-forgetting delirium. Festivals take us out of the workaday world and out of ourselves. They bathe us in the timeless light of original creation, link us to the natural world and to each other.

If history and anthropology have anything to teach us, it is that human beings, from the tribe to the traditional cultures of the modern world, have among their most basic needs the need to celebrate, to pay their respects to the invisible powers of the world. We celebrate birthdays, weddings, marriages, anniversaries, even deaths where lives have been fully and fruitfully lived. We mark the holy religious days of all the great faiths of the world. It is in our nature to do so. Without the power to celebrate, we are greatly diminished. We suffer a kind of illness of the soul.

All right. Let us assume that celebrations and festivals touch us on the deepest levels of our being, exalt us, and heal us, and the absence of them often leaves us isolated and neurotic. What has that to do with higher education? Well, we were talking about the true person at home in the world, so the connection should be obvious. Students should be reminded of the centrality of celebration and the necessity of festivals throughout human history. More than that, they should experience both. They do, to be sure, have commencement exercises, celebrations of the completion of their college careers, but the black-clothed processions of professors and graduands with tedious and repetitious addresses are dispiriting affairs. The closest thing to a festival most campuses can offer are football or basketball "pep rallies." But can festivals simply be introduced into the gray and somber atmosphere of the average institution of higher learning? How about the summer and winter solstices for starters? They already have a respectable history as festivals in many cultures, and they would provide ideal opportunities for emphasizing humankind's dependence on the natural world.

Imagine a campus (perhaps one exists or has existed) where members of the so-called-but-seldom-existing-in-reality academic community—faculty, students, and even administrators—gather together to dance and sing and dine! Is that so bizarre, so unacademic, so "emotional" that it cannot even be imagined? How are we to learn to celebrate life and lift our spirits in festivals if we are not taught? How are we to get "in tune with the world"?

How do you think the academic world would react to the notion that it had some responsibilities in such matters? Not the proper business of any respectable university. It may be that at the heart of the primness, the austerity, indeed, of the puritanical temper, of the academy is the uneasy awareness that such rituals contain in themselves the message that "scientific objectivity" does not rule the world, that its hegemony is being challenged, its dominance over our consciousness, our view of ourselves, and our relation to the world. Celebrations and festivals are, after all, primitive and emotional. They are eminently unreasonable, thoroughly irrational. If students want to sing and dance, let them take "Choral Music 101" or "Modern Dance 6B." They can thereby get six units of credit. Or let them sing and dance extracurricularly. Some years ago, on the campus of the University of California, Santa Cruz, the professor in charge of the Western Civilization segment of the World-Civilization course, the college's required "core course" that everyone was expected to take, prevailed on the entire class to sing Handel's *Messiah*. They did not, it must be confessed, sing it very well, but the point was that, in struggling to sing it at all, the members of the class gained an insight into the spirit of eighteenth-century Christendom that I believe they could never have gotten in routine classroom exercises.

I came away from my years of teaching on the college and university level with a conviction that enactment, performance, dramatization are the most successful forms of teaching. Students must be incorporated, made, so far as possible, an integral part of the learning process. The notion that learning should have in it an element of inspired play would seem to the greater part of the academic establishment merely frivolous, but that is nonetheless the case. Of Ezekiel Cheever, the most famous schoolmaster of the Massachusetts Bay Colony, his onetime student Cotton Mather wrote that he so planned his lessons that his pupils "came to work as though they came to play," and Alfred North Whitehead, almost three hundred years later, noted that a teacher should make his/her students "glad they were there."

Since, we are told, 80 to 90 percent of all instruction in the typical university is by the lecture method, we should give close attention to this form of education. There is, I think, much truth in Patricia Nelson Limerick's observation that "lecturing is an unnatural act, an act for which providence did not design humans. It is perfectly all right, now and then, for a human to be possessed by the urge to speak, and to speak while others remain silent. But to do this regularly, one hour and 15 minutes at a time . . . for one person to drone on while others sit in silence? . . . I do not believe that this is what the Creator . . . designed humans to do."

The strange, almost incomprehensible fact is that many professors, just as they feel obliged to write dully, believe that they should lecture dully. To show enthusiasm is to risk appearing unscientific, unobjective; it is to appeal to the students' emotions rather than their intellect. Thus the ideal lecture is one crammed with facts and read in an uninflected monotone. Witness the testimony of the eminent sociologist Daniel Bell.

When Bell gave a talk to the faculty and staff and some graduate students at the Leningrad State University during a trip to Russia, he spoke extemporaneously (which professors seldom do) and with evident emotion, which clearly moved his listeners profoundly but which left Bell feeling "an odd turbulence. . . . For years," he writes, "I had fought within myself against giving emotional speeches. They were easy, cheap, sentimental, lachrymose. . . . In the lectures I usually give . . . I have tried to be expository, illustrative . . . resenting the cheap jibes to get a rise out of the audience." Here, to his discomfort, he had let emotion get the best of him and, plainly, of his audience. I would only note that the kind of austerity and lack of emotion that Bell normally strove for is the classic mode of the American professor lecturing to his class.

The cult of lecturing dully, like the cult of writing dully, goes back, of course, some years. Edward Shils, professor of sociology and social thought at the University of Chicago, recalls the professors he encountered at the University of Pennsylvania in his youth. They seemed "a priesthood, rather uneven in their merits but uniform in their bearing; they never referred to anything personal. Some read from old lecture notes—one of them used to unroll the dog-eared lower corners of his foolscap manuscript and then haltingly decipher the thumb-worn last lines. Others lectured from cards that had served for years, to judge by the worn and furry edges. . . . The teachers began on time, ended on time, and left the room without saying a word more to their students, very seldom being detained by questioners. . . . Almost all male students wore suits, all wore neckties. . . . The classes were not large, yet there was no discussion. No questions were raised in class, and there were no office hours."

William Lyon Phelps described the Yale faculty in the 1890s thusly: "nearly all the members of the Faculty wore dark clothes, frock coats, high collars; in the classroom their manners had an icy formality. . . ." The clothes and manners have become informal, but the aloofness and impersonality, I fear, remain.

Karl Jaspers makes the point that the lecture, like research, must never become routine. It is the opportunity for the teacher to present in dramatic fashion, highlighted by his/her own insight and enthusiasm, material that cannot be conveyed with the same potency on the printed page. In the lecture the student must see *enacted* the power and excitement of ideas. The posture, gestures, and intonations of the lecturer carry as much force as the words themselves, words that, when reduced to notes, often lie quite inert on the page.

The lecture has a quasi-religious character about it, since exalted speech partakes of the sacred. Every lecture, listened to by dozens or hundreds of students, should partake of art (dramatic art being perhaps the closest). The lecturer who reads his notes dutifully is performing an act that the students can do better for themselves. Such an instructor gives up the very element of spontaneity which alone justifies the lecture as a form of teaching. The lecturer must *address* students. He/she is, after all, asking a good deal of them. If there are two hundred students in the class, the lecturer is saying to them, in effect: What I have to say is of such considerable consequence that I feel entitled to take up two hundred precious hours of your collective time in order to explain it to you, or, even better, in order to enlarge your sense of the possibilities of human existence in relation to this topic we are considering together. "Lectures which aim to sum up an entire subject are in a class by themselves," Jaspers writes. "Such lectures should be given only by the most mature professors drawing upon the sum total of their life's work. . . . Such lectures belong to what is irreplaceable in tradition. The memory of outstanding scholars lecturing, accompanies one throughout life. The printed lecture, perhaps even taken down word for word, is only a pale residue." The inspired lecture evokes, again in Jaspers' words, "something from the teacher which would remain hidden without it. . . . He allows us to take part in his innermost intellectual being." The great lecture is thus a demonstration of something precious and essential in the life of the spirit and the mind, and the dramatic power that inheres in that unity. Such lectures link us with the sermons and political addresses that have played central roles in the "great chain of being" that links classes and generations and nations together in "the unity of spirit." Thus the casual, the perfunctory, the oft-repeated, the read lecture, the *dead* lecture, is a disservice both to the students and to the ideal of learning that presumably holds the whole venture together.

William Lyon Phelps at Yale was a "great teacher," in the classic tradition. "If a teacher wishes success with pupils, he must inflame their imagination," he wrote. "The lesson should put the classroom under the spell of an illusion, like a great drama." The abstract should be avoided. "If a pupil feels the reality of any subject, feels it in relation to actual life, half the battle is gained. Terms must be clothed in flesh and blood . . . ," Phelps wrote. The modern professor often takes a contrary turn. The real things are the abstractions; the personal, the individual, the anecdotal are all distractions and indulgences. A professor may give the same course, covering the same material, year in and year out (it is, after all, his "field," and he is actively discouraged from stepping outside it). He/she may go so far as to incorporate in the lectures the latest "researches," to the degree that they are relevant to undergraduate students, but unless he/she rethinks each lecture, reanimates it, *reappropriates* it, and thereby makes evident to his listeners why they should take their valuable time to listen, the lecturer is discrediting the lecture system and the process of learning that the lecture system represents. The lecturer is putting forward a "negative stereotype," as we say, not just of himself and of lectures in general, but of the whole edifice of higher education. If the lecturer is bored by the constant repetition of familiar material, he may be sure that his auditors are even more bored. The comedian Professor Irwin Corey had a popular routine in which he fell asleep while lecturing; it was invariably greeted with enthusiastic applause.

In his fourteen-week survey of the great universities in 1910, the journalist Edwin Slosson attended more than a hundred classes. His strongest impression was "the waste of time and energy in the ordinary collegiate instruction." There was "no lack of industry, devotion, and enthusiasm on the part of the teachers, but the educational results," Slosson wrote, "are not commensurate with the opportunities afforded and the efforts expended." One's strongest impression was of "lost motion." There was "no general appreciation of the fact that the printing press had been invented in the years since the rise of the Medieval university." Most of the professors lectured poorly, and many did not "even take pains to speak distinctly enough so that they can be heard in their small classrooms without strained attention." Conveying information by ear was a strikingly inefficient way of transmitting it, especially to passive, note-taking students who often showed little comprehension of what they were hearing. "The lecture," Slosson concluded, "is useful for inspiration and demonstration, but not for information." It was apparent to Slosson that, despite its obvious and, in the main, undisputed shortcomings, the lecture was persisted in because it was the quickest and easiest way for a professor to discharge his nominal obligations as a teacher of undergraduate students. One of the unfortunate consequences was that the professor commonly indulged himself in excessively detailed information in the field of his academic specialty, often scanting or ignoring issues of the greatest importance and interest to his captive auditors.

I must confess that my own attitude toward lecturing was deeply influenced by my experience in teaching Dante's *Divine Comedy* in a seminar. When I suggested to my students that they devise some modern hells for modern sins, two students in the seminar offered interesting hells for professors-who-neglected-their-students. They proposed that the professors be required to listen to lectures for all eternity. The only point of dispute between them was whether it would be worse torment for professors to have to listen to their own lectures or to those of an especially dull colleague. I have never been able to feel the same way about lecturing since. Every time in the intervening years that I have undertaken to lecture, I have suffered from post-traumatic stress syndrome.

I think it is fair to say that the lecture system is the most inefficient way of transmitting knowledge ever devised. It would be much more effective, in most instances, simply to print up a lecturer's notes and distribute them to the students at the beginning of the course. Or students might be given reading lists of important books to pursue on their own initiative. In many instances it would be more useful to let the students give the lectures. All this is not to say, of course, that particularly inventive and enterprising professors can't overcome the most negative aspects of the lecture system, but only to point out that very few do. Indeed, it is the nature of things that there are only a few great lecturers. In the thirty-some years in which I had contact with the academic world, I knew only five or six. They were individuals who had passionately held views of life as well as deep knowledge of their subjects. They took every lecture with the greatest seriousness and spoke as though they realized that to speak was both a privilege and a responsibility. Eugen Rosenstock-Huessy, William Hitchcock, Mary Holmes, Norman O. Brown, Donald Nichol, and Paul Lee all fell into that category.

The most conclusive argument against the lecture system is that all true education must involve response. If there is no dialogue, written or spoken, there can be no genuine education. The student must be lured out of his or her instinctive passivity. This can only be done properly if an atmosphere of trust is built in the classroom or seminar. The professor cannot ask his students to expose their innermost hopes and feelings unless he is equally candid with them and allows them to see him as a fallable, searching individual.

The best discussion of the relationship between professors and their students (which, of course, is at the heart of all true teaching) is, I am pleased to say, by a former student of mine, Patricia Nelson Limerick, a professor of history at the University of Colorado. After describing a number of imaginative ways to involve students in classroom exercises designed to break down the barriers between "aloof professors" and "shy students," Limerick writes: "In all these exercises, my goals have been the same; to bump students out of passivity, and to bump myself out of self-consciousness and sometimes out of complacency. . . . By contrast, the more conventional tensions of the classroom cause students and professors to fear making fools of themselves. . . . The underlying reason for holding class, whatever the subject or the course, has to involve the project of inviting students to think for themselves, to ask their own questions, and to pursue the answers with both freedom of thought and discipline of argument." If a professor tries to promote such a notion in the conventional classroom, "there is such a disjunction between the medium and the message," Limerick writes, "that the project will work for only a few. . . . The trial and burden of adventurous teaching is that it never feels safe—you never sign a contract with the universe guaranteeing success in all your experiments."

That, of course, is the essence of teaching—taking chances. And you can only do that if you are willing to come down from your perch as a professor of this or that and be as vulnerable (or almost as vulnerable) as your students. No professorial vulnerability, no real teaching.

Karl Jaspers wrote, "The reverence and love rendered to the master's person have something of worship in them," but Jaspers goes on to point out that the master must turn this "reverence and love" into the channels of learning in a manner perhaps akin to the analytic "transference," wherein the scrupulous analyst directs the patient's instinctive attachment to the analyst back toward the process of healing. Jaspers' ideal in the teaching relationship is the Socratic method, whereby teacher and student "stand on the same level. . . . No hard and fast educational system exists here, rather endless questioning and ultimate ignorance in the face of the absolute."

The geologist Israel C. Russell wrote in the journal *Science* in 1904: "In the school of research . . . professor and student should be co-workers and mutually assist each other. From such comradeship, that intangible something which is transmitted from person to person by association and contact, but cannot be written or spoken—we may term it 'inspiration,' or personal magnetism, or perhaps the radium of the soul—is acquired by the student to a greater degree than at any previous time in his life after leaving the caressing arms of his mother."

Alfred North Whitehead's wife, Evelyn, told Lucien Price: "When we first came to Harvard, Altie's [Whitehead's] colleagues in the department said, 'Don't let the students interfere with your work!' Ten or fifteen minutes is long enough for any conference with them." Instead of following his colleagues' advice, Whitehead, who lectured three times a week, would give his students "a whole afternoon or a whole evening. . . . The traffic was two-way, for Whitehead felt that he needed contact with young minds to keep his own springs flowing. 'It is all nonsense,' he said, 'to suppose that the old cannot learn from the young.'"

Contacts between professors and their students outside the classroom, ideally in walks or sports or social occasions, are as important as or perhaps more important than classroom contacts, because they reveal something to the student about reality that can, I suspect, be learned no other way. Such contacts demonstrate that ideas are "embodied." They do not exist apart from a person, remote or near at hand, who enunciates, who takes responsibility for them by declaring them, by speaking about them. It is not only that ideas have consequences; they are held, passionately or perhaps frivolously, by individuals; otherwise they could not survive; they would die of inattention, and of course many do. We are all dependent, in the last analysis, on readers or listeners (and responders) who by responding remind us that we are talking to living souls.

In Woodrow Wilson's words: "The ideal college . . . should be a community, a place of close, natural, intimate association, not only of the young men who are its pupils and novices in various lines of study but also of young men with older men . . . of teachers with pupils, outside the classroom as well as inside. . . ."

When it became evident beyond question or cavil that professors were determined to ignore the "moral and spiritual" needs of their students, a new academic order called "counselors" was created. Counselors were in essence men and women employed to do what the traditional college education had professed to do (but which it had seldom done)—that is to say, care for what we would call today the psychological needs of the student, what, indeed, John Jay Chapman's ladies and bishops and teas had done at Harvard: provide some human contact, some counsel and advice. I suspect "ladies, Bishops and tea" were a sounder remedy for the distress of undergraduates not simply ignored but positively rebuffed by their instructors. The trouble was (and is) that most of the students who find their way to counselors are near the end of their rope. They have, as we say today, serious "problems." One can only speculate that there might be far fewer such "problems" if faculty members were willing to lend sympathetic ears to the trials and tribulations of the young men and women they are supposed to teach. Their defense, as one might suspect, is that they are not "experts" in matters pertaining to the psychological needs of students, they are only experts in Sanskrit, or economics or abnormal psychology or chemistry. I have long maintained that Ionesco's *The Lesson* should be performed each year for entering freshman at our institutions of higher learning to prepare them for the years ahead. The reader may recall that in *The Lesson* the student arrives to interrupt the professor in his researches on the origin of ancient Spanish verbs. While he is lecturing on the subject, she experiences acute pain from a toothache. The professor ignores her cries until they become too obtrusive, at which point he strangles her. The play ends as another student arrives.

Testimony to the bad consciences of universities about the sorry state of the teaching function is the widespread practice of awarding, with much fanfare, cash prizes to the "teacher-of-the-year." This is supposed to demonstrate the institution's commitment to "excellence in teaching." What it does, in fact, is to distort and demean the true nature of teaching. It is also often the case that untenured winners of such awards soon disappear from the scene, victims of the publish-or-perish rule. So often has this been the case on some campuses that there has been pressure from the administration to make the award only to faculty who have already attained tenure, thus sparing the university the embarrassment of firing someone who has just been recognized as an outstanding teacher. Moreover, although the awards doubtless go, in the main, to deserving individuals, the winners are often those lecturers whom the students simply find the most entertaining. William Arrowsmith, the classics scholar, has written: "At present the universities are as uncongenial to teaching as the Mojave Desert to a clutch of Druid priests. If you want to restore a Druid priesthood you cannot do it by offering prizes for Druid-of-the-year. If you want Druids, you must grow forests. There is no other way of setting about it." In other words, if you want good teaching, you have to create an academic atmosphere where good teaching is encouraged, recognized, and rewarded with something more substantial than "prizes."

It should also be said that one of the greatest obstacles to effective teaching is the grading system ("de-grading system" would be a better name for it). It treats the students as isolated individuals. It pits them against each other and, in a sense, against their teachers in a competitive struggle for survival. Only the fittest survive. I have heard not a few professors boast of the severity of their grading. How many students flunked a course was a measure of their tough-mindedness. In addition to discouraging cooperation among students, grades falsify the relation between teacher and student. The teacher's task is to win the student's confidence and to create an air of trust congenial to learning, but over this rather tender relationship there hovers the cloud of that grade. Professors often fall into the habit of thinking of students less as people in need of help and guidance than as A students or C students, a very bad frame of mind indeed.

Finally, there is an important point, I think, to be made about students *en masse,* so to speak. We are inclined to think that the best students go to the most prestigious institutions—that the students at Harvard, for instance, are inherently superior to the students at Towson State. That that is not necessarily the case is suggested by an interesting by-product of E. Alden Dunham's 1969 report for the Carnegie Commission on Higher Education. Dunham made a survey of three categories of freshmen students: those in all four-year colleges, those in public four-year colleges, and those in public universities. What was most striking about the survey was the general uniformity of views and backgrounds between the students in the different categories. For example, between 20 and 23 percent of all entering freshmen had been elected "president of student organizations"; between 10 and 12 percent had "high rating" in state music contests; between 17 and 19 percent (that was the high-low spread) had had "a major part in a play"; between 5.1 and 9.8 had "National Merit recognition"; between 9.6 and 12.6 planned to get a Ph.D. Forty percent across the board planned to get master's degrees. Even in "major influence in deciding to attend" a particular college there were only a few percentage points between students attending four-year colleges and those in state universities.

The fathers of between 26 and 33 percent of freshmen students were businessmen. Between 11 and 14 percent of fathers were skilled workers. Sixteen percent of the fathers of students at state colleges were semi-skilled or unskilled workers.

Under "objectives considered to be essential or very important" in attending college there was, again, surprising uniformity in students' responses in "high"- and "low"-prestige institutions. Between 59 percent (all four-year colleges) and 60 percent (state universities) said that being "an authority in my field" was "essential or very important." Six or 7 percent wished to "compose or perform music" while 12–14 percent hoped to "write original works" and 13–14 percent wished to "create works of art"; 18 to 20 percent expressed the intention of joining the Peace Corps or VISTA; roughly 40 percent wished to succeed in business and 83 to 85 percent listed as "essential or very important" developing "a philosophy of life." Ninety percent had "attended a religious service during the past year," 40 percent had played a musical instrument, and some 58 percent had "read a poem not required for a course" in the past year. Forty percent had played chess, and 50 percent had tutored another student. Seventy-plus percent had visited an art gallery or museum in the past year. Three times as many (some 16 percent) students had protested the "school administration" as had protested the Vietnam War.

Not by any means incidentally, 90 percent of the students in the three categories agreed "strongly or somewhat" that students should be actively involved in the "design of curriculum" (certainly an indication of dissatisfaction with the curriculums as they existed), and 62 to 65 percent believed that faculty pay should be based on student evaluations.

I am not generally enamored of statistics, but two items seem striking (and poignant) to me. First, despite the differences in prestige between public and private four-year colleges and state universities, the abilities, aspirations, and backgrounds of the students in those respective institutions are virtually indistinguishable, and it could be argued that where there is a noticeable difference it is in favor of the "lesser" institutions—i.e., 4.1 percent of the state-college students protested the Vietnam War as opposed to 3.7 percent of the state-university students. The other striking statistic is the roughly 85 percent of freshmen who listed developing a "philosophy of life" as an "essential or very important" part of their college experience. As they say, "Lots of luck!" The one thing that more freshmen agree is more important than anything else—more than material success, being "an authority," "becoming a community leader," etc.—is the one thing that the university is most indifferent to, or least equipped to help the student achieve.

It seems reasonable to say that, although the prestige conferred on graduates of high- and low-status institutions varies widely, the human beings who pass through them are astonishingly similar by the almost three hundred indices that an ingenious surveyor dreamed up. We have, of course, relatively few data on "what comes out the other end"—that is to say, how the entering freshmen, so similar in talent, background, and expectations at their entrance, compare as seniors or alumni. It is the major thesis of this work that the great majority of them, whatever their capability, are short-changed by the system. The principal exceptions would, of course, be those who attend small, private, once-denominational colleges and community colleges, where there is a strong tradition of placing the needs of students rather than the ambitions of professors at the center of the institutions.

Good teachers are, fortunately, far more numerous than great (or good) lecturers. They are men and women who know their subjects well, feel enthusiasm for conveying the subjects to their students, and, equally important, know their students as individuals and care for them. Good teachers do not have to be geniuses, or great scholars, or publishers of monographs. They have to have lively minds and broad interests.

We live on a number of levels; we are sensuous, intelligent, believing, celebrating, self-contemplating, world-resolving, problem-solving beings. We need to be able to move from one level (or one pole) to another. We breathe, respond, sing, worship. The academic world has not adequately represented what Rosenstock-Huessy has called our "multiformity." We need to establish new rhythms, new ways of learning, new ways of celebrating. We need alternation and alternatives; action and response; freshening of the spirit and lightening of the mind. We need to teach.

15
THE SOCIAL NONSCIENCES

"Thought divorced from responsible action is sterile, and a purely theoretical analysis is liable to lead to impotence."

—SIR WALTER MOBERLY

We have traced rather cursorily the process by which the social sciences became part of the modern curriculum. The initial expectation was clearly that they would each make important contributions to the solution of the crisis that, it was generally agreed, faced the country in the post–Civil War period. At this point it may be well for us to take some account of the fate of the various social sciences as well as the humanities.

First, sociology. History records that Auguste Comte, the French philosopher, first used the term "sociology" in his six-volume work, *Positive Philosophy,* which began to appear in 1837. For Comte, sociology comprehended all knowledge. The Frenchman wished to establish sociology as a basis for a "religion of humanity," a unifying theory based on observation and experimentation. In light of the subsequent history of academic sociology, it is important to note that Comte called sociology "the *religion* of humanity [italics mine]." The sociologist Peter Berger makes the point that, once the world had been divided up along scientific and nonscientific lines, sociology became a much more formidable enemy of religion than science *per se,* since sociology claimed jurisdiction over social man, over the whole realm of experience outside of the sciences, and thus became the natural opponent of religion. In Berger's words: "The challenges of the human [or social] sciences . . . have been more critical, more dangerous to the essence of the theological enterprise [than science]." The social sciences claimed, in practical fact, to supersede history and psychology by giving a more up-to-date account of the nature of social man. Even before the appearance of academic sociology, history and psychology, according to Berger, had done much to undermine a theistic view of the world: history by suggesting the historical character of religions—i.e., that they "arose out of particular historical circumstances and not as a consequence of divine intervention in the world" (and were thus "relative"); psychology because, at least in the Freudian version, it took the line that religion was simply a "gigantic projection of human needs and desires," a notion "all the more sinister because of the unedifying character of these needs and desires. . . ."

There was clearly a strong utopian element in Comte's thought, and a number of utopian communities were founded along Comtian lines with the avowed intention of testing his philosophical (or sociological) assumptions. Sociology was thus a direct and specific product of the Enlightenment temper. The science of society, like any proper science, should develop laws of social behavior that, if followed, would produce close to ideal conditions of life for the faithful. If enough information was collected on diverse cultures, patterns must emerge that could be used in the reformation of society in general.

In the United States there were two main currents of sociology. One was originated by John Humphrey Noyes, the founder of the Oneida Community and leader of the so-called Perfectionists. Perfectionism was a Christian dogma that held that mankind was actually living in the millennium predicted in the Gospel of Saint John, wherein Christ was to return to reign on earth for a thousand years before all the saints were taken up to heaven. All that was wanting was for the faithful to band together and live according to God's word. It was, in Noyes' view, the task of Christian sociology to determine the principles by which God wished his followers to live. The result, in Noyes' thought, was a combination of ideas derived from New Testament accounts of the early Christian communities, plus an Enlightenment faith in rational planning and the power of reason when based on Christian faith. Men and women were equal in the eyes of the Lord and in most of the activities of the community—in work, in sports, in sexual matters, and in such social issues as child-rearing.

Noyes wrote a fascinating book entitled *The History of American Socialisms* in which he listed some eighty utopian or socialist experiments. Thirty-four of these were Fourier phalanxes based on the theories of another French utopian, Charles Fourier (Frenchmen usually thought up the utopias, and Americans tried them out). Noyes was convinced that all secular utopias must fail. Only Christianity could tame the unruly impulses of the human heart and thus provide a base for social cooperation. On the other hand, mere religious enthusiasm, without some "scientific" social and political structure to organize and support it, must also collapse.

Since, according to the Scriptures, there was no marrying or giving in marriage in heaven, Noyes invented what he called "complex marriage," whereby men and women in the community could express their "amative" inclinations and on occasion, with permission, their "propagative" instincts (to have children). Young men were instructed in the correct sexual techniques by older women who had gone through menopause. "Every woman was free to refuse any, or every, man's attention." "It is the theory of the equal rights of men and women," Noyes wrote, "and the freedom of both from habitual and legal obligations. . . . It is the theory that love *after* marriage and always and forever, should be what it is *before* marriage—a glowing attraction on both sides, and not the odious obligation of one party and the sensual recklessness of the other." A member of the community wrote: "We believe that the great secret in securing enthusiasm in labor and producing a free, healthy, social equilibrium, is contained in the proposition, 'loving companionship, and labor,' and especially the mixing of the sexes, makes labor attractive." Noyes wrote that the community treated all work done in the Lord's name as equally honorable. Members were taught that it was not "the kind of work that dignifies a man, but that by good spirit and good manners the man dignified *every kind* of work; and that he is the truest gentleman who is capable of doing the most useful things."

The main-line development of academic sociology in the United States derived from Lester Ward, a veteran of the Civil War, an ardent admirer of Herbert Spencer's Social Darwinism, a founder of the National Liberal Reform League and a dedicated enemy of anything even vaguely associated with religion in general and Protestant Christianity in particular. The reader may recall that the league was opposed to "all fallacious moral and religious doctrines." The principal targets of the league's disfavor were "the leading doctrinal teachings of the so-called Catholic and Evangelical Protestant Churches. . . ." The league wished to promote "the triumph of reason and science over faith and theology."

Lester Ward's religion was education, and specifically sociology. Intellectually, Ward was a lineal descendant of Comte (who did not die, incidentally, until 1857) in that his intention was to use sociology to reform society. Although he believed that sociology was, or could be made into, a science, his real interest was in using that science for the betterment of mankind. In this respect, Ward was in the by now well-established tradition of American utopian reformers. The basic difference between John Humphrey Noyes and Lester Ward was that Noyes believed that society could only be redeemed by "scientific Christianity," by Christianity applied to scientific inquiry, whereas Ward considered religion an anathema and believed that the path to reform was that indicated by scientific sociology. The state universities were, Ward believed, the true channels of redemption. He was confident that in time they would "supersede" the older, "endowed" universities. They were "freer and more democratic," more able to lead the way to "the complete socialization of education throughout the civilized world"—not socialization as in "socialism," but socialization in the sense of serving the needs of society for progress and reform. Sociology, in Ward's words, meant "nothing less than the complete social appropriation of individual achievement which has civilized the world. It is the crowning act in the long list of acts that we have only partially and imperfectly considered, constituting the socialization of achievement." Behind Ward's rather vague formula lay the Enlightenment-cum-Darwinian faith in the ability of reason and science to take charge of the evolutionary process and guide it toward the fulfillment of humanity's ancient dream of a just and harmonious world—the Christian dream of universal brotherhood now flying the banner of science. Jefferson would have approved.

Ward, of course, did not go unchallenged. His rival in influence was William Graham Sumner, a former Episcopal minister turned sociologist. Sumner was a hard-line Darwinian who believed that the evolutionary process, human or animal, should not be tampered with. The fittest should survive and the less fit fall by the wayside. To help the poor and needy was to intervene vainly and foolishly in the process. In a famous essay entitled "What Social Classes Owe to Each Other," he declared "nothing." Sumner wrote: "Constraint, anxiety, and possibly tyranny and repression characterize all social relations." It was when "the social pressure due to an unfavorable ratio of population to land becomes intense that the social forces develop increased activity. Division of labor, exchange, higher social organizations, emigration, advance in the arts, spring from the necessity of contending against the harsher conditions of existence which are continually reproduced as the population surpasses the means of existence. . . . The law of population, therefore, combined with the law of diminishing returns, constitutes the great underlying condition of society. . . . Progress is a word that has no meaning save in view of the laws of population and the diminishing return. . . ." These laws were "the iron spur which has driven the race on to all which it has ever achieved. . . ." Sumner was a skeptic about the values of "democracy" and "equality." "No philosophy of politics or ethics makes human beings prosperous. Their prosperity makes their political philosophy and all their other creeds." For Sumner, "Hard work and self-denial (in technical language, labor and capital)" were the only qualities that served to advance "the welfare of man on earth." It was the "Forgotten Man" and the "Forgotten Woman" on whom, in the last analysis, "the very life and substance of society" rested. "They are always forgotten by the sentimentalists, philanthropists, reformers, enthusiasts, and every description of speculator in sociology, political economy, or political science."

Still a third sociologist had considerable influence in the 1890s, although his name is hardly known now. George Herron was a Christian socialist as well as a Christian sociologist, a member of the faculty at Iowa College (later Grinnell). Herron's lectures on Christian socialism were so popular with the students that the only space big enough for him to lecture in was the college chapel. He went on tour with his doctrine of reform through Christian sociology and at Ann Arbor drew three thousand people, one of the largest audiences ever assembled there. He had similar success at DePauw, Indiana State, the Union Theological Seminary, and, of all places, Princeton. When Herron lectured in Montreal, a reporter compared his impact to "the explosion of a bomb in a public square." "The church," Herron told his listeners, "was not sent to be an institutional dominion, but a sacrificial and redemptive life in the world." The United States was facing a revolutionary upheaval because it had failed, not in material things, but in faith. Revolutions were caused by "seeking to substitute expediency for justice." The dangerous social tensions in the country were caused by "the wicked moral blindness of our industrialism." The nation was in the throes of a devastating depression—"this winter of unemployment and want." There had been no war, no pestilence, no crop failures. "Yet this richest nation of the world, in the midst of a material prosperity so marvelous as to become the object of political worship, suddenly finds a vast population face to face with famine, dependent upon some quality of public philanthropy. . . ." America had betrayed its trust. "God is not in this nation. We are a fallen nation, an apostate people. We have used the liberty wherewith [our fathers'] sacrifice made us free to rob and oppress another. . . . Except our nation repent, turning from political sin to social righteousness, it cannot be saved, and will lose its divine place in the earth."

Herron's teaching resulted in a utopian Christian colony in Georgia—the "Georgia Commonwealth"—a journal—the *Kingdom*—and, not surprisingly, since colleges were so readily founded, a college—the College of Social Science—which was started to teach Herron's brand of sociology. Herron was not helped in the eyes of the orthodox by embracing the doctrines of free love, abandoning his wife, and taking up with the daughter of his principal benefactress.

Herron's crusade won a number of Protestant ministers to the discipline of sociology, men who, like Herron, yearned to redeem a fallen nation. Typical of this breed was John Mecklin, professor of sociology at Dartmouth College. In his *Passing of the Saint,* Mecklin wrote: "[O]ur unhappy world, in spite of its scientific triumphs, its endless multiplication of superfluous gadgets, its farflung machinery for the exploitation of nature, its aimless pilingup of wealth, and its devastating wars, has found no substitute for the saint." At the end of his book, Mecklin reflects upon the "mysterious but insidiously dangerous disease" of modern Americans, "a disease that kills the soul and not the body."

The point that should be clear is that both secular sociology, as exemplified by Lester Ward, and Christian sociology, in the person most dramatically, but of course by no means exclusively, of George Herron, shared the common goal of chastening a rampant industrialism and creating a just social order. The purpose, in both instances, was radical social change.

As sociology became more academic, its idealism, one might say, was squeezed out of it. Its ambitions were lowered, its claims moderated. On the one hand, it became clear that outspoken political advocacy of radical causes could (or inevitably would) imperil one's professional career. It turned out that trustees were less interested, in the final analysis, in a professor's religious orthodoxy than in his political opinions. In addition, the convention grew stronger every decade that real science was "neutral" in all matters. Its responsibility stopped when it had mustered all the relevant facts. That facts should lead to action was a notion less and less regarded.

In the period from the late 1920s to the early 1960s, sociologists, perhaps influenced indirectly by Marxist theory or with nothing better to do, became infatuated with the question of class in the United States. All their informants insisted that the U.S. was a classless society (when the sociologists descended on various towns to quiz their bemused citizens, they gave them such names as Yankeetown, Hometown, Middletown, although everyone in the know knew just what towns they had invaded with their questionnaires and tape recorders) but since virtually everyone denied the existence of class, the ingenuity of the sociologists was tested. They selected things they considered to be indices of class—the magazines a family subscribed to, the newspapers they read, the plays or movies they attended—and once they had gotten the replies down, assigned the respondents to the class the researchers decided they belonged in.

Class and Caste in a Southern Town, Class and Mental Health—almost any book with the word "class" in it was guaranteed notice, and some, like *Middletown,* became best-sellers. There was about such works something of the quality of a novel by Sinclair Lewis with a touch of voyeurism, as we peeked with the professor through a neighbor's windows or compared the magazines on our coffee table with the ones on the subjects'. Were we upper-middle or lower-upper (a good many refinements appeared)?

Now class seems to have had its day. Contemporary sociology has gone on to other matters. And one may be permitted to wonder if anything very useful resulted from the pile of monographs on the subject of class. It might be argued that, although we know more about class in America, we care less. It is also true that the perceptions and definitions of class seem to be in flux, which may mean we are due for an update.

As sociology developed in the middle decades of the twentieth century, two major schools emerged that were identified by the sociologist C. Wright Mills as the Grand Theorists, led by Talcott Parsons (at Harvard), and the Radical Empiricists. The Grand Theorists turned out to be *too* grand, and eventually their systems collapsed of their own weight, leaving the field to the empiricists, who, like the historians and the psychologists and political scientists, went about verifying the obvious and the commonplace. (One notable study revealed that the population density in poor neighborhoods was higher than that in rich neighborhoods. This was before the Donald Trumps of the real-estate world started piling rich people on top of each other.)

It should also be said, parenthetically, that the second-generation sociologists, unlike their predecessors, paid little attention to history. For this they were taken severely to task by the critic George Lichtheim in the spring 1960 issue of the *Partisan Review*. Reviewing a spate of books in the field, Lichtheim pointed out how seriously the authors' conclusions were compromised by their inattention to history, as well as by their addiction to the obvious. He quoted Leonard Reissman as observing of "Hometown" that the "number of classes that is recognized [by the citizens of Hometown] varies, depending on the number of social differences that Hometowners can detect and agree upon."

Whereas Reissman, in Lichtheim's view, had been careful "to guard against misunderstanding by a triple layer of impenetrable academic prose," Seymour Martin Lipset showed a distressing lack of historical knowledge and the critical sophistication to deal with what he did know. Lichtheim quoted one of Lipset's riskier generalizations: "[T]he lower-class individual is likely to have been exposed to punishment, lack of love, and a general atmosphere of tension and aggression since early childhood—all experiences which tend to produce deep-rooted hostilities, expressed by ethnic prejudice, political authoritarianism, and chiliastic transvaluational religion." (That's the way sociologists like to talk, and it is one of the reasons they have relatively few readers, which, as I have indicated elsewhere, is all right with them since it spares them the danger of becoming "popular" and thus a byword among their colleagues.)

It was Lichtheim's sardonic observation that "sociology offers the layman more entertainment, and a wider range of bizarre contrasts in tone and substance, than any other intellectual discipline, not excluding psychoanalysis." To Lichtheim the real trouble with academic sociology "has to do with the uncritical veneration of quantitative measurement and the resulting superstitious belief that meaningful conclusions can be extracted from the juxtaposing of heterogeneous evidence—if this reviewer may for a moment be permitted to lapse into jargon."

A brief four years after Lichtheim's acidulous review, academic sociology was put to its severest test. It involved, to be sure, a relative handful of sociologists, but it seems safe to say that the sociology department of the University of California, Berkeley, was the most distinguished in the country by the early 1960s. What it was doing at the moment the Free Speech Movement began and Mario Savio made his famous remark that the Berkeley campus had become "a community of love" is, so far as I know, not recorded, but it can be said that the effect on the department was devastating. In the face of a "sociological event" of the first magnitude, the members of the department could not agree on the meaning or significance of something that was taking place right under their noses, or even on where they stood personally in regard to these unsettling episodes. They fell out among themselves in bitter personal ways, and the whole pod of sociologists exploded, with noted professors scattering to campuses all over the country. Two of the best known sought refuge at Harvard, where, to their dismay, the students began behaving almost as badly as those they had left behind.

No fair observer would blame the members of the Berkeley sociology department for failing to agree on a common stance in the face of such a strange and unforeseen upheaval, but the whole affair was bound to raise serious questions about how scientific sociology was and exactly what its overall utility was, both to the world of learning and to the world outside. There was a marked swing of some of its once-radical leaders to the right (most are now described as neo-conservatives, and some have openly allied themselves with the Reagan right).

It would be rash to say that academic sociology has been dealt a body blow or blows from which it is unlikely to recover, but it is clear that it shares the most acute problem of the other social sciences. It is not a science and is never going to be one. Moreover, it lacks a clear vision of its mission as a less pretentious "study." It has little to say about the restructuring of our common social life, which, it is widely argued, is in a state of crisis. Unlike history, it has no real body of literature to fall back on. After a student has read Max Weber, R. H. Tawney, Emile Durkheim, C. Wright Mills, Auguste Comte, and a few others, he or she has pretty much exhausted "the literature."

The most serious problem facing academic sociology may be

similar to that facing anthropology: we have come to look at human beings differently in recent decades. It is increasingly distasteful to many people to look at other people (or peoples) as objects of study and observation. We are becoming aware that there is something dehumanizing to both observer and observed in looking at individuals (or social groups) like creatures under a scientist's microscope. We enter into sacred precincts when we approach the "other." By what right do we "study" *them?*

According to Peter Berger, sociology is the "dismal science par excellence of our time, an intrinsically debunking discipline that should be congenial to nihilists, cynics, and other fit subjects for police surveillance." Thus the popular suspicion of sociology is based on "a sound instinct for survival." Well, a sociologist said that, not me.

Anthropology is a more organized expression of our natural curiosity about other peoples, races, nations, tribes. As such it is at least as old as the Greek Herodotus. Academic anthropology is, if anything, even more of an academic Johnny-come-lately than sociology. By and large, anthropologists have concentrated their attention on primitive tribes and "other" cultures. The physical anthropologists collected bones and measured skulls; the cultural anthropologists investigated primitive sexual rites and such matters.

Anthropology is, arguably, the funniest academic discipline. There is something faintly ridiculous about a sober white anthropologist asking impertinent questions of quizzical aborigines and writing down the answers. Sometimes the interrogators were misled deliberately by fun-loving natives. Such rebuffs did not dim their enthusiasm. They swarmed around the world searching out primitive (and not-so-primitive) peoples and giving away their most dearly held secrets.

As it turned out, anthropology had certain practical applications. In the post-Darwinian period, "applied" anthropology made its appearance. It was at least potentially useful to colonial administrators, for example, by suggesting (often incorrectly) how they might best deal with native populations. Unfortunately, such services had the effect of identifying anthropology with colonialism. In a different spirit, Ruth Benedict's *The Chrysanthemum and the Sword,* a study of Japanese culture, was originally intended to provide certain insights into Japanese character that might prove useful in confronting the Japanese as America's wartime enemies.

The most powerful figure in American anthropology—indeed, the founder of academic anthropology—was Franz Boas, a German Jew who emigrated to the United States after studies at Heidelberg, Bonn, and Kiel. In 1883 he spent a winter with Eskimos at Baffin Land. The Eskimos seemed to Boas much superior to his fellow Germans, and his love affair with them may be said to have laid the foundation for modern academic anthropology. His next area of research was among the Indian tribes of the Pacific Northwest. Since there was, as yet, no academic anthropology as such (just some ethnographic studies), Boas enrolled at Clark University in Worcester, Massachusetts, in 1889 and three years later was awarded the first American Ph.D. in anthropology. In 1896 he was appointed a lecturer at Columbia, and the most fruitful period of his career began. Academic anthropology can be seen, in its initial phase at least, as a kind of projection of Boas' own personality and thought. His approach was basically historical, and it soon came into conflict with a statistically and "scientifically" oriented counter-revolution, determined to validate anthropology as a social science rather than as a "humanistic" study. (It is perhaps worth noting that a number of brilliant women gravitated to Boas. His student Ruth Benedict was one of the most important figures in academic anthropology. Margaret Mead was another. The black novelist Zora Neale Hurston was one of his students and an excellent anthropologist as well as a novelist.)

The leading contemporary anthropologist Clifford Geertz has recently described the current dilemmas of the academic anthropologist with characteristic panache. Geertz, who holds a chair at the exalted Institute for Advanced Studies at Princeton, is himself famous as the formulator of extremely recondite theories of anthropology. Now near the end of his academic career, he appears, in a somewhat chastened mood, to reflect upon a lifetime of work in his field. He is impressed by the incongruity of an anthropologist's life, "a few years, now and again, scuffling about with cattle herders and yam gardeners, a lifetime lecturing to classes and arguing with colleagues. . . ." Geertz is struck by the innocence of it all, the naïve assumption that one could, with the tools of the anthropologist in hand, forms and questionnaires, penetrate to the heart of other cultures. That age "now seems very far away." "What is at hand is a pervasive nervousness about the whole business of claiming to explain enigmatical others on the grounds that you have gone about with them in their native habitat or combed the writings of those who have." The worlds of "primitive, tribal, traditional, or folk," now called "emergent, modernizing, peripheral, or submerged," have changed, and so has the world of the observers. The end of colonialism has "altered radically the nature of the social relationship between those who ask and look and those who are asked and looked at."

Perhaps more than the other so-called social scientists, who, as we have seen, have been extraordinarily ingenious in sealing themselves off from the outside world, the anthropologist is faced with the possibility of having to greet his former subject at an international conference on social change. Geertz believes that the old imperial attitudes of colonialism fell "at the same time that the belief in the universal applicability of science to every field of knowledge collapsed." (We have discerned a far more tenacious grip on science than Geertz' remarks suggest and, frankly, far more than we expected to find.) Geertz' central point seems indisputable, however: "the moral context within which the ethnographical act takes place" has changed strikingly and in a way that to Geertz, and certainly to me, appears almost entirely exemplary. The treatment of people as objects of scrutiny, scientific or not, is, when one thinks about it, pretty deplorable under whatever academic rubric that scrutinizing is carried on.

Geertz mentions, among the factors that have overturned the anthropological applecart, "jet-plane tourism" as well as the remarkable diffusion of cultures into other, quite different cultures (a wonderful opportunity, of course, for sociologists to study cognitive dissonance). Who, Geertz asks, is now the student and who the teacher: Africanists or Africans? Americanists or American

Indians? Japanologists or Japanese? Are we to study the heroic African men and women who risk their lives against apartheid or try to emulate them? Suddenly the whole world seems topsy-turvy. We are conscious of what we can learn about some of the most profound aspects of our common humanity from those whose inferiority we not so long ago took for granted. Geertz quite rightly asks whether the "very right write—to write ethnography—" is not itself at risk. Anthropologists, he notes, have "added to their 'Is it decent?' worry (who are *we* to describe *them?*) an 'Is it possible?' one. . . ." Geertz goes on to suggest the complex and almost interminable dialogue that anthropologists have carried on within their own circles. "Like any cultural institution, anthropology—which is a rather minor one compared with law, physics, music, or cost accounting—is of a place and in a time, perpetually perishing, perpetually renewing," Geertz writes.

For me, the first intimation of a new kind of consciousness on the part of anthropologists came with the publication of a book called *Return to Laughter* by Ruth Bohannon. The book was a work of literary merit in addition to giving a charming, personal, and, at least on the face of it, unscientific (but nonetheless persuasive) portrait of the African tribe that had been the subject of the author's study. What was clear from the text was that she had fallen in love with the members of the tribe and that this falling in love had both opened her eyes and made it impossible for her to treat her new friends with the objective detachment required of a "true" scientist. Fearful that the publication of the book under her own name might wreck her career as an academic anthropologist, Bohannon used a pseudonym. When a new edition was printed some ten years later, it was clear that the work was a classic (as well as a watershed in anthropology), and she felt free to confess to having written it. I think it is safe to say that anthropology has never been quite the same since. To put the Bohannon matter as simply as possible: like Franz Boas, Ruth Bohannon fell in love with her subjects and discovered to her surprise that love was a better guide than scientific objectivity. One is reminded of William James' observation that loving is a deeper form of knowing than detachment.

In the words of Clifford Geertz, "What, now that the proconsuls are gone and the socio-mechanics implausible, is the next necessary thing?" I have some suggestions, but I think it more modest to keep them, at least for the moment, to myself. What is important in the context of this chapter is the point that anthropology, no less than sociology, economics, history, psychology, and political science, has run out its string. It might be said that the principal inhibition to the discipline has been the growing awareness that it is *rude to stare*.

Which brings us to academic psychology. Psychology was founded as a study of the psyche—the soul. Properly speaking, then, psychology is the study of the human soul, but the soul is something never mentioned in a proper psychology class, because academic psychology does not believe that human beings have souls. "Soul" is a word, like "love" or "faith," that is patently unscientific. Just as no one has ever seen love in a form that can be examined under a microscope, no one has dissected an individual and found a soul. Nonetheless, psychology is one of the most popular of all undergraduate majors in the United States. Here at least we should find, if not agreement, some common principles regarding human behavior that have stood the test of time and can be used to understand the motivations and psychological (I almost said "spiritual") needs both of individual men and women and, ideally, of society, so-called social psychology. But here again the confusion that we find in other academic disciplines prevails. There is, of course, the classic division of psychology into "experimental" psychology, in which rats and to a lesser extent chickens (the pecking order) are prominent subjects, and clinical psychology, which focuses attention on human beings. Clinical psychology is at present in the ascendancy, in part because of a well-justified skepticism about the applicability of experiments with rats to human subjects. This skepticism, always evident in the general population, has put down roots in the academic world as well. The reasons are various, but one unforgettable newspaper headline remains in my mind: "Rats Hint Man May Be Wilder Than Psychologists Suspect." The basis of this marvelous headline was an experiment conducted with wild rats, instead of the meek and downtrodden laboratory rats usually used in such experiments. The wild rats behaved in wild and un-inhibited ways that astonished and confused the experimenters and indeed raised serious questions about all previous experiments conducted with laboratory rats. I am not prepared to argue that this specific experiment or any number like it put a spoke in the wheel of experimental psychology—a much broader and deeper change in the general public consciousness was doubtless responsible for that—but it makes an irresistible reference point.

On the clinical side, psychology had to come to terms eventually with Freudian psychology, although the penetration of Freud into the world of academic psychology was far slower than one might have anticipated. In many instances, professors of history and literature, for example, proved far more susceptible to the doctrines of the Viennese doctor than psychologists themselves. The resistance to Freud came in part from the influence of William James as the founder of "American" psychology with his famous two-volume *The Principles of Psychology*, and from the work of Harry Stack Sullivan, whose personal influence was strong and who stressed the role of the wider cultural context in mental illness, particularly schizophrenia.

Generally speaking, psychology proved peculiarly suited to the American temperament. The reasons for the American infatuation with psychology I take to be the following: From the earliest days, Americans have been a highly introspective people. This trait is, in large part, a consequence of the Protestant Reformation, which shifted the burden of salvation from the church and priesthood to the individual believer or sinner. He/she was thus inclined to be constantly taking his/her moral temperature or, perhaps better, auditing his/her state of grace. This disposition survived the decline of the Calvinist version of the Reformation that gave birth to it; it is evident today in our various therapies. Do we like ourselves? We must say to ourselves (we are told): "I am a good person. I am a worthy person." This is, of course, only an up-to-date version of the question: "Am I in a state of grace? Am I saved? Does the Lord love me?"

In large part as a consequence of our perpetual introspection, we are a notably "nervous" people. This has been true since the days of the Puritans. After all, we originally landed in a "wild and desolate wilderness . . . surrounded by savages" of unpredictable disposition. Successive waves of immigrants left all that was known and familiar and came to a country where most of the inhabitants seemed scarcely less savage than the aborigines themselves. "Stress" is only a modern word for the American nervousness that European travelers so often commented on when they visited the United States. When S. Weir Mitchell, a writer of novels and an early "alienist," wrote a book of advice in 1871 about how to reduce the stress of daily life in America with the title *Wear and Tear,* it sold out within a few weeks and went through a number of editions.

George Templeton Strong, a New York lawyer, complained in the 1850s of the strains of life in that city. He kept going by drinking numerous cups of coffee during the day and taking sleeping potions at night. Like many of his contemporaries, he experimented with marijuana and cocaine and tried sniffing chloroform as antidotes to nervousness.

There were other popular remedies, among them bicycling and walking as well as taking warm baths, but nothing seemed to help much, and Americans kept wondering why. They wondered why alcoholism was so conspicuous in the United States and speculated that it and other addictions were related to the fast pace of American life, to getting ahead and staying ahead. By the 1890s alienists (later to be called "psychiatrists") were in great favor with the well-to-do. To Henry Adams, devastated by the disappearance of religious belief in his class, the rise of psychology was a mixed blessing at best. "Of all studies," he wrote in his famous *Education,* "the one he [Adams] would rather have avoided was that of his own mind. He knew no tragedy so heartrending as introspection. . . . Ever since 1870 friends by the score had fallen victim to it. There was a whole new discipline—psychology—derived from it. There were hospitals, libraries, magazines devoted to it. . . . Nothing was easier than to take one's mind in one's hand, and ask one's psychological friends what they made of it. . . ." It was Adams' opinion that, to all the truly important questions, psychology seemed to have no answer. "Were soul and mind, for example, a unit?" Psychologists declared that they had been able to distinguish "several personalities in the same mind, each conscious, individual and exclusive. . . . The new psychology," Adams wrote, "went further and seemed convinced that it had actually split personality into dualism, but also into complex groups, like telephonic centres and systems, that might be isolated and called up at will. . . ." The individual seemed to be "mechanically balancing himself by inhibiting all his inferior personalities, and sure to fall into subconscious chaos below, which everyone could feel when he sought it." Although the word "schizophrenia" was not coined until 1911 by Eugen Bleuler, the condition it described seems to have flourished in the United States.

Academic psychology has long had the advantage of offering a booming job market for psychologists, especially those with advanced degrees. To be sure, this has been a mixed blessing, because academic psychology has had to some degree to answer to this constituency. The performance of professional psychologists has reflected both positively and negatively on academic psychology. If practicing psychologists, who, incidentally, are to be found at virtually every level of American life—screening candidates for jobs, counseling schoolchildren and their parents, and advising college students, testifying as to the mental state of criminals accused of crimes, advising prison authorities on whether inmates have been rehabilitated or not—if the practitioners fall down on the job, questions are bound to be raised about the scientific credentials of the discipline itself. Recently such questions have been raised specifically about the performance of psychologists in two areas: as expert witnesses in court cases, and as judges of whether a criminal with a record of violence can be safely released from prison. On the latter issue, a former inmate wrote a book entitled *The Fox Is Smarter,* detailing the ways in which inmates deceive prison psychologists and psychiatrists by giving answers that the inmates know will dispose the psychologist to recommend that they be released.

A recent study in the *Journal of Consulting and Clinical Psychology* purported to show that normal children between the ages of nine and twelve were able to convince psychologists that they were suffering from neurological problems. The conclusion was that trained psychologists would not be able to tell "if someone who sought damages for a brain injury was in fact faking." .

Two psychologists—David Faust, a psychologist at Brown University, and Jay Ziskin, a lawyer and clinical psychologist—argue in a recent issue of *Science* that the testimony of psychologists and psychiatrists as to the mental state of individuals on trial reveals "an immense gap between experts' claims about the judgmental power and the scientific findings" about the accuracy of their diagnoses. According to Faust and Ziskin, in one test high-school students demonstrated roughly the same degree of accuracy in judging which individuals were apt to be violent as did trained psychologists. In the words of *The New York Times'* reporter, the new studies "seem to show that, in effect, the 'expert testimony' of psychologists and psychiatrists has little scientific validity." A judgment that, for the most part, confirms popular prejudices on the subject.

Experimental psychology has been subject to some of the same misgivings that anthropologists are experiencing. The basic issue is whether it is appropriate, or perhaps, more accurately, moral, to experiment with living creatures, animal or human. First there were considerable doubts as to whether experiments with rats or chickens produced responses applicable to human beings. Then there is the uncomfortable fact that the Nazis performed both medical and psychological experiments on human beings in concentration camps. Finally, the news has filtered out that the CIA funded research by psychologists using LSD on unwitting subjects. This was the most unsettling of all. A Canadian psychiatrist, D. Ewen Cameron, in the words of the lawyer for plaintiffs against the Canadian government and the CIA (which funded Dr. Cameron's experiments), "tested the theory that a person could have some of the concepts of the mind obliterated and replaced by ideas of the researcher's choosing."

Once the centerpiece of academic psychology, personality psychology is definitely on the wane. The most popular area for undergraduate majors, especially those planning to become professional psychologists, it has been eclipsed on many campuses by the more fashionable fields of cognitive and developmental psychology. Developmental psychology is, in essence, a more up-to-date form of child psychology. Social psychology shades off into applied sociology and is increasingly disposed to concern itself with such problems as how to develop instructional programs on AIDS. The great "humanistic" psychologists like Henry Murray, for many years the chief ornament of the Harvard psychology department, and Erik Erikson, inventor of the "identity crisis" and biographer of Martin Luther, have passed from the scene (Murray is dead and Erikson retired) and have no successors.

A detailed analysis of the relationship between personality psychology and social psychology by Seymour Rosenberg and Michael Gara that came out in 1983 concluded that "both areas are in a period of great transition or are at the end of a major cycle of development." Although some of the psychologists whom the authors contacted expressed the view that "researchers would adapt the idiographic models," others were convinced that "the nomothetic tradition will continue to dominate research in social psychology. . . ." A key phrase in an article by Theodore Sarbin was "contextual perspectives," which I take to mean the social and historical context within which the individual exists.

Psychonomics is a flourishing branch of academic psychology that still clings to the illusion that psychology is or can become a science. Cognitive psychology is all the rage in psychonomics—studies of the brain, how we learn, etc. The cognitive psychologists work with the "information sciences" to help refine artificial intelligence and create computers that function as much as possible like the human brain. Psychobiology is another field "hot" at the moment.

Although William James, the father of American psychology, was confident that psychology could never become a "science" in the proper sense of the word, this did not deter psychologists from making such a claim. After deriding the claims of psychology to be scientific, Ludwig Wittgenstein noted in *Philosophical Investigations,* published in 1953: "The confusion and barrenness of psychology is not to be explained by calling it a 'young science'; its state is not comparable with that of physics, for instance, in its beginnings. . . . For in psychology there are experimental methods and *conceptual confusion*. . . . The existence of experimental methods makes us think we have the means of solving the problems which trouble us; though problems and methods pass one another by." Wittgenstein's description of the dilemma of psychology, although made more than forty years ago, is today as true as (or truer than) it was when he made it. Unlike mathematics, psychology has, in effect, no "method of proof." Physics, by contrast, can endure considerable "conceptual confusion," because it, like mathematics, has methods of proof sufficient to sustain its day-to-day activities.

The fact is psychology has much to answer for. Pre-frontal lobotomies, shock therapy, the Neuro-Linguistic Institute in its various forms, Esalen, est, techniques for manipulating people in a wide variety of areas, such as developing methods for selling inferior products to foolish consumers. During the Vietnam War psychologists advised the military on how to win the "hearts and minds" of the Vietnamese people by such techniques as dropping leaflets over Vietnam villages (and when that technique failed, in part because many villagers were illiterate and could not read the leaflets, broadcasting messages about American beneficence from helicopters). The operation was called "psy-op," short for "psychological operation."

The appearance of political science as an academic discipline was relatively recent. It was in essence a spin-off from political economy. The year 1903 is identified as its birthdate, and from the first it had as a subfield "political theory," borrowed from history. In a real sense it was, like most of the late-nineteenth-century academic disciplines, simply another way of slicing up the pie. Francis Lieber, a German refugee from the upheavals of the 1840s, is generally accounted the father of American political science. In 1857 he became professor of history and political economy at Columbia.

Moral philosophy (or ethics) was another ancestor of political science. In the words of John G. Gunnell of the State University of New York at Albany, the first generation of political scientists believed in "the relativity of ideas and institutions, the evolution of political thought toward science and democracy and the practical mission of political science." Like Frederic Howe and the pioneers of graduate study at Johns Hopkins, the founders wished to use the study of politics in a scientific spirit to broaden, deepen, and reform American democracy. Charles E. Merriam, himself actively involved in the considerable task of reforming Chicago politics, emphasized the importance of drawing on all the related social sciences, including anthropology, psychology, and economics, in order to develop "scientific" political principles. In his 1924 "Report of the National Conference on the Science of Politics" it was stated that "the great need of the hour is the development of a scientific technique and methodology for political science." But it was emphasized that the purpose of such a development was still to improve the character of practical politics. Merriam insisted that "the perfection of social science is indispensable to the very preservation" of the civilization that had "given rise to modern science."

Decade after decade, the same theme recurred. Political scientists, if they were to deserve the name, must establish "a body of testable propositions concerning the political nature and activities of man that are applicable throughout the world" and "at all times" resulting in a predictive science of "human political behavior."

The 1950s have been called the era of the "Behavioral Revolution" in political science. The Behavioralists put their emphasis on developing political theory in a systematic, scientific spirit. Influenced by the British philosophical school of logical positivists, they wished to sort out those ideas that were simply sentimental or idealistic from those that could be subjected to close examination. Again in Gunnell's words, the Behavioralists brought to their researches—or, perhaps more accurately, to their reflections—"an unprecedented metatheoretical consciousness about scientific theory and scientific explanation." In other words, they debated what a scientist actually does. What entitles him to be called "a scientist"? How does scientific method differ from looser forms of generalization? Along with the newly fashionable concern for the philosophy of science came a turning away from what was referred to patronizingly as "the idea of liberal reform and social control." It was, in this respect, a critically important moment. A bold if sometimes imprecise line was drawn between "pure" research and "applied" research. The notion that the study of politics should have more or less immediate practical results in the "outside" world was dismissed as old-fashioned. That was not the way "hard" science functioned. No one rushed into the physicist's laboratory and importuned him to wind up an experiment so that the practical results could be utilized.

One of the most vocal champions of Behavioralism claimed that it had dispensed with "the last remnants of the classical heritage in political science." At the same time, it had finally resulted in "the integration of the methods of science into the core of the discipline [of political science]."

I believe we must look for the key to this transformation from the practical to the theoretical in the changing culture or consciousness of the larger society. The New Deal had been, in many ways, the fulfillment of the dreams of the reformers for fifty years (many of them turned up as old men in Washington, hoping to play some part in the great transformation that they had dreamed of, then despaired of, and now could dream of once more). The intellectual class inside and outside the university had suffered a profound disenchantment with the most compelling political theory of modern times—Marxian socialism. After the war, in an unnerving reaction against the New Deal and the anxieties produced by the Cold War, hundreds of "leftists," some of them university professors, had been hauled before the Dies Committee and abused and humiliated. Suddenly practical politics appeared to be a risky game. This is doubtless too simple an explanation, but one cannot doubt that it played a role. The most widely touted book of the era was Daniel Bell's *The End of Ideology*. That was the mood. What was borrowed from Marxism was the conviction that political theories (except for Marxism) were simply rationalizations of the economic interests of the ruling class, the capitalists, the elite, or whatever. The Founding Fathers, as Charles Beard had argued earlier, were not so much developing a great constitution dedicated to preserving liberty and creating republican institutions as protecting their investments in land and slaves. The effect was to deflate political theory. If the *Federalist Papers* could best be read as a brilliant cover-up for class interests, it was obviously more important to probe those interests than to study and celebrate the Constitution itself. Political theory, in Gunnell's words, "was characterized as teleological, moralistic ["moralistic" became one of the nastiest words in the lexicon of all the social sciences], historical, ethical [another bad word], and, in general, in about the same state that Aristotle left it." The call was for "interdisciplinary model construction that would yield predictive generalizations and observably testable propositions"—the way the hard scientists did it. Political science must be based on "logical positivism, operationalism, instrumentalism," according to an influential book of the time.

By the 1970s the "Structural Realists" were in the limelight. They stood on the proposition that "if there is any distinctively political theory of international politics, balance of power theory is it." But they had hardly made themselves known before they were under fire. A critic wrote unkindly (if obscurely) that the effort to "deduce national interests from system structure . . . has been unsuccessful [apparently a reference to the so-called rational-choice model]. . . . [T]he attempt to predict outcomes from interests and power leads to ambiguities. . . . The auxiliary theory attributing this failure to conversion-processes often entails unfalsifiable tautology rather than genuine explanation. Ambiguity prevails on the fungibility of power. . . . Thus the research program of Realism reveals signs of degeneration."

It would be unfair to the writer of the above and to the reader to undertake to unravel these sentences. The Structural Realists like such phrases as "trivial animating law," "a priori utility functions for actors [not real "actors," it should be noted, but individuals who act]." It is small wonder that practicing politicians, if they came across such speculations, might be skeptical of their utility.

Two main fields, at least in what I suppose could be called neo-Marxist political science, would seem to be those who favor "rational-choice models" and "methodological individualism." The dominant tone is one of irony, as in analytic philosophy itself. The holistic school holds to the theory that "the whole expresses the whole." Both schools of Marxist political science are apparently characterized by a disenchantment with the working class as the instrument of radical social change (about time, one would think) and by enchantment with the writings of the Italian communist Antonio Gramsci.

As matters were explained to me, within academic Marxism (which has remarkably little relation to the Old Time Religion of Marxism) the so-called deconstructionists are to be found in the holistic branch. What used to be at the center of political science—namely, political theory, starting, say, with the Greeks—has now been crowded to the margins of the discipline and ekes out a precarious existence by reflecting on its own "terms of discourse"—in short, how political theorists are actually functioning. Here, too, the deconstructivists are found, deconstructing the assumptions and language of political science and studying the "professionalization" of the field. Not only is the battle joined between the two dominant schools of Marxist political science; there is a "Straussian" wing, named after the German refugee scholar Leo Strauss, of whom Allan Bloom is a follower. Strauss himself was a follower of the German philosopher Martin Heidegger and the so-called Frankfurt or Continental School. Also strongly influenced by Heidegger was Hannah Arendt, a "centrist" in her thinking. What trickled down to the general public from all this was an opposition to modern relativism (and it is this, doubtless, that strikes a responsive chord among Allan Bloom's many readers). Strauss—and Bloom—believe in final or "ideal" truths which can be discovered by reason. The Straussian illuminati, like the Masons, think of themselves as a secret order advancing their ideas subtly and indirectly, from the academic underground, so to speak. Hannah Arendt put her faith not in secrecy but in making the public a central part of the dialogue about the nature of reality. What is also evident is that the "rational-choice-model Marxists" are far closer to the economists (and the anthropologists) than to what's left of the political theorists. Moreover, since the Straussians incline to the political right, any number found lodgments in the Reagan administration, where they were almost impossible to distinguish from other run-of-the-mill reactionary ideologues.

Meanwhile, calls for the discipline (if indeed at this point one could call it that) to find some common ground were reiterated at every official gathering, but to no avail. One political scientist, Brian Barry, confessed "the nightmarish feeling that 'the literature' has taken off on an independent life and now carries on like the broomstick bewitched by the sorcerer's apprentice." Another respected political scientist suggested that the discipline was "coming to the end of an era . . . a slow, whimpering end," since "the hoped for cumulation of knowledge into a coherent body of theory has not occurred."

At this point I cannot resist inserting the words of the most famous political economist of the last century, Henry George, the prophet of the single-tax. George told an audience of University of California professors and students that the true law of social life was "the law of love, the law of liberty, the law of each for all and all for each. . . . [T]he highest expressions of religious truth include the widest generalizations of political economy." "For the study of political economy," he told his audience, "you need no special knowledge, no extensive library, no costly laboratory. You do not even need textbooks and teachers, if you will but think for yourselves. . . . All this array of professors, all this paraphernalia of learning cannot educate a man. Here you may obtain tools; but they will be useful only to him who can use them. A monkey with a microscope, a mule packing a library, are fit emblems of the men—unfortunately there are plenty—who pass through the whole educational machinery and come out but learned fools, crammed with knowledge that they cannot use. . . ."

George was being considered for an appointment at the university. He did not get it.

Finally, there is economics. Richard Ely was considered the father of political economy. Here the determinative word was "political." Ely and his followers believed that government should intervene in the economy in order to ensure justice; hence the "socialist."

Like John Humphrey Noyes, he took the line that Christian ethics must be applied scientifically to rectify the manifold inequities in American society. The issue was thus both economic and political. The phrase was not new. When it was first used in an academic sense at Heidelberg in 1803, it incorporated urban and rural economics, forestry, civil engineering, architecture, mining and surveying, police organization, and "everything that concerns the knowledge, preservation, development and proper maintenance of public administration."

By the end of the century it had split into political science *and* economics. Economics came to have great prestige, in large part because the arguments about the nature of the national economy occupied the center of the stage. Many of the first generation of economists were unabashed socialists. To trace the transformations and permutations of economic theory from the inception of the discipline to the present would be tedious in the extreme. With the triumph of Keynesian economic theory, the role of the government in managing the economy became accepted practice. The task of the economists was then understood to be that of telling the government *how* to manage the economy. This proved more complicated, and the credentials of economists as scientists appeared increasingly shaky.

Econometrics was the hot field of the 1930s. It made the most impressive claims of being scientific through the empirical testing of economic theories and "the expression of economic relationships in mathematical forms." Economic anthropology involved the "comparative study of societies of various types and the structure and values of such societies." The economic consequences of magical beliefs, for example, was an appropriate subject for such study. Economic development, forecasting and studies of the relationship of population growth to economic expansion, became an important field within the general framework of economics. The author of the article on economics in the *Encyclopaedia Britannica* lists as major fields "welfare economics," "the theory of monopolistic competition," "the theory of the determination of national income and employment," and "econometrics." There is also "microeconomics" and "macroeconomics." In addition, there are, as one might surmise, various schools of thought in all the major areas of economic theory; "game theory" has a place. Even the old laissez-faire economics against which Richard Ely and John Commons revolted has crept back into the picture, under the auspices of the University of Chicago and Milton Friedman, Ronald Reagan's favorite economist.

But the problem with economics is the same as that of the other social sciences. Although economics has far more direct impact in the real economic and political world than the other social sciences, it is as far as ever from being a science. It has, in the final analysis, to deal with human behavior, and human behavior remains maddeningly unpredictable, fortunately.

Since social scientists from the 1950s had been stressing the fact that their real mission was not to effect positive political change but to theorize about the scientific nature of their researches, they should not have been surprised when, in 1982, the National Science Foundation made a substantial cut in research funds available to the social sciences. The action sent a shiver of apprehension through social-science departments all over the country. The drastic cut in funding was justified by those in charge of funding allocations on the grounds that the social sciences were not really sciences in the strict meaning of the word and that the usefulness of their researches to the general public was questionable.

In reply, the Reagan administration was accused of a "frontal attack on the budget of the Division of Social and Economic Science." The attack set off a "train of events . . . perhaps unprecedented in the history of the social sciences." The social-science group of the National Science Foundation had, Donna Shalala wrote, "consistently rebuffed any efforts by Congress and cabinet agencies to make its work more applied." Irving Louis Horowitz pointed out, rather tactlessly, that the situation in the social sciences as a whole could best be described "as one of Balkanization, fragmentation so severe that no unified paradigm prevails. In place of a uniform sense of social science research are a series of belief-systems of little concern at the level of presidential decision-making. The inner resolve of social scientists has been sapped not only at the periphery, but at the core."

"Belief-systems" was an especially cruel phrase, considering that the social sciences consistently denounced all "belief-systems" and insisted they were just around the corner from being scientific. Professor Philip Converse, trying some spin-control, told a congressional committee that the "serious social scientists" had "progressively drawn the main stream of social science away from loose speculation and various social advocacies, in the direction of true basic science. . . ." The president of the Carnegie Foundation tried to come to the rescue by insisting that "science is a seamless web," apparently implying that the difference between political science and, say, physics was more apparent than real.

Although Shalala confessed that "social science research is at a turning point in its history" that would affect its "ability to attract substantial public and private monies," she insisted that it was time to go on the offensive. She called for a "born-again social science." "We need," Professor Shalala wrote, "to make the case that, like the natural sciences, this nation—indeed the world—cannot and does not survive without us." This is, I fear, a case that it is getting increasingly difficult to sustain, especially in the face of the scorn of the academics for the "real world." I am inevitably reminded of the 1920s song: "Got along without you before I met you, Gonna get along without you now."

Alston Chase has written critically of what social scientists conceive of as their "methodology," "borrowed from the teachings of the logical positivists. . . . Logical positivism," Chase writes, "was given up long ago by most scientists and philosophers, including many of the positivists themselves. Yet this positivist doctrine . . . has taken firm root in the social sciences. It has done so because it . . . allows social scientists to make the (sometimes bogus) claim of scientific objectivity."

In Robert Hutchins' words, modern man "believes . . . that if we can gather enough information about the world we can master it. Since we do not know precisely which facts will prove to be helpful, we gather them all and hope for the best. This is what is called the scientific spirit. . . . A large part of what we call the social sciences is large chunks of such data, undigested, unrelated, and meaningless." It would be hard to find a more accurate and succinct description of current academic research on the social sciences. Most of it is, quite literally, the mindless accumulation of data in the hope that these data will prove relevant. It is guided by no comprehensive view of the nature of man and woman or of the society in which they live. It is directed by no "metaphysic," by no integrated world view (except the exclusion of all things having to do with what was once called "the soul of man"). It is an activity ant-like in its industry but barren of accomplishment.

The question that remains is, why do the social sciences, now that it is abundantly evident that they are not sciences, cling to this pathetic fallacy? Very few people outside the social sciences give them credit for being scientific, and many of their practitioners are quite ready to confess that their disciplines are not scientific in any proper sense of that elastic word. Why this strange tenacity?

Perhaps the answer is the old "identity-crisis" answer. If we are not scientists, then who are we? And what is our mission? To admit publicly to being not sciences but merely "studies" would presumably bring a loss of face but, more important, it would mean opening the door to all the questions, the "Big Questions," the "Burning Questions," that have been so long and so resolutely excluded. That must be an alarming if not terrifying prospect.

16
THE INHUMAN HUMANITIES

"Either the university of the future will take hold of the connection between knowledge and human values, or it will sink quietly and indiscriminately into the non-committal moral stupor of the rest of the knowledge industry."

—CHARLES MUSCATINE

The so-called humanities are as inhuman as the social sciences are nonscientific. Like the social sciences, they, too, have lusted after the accolade Science. They have sold their souls to the company store, the Big S. First philosophy, whittling down that ancient and honorable study from logical positivism to analytic philosophy until nothing is left; then history; and finally literature.

"[M]odern society," Peter Berger writes, "has not only sealed up the old metaphysical questions in practice, but . . . has generated philosophical positions that deny the meaningfulness of these questions. 'What is the purpose of my life?' 'Why must I die?' 'Where do I come from and where will I go?' 'Who am I?'—all such questions are not only suppressed in practice, but are theoretically liquidated by relegating them to meaninglessness."

The great venture that William James had launched at Harvard with Royce as his principal ally, no less than an effort (in which, incidentally, Charles Sanders Peirce was also a supporter) to create some space in the new academic order of things for faith, was marked with failure by the time James retired. The tide of scientific philosophy was already rising about him, and the "gray-pated" young professors, old beyond their years, were busy dismantling the spacious house that James had labored so diligently to construct.

The influx of German refugee scholars from Hitler's Germany completed the rout of what we might call the humanistic philosophers. Whitehead was the last of the breed. Hans Reichenbach's *Rise of Scientific Philosophy,* published in 1951, was taken as the death knell of metaphysics. It was also the death knell of the philosophy of history. If all philosophy prior to the rise of scientific philosophy was now obsolete, it was obviously a waste of time to read the classic philosophers. Reichenbach maintained that "philosophic speculation is a passing stage, occurring when philosophic problems are raised at a time which does not possess the logical means to solve them. It [his book] claims that there is, and always has been, a scientific approach to philosophy. And it wishes to show that from this ground has sprung a scientific philosophy which, in the science of our time, has found the tools to solve those problems that in earlier times have been the subject of guesswork only. To put it briefly: this book is written with the intention of showing that philosophy has proceeded from speculation to science."

That Reichenbach's claims were initially received as revelation should not, at this point, surprise us. The basic notion of the analytic philosophers was that "positivistic philosophy was pathology" and that the pathology could only be cured through analytic philosophy. In the words of Richard Rorty, professor of humanities at the University of Virginia: "in the early 1950s analytic philosophy began to take over American philosophy departments. . . . As a result, most of today's teachers of philosophy in American colleges and universities assimilated some version of Reichenbach's picture of the history of philosophy in graduate school. They were brought up to believe themselves the lucky participants in the beginnings of a new philosophical age—an Age of Analysis—in which things would finally be done properly. They were often led to despise the sort of person who was interested in the history of philosophy, or more generally in the history of thought, rather than in solving philosophical problems." Those hardy souls who clung to some elements of classical philosophy, who continued to express an interest in the metaphysical thinkers and those modern philosophers grouped under the title "Continental philosophy," men like Husserl, Heidegger, Jaspers, et al., were pushed to the margins of the academic scene. Since the "Existential" philosophy of Jean-Paul Sartre and Heidegger sprang up in unlikely places and showed surprising tenacity, most departments took on an Existentialist or at least a Phenomenologist, but these poor souls were like fish out of water or, if still in the water, out of the mainstream. They held their chairs by sufferance and could only watch bemused as time began to reveal numerous cracks in the structure of analytic philosophy.

In Rorty's words: "In 1951 a graduate student, who (like myself) was in the process of learning about, or being converted to, analytic philosophy, could still believe that there was a finite number of distinct, specifiable, philosophical problems to be resolved, problems that any serious analytic philosopher would agree to be *the* outstanding problems." What resulted instead was a general unraveling of analytic philosophy itself. Fad followed fad in bewildering succession. "Any problem," Rorty writes, "that enjoys a simultaneous vogue in ten or so of the hundred or so analytic philosophy departments in America is doing exceptionally well." Since Reichenbach's triumphant proclamation, "Oxford philosophy" has come and gone, followed by "West Coast Semantics" and a vogue for several philosophies of language. Ved Mehta quotes the British philosopher Ernest Gellner as saying, "Linguistic philosophy is nothing more than a defense mechanism of gentlemen intellectuals, which they use in order to conceal the fact that they have nothing left to say."

One of the reasons professors go to meetings of the American Philosophical Association, according to Rorty, "is to find out what the fashionable new problems are—what the 'good people in the field' are talking about nowadays." "Structuralism" and "deconstructionism" have had their day and their "schools," but the analytic philosophers, in the main, persevere in their efforts to "get philosophy out of the humanities into the sciences." All they have accomplished, in Rorty's opinion, is to be "able to spot flaws in any argument" and, as a corollary, "able to construct as good an argument as can be constructed for any view, no matter how wrongheaded," a gift that used to be called sophistry. Rorty compares the analytic philosopher of the current moment to a lawyer able to argue any case with considerable skill. "The problem that confronts academic philosophy is lack of any clear content for analysis, a feeling exacerbated by the increasingly short half-lives of philosophical problems and programs [which] make the home territory shifting ground. The rest of the academy has . . . become puzzled about what philosophical expertise might be."

I suppose at this point it would be unfair to inquire what undergraduate students of philosophy have been able to make of all this. Even if they have mercifully been spared the more sordid details, they must, one suspects, have suffered from the fact that the interest and energies of their younger instructors were flowing into fields too esoteric for them to follow. It is Rorty himself who suggests that present-day philosophy may have finally arrived at the position so presciently held by Henry Adams, who, a century or so ago, saw the new "religion of science . . . as being as self-deceptive as the old-time religion," and believed that the "scientific method" was simply a "mask behind which lurks the cruelty and despair of a nihilistic age."

J. Bronowski, a biologist at the Salk Institute for Biological Studies, found it "particularly sad that philosophy has remained remote from any genuine inquiry into the human mind and the dilemmas of personality. At a time when young men hunger for principles to guide their lives, philosophy has been preoccupied with forms of analysis in which, it rightly assures them, there surely are none [no principles to guide their lives] to be found." Bronowski's remedy was to put together a "core curriculum for all students, whose parts truly represent the constituents of modern culture." His core would have three parts: science, anthropology, and literature.

The problem with all such core curriculums, as I noted earlier, is that they run counter to the basic assumptions underlying the modern universities. Can you teach things that are denied by the whole organizational structure of the institution in which they are taught? The problem is not, in essence, with the curriculum: it is with the intellectual assumptions of those individuals who constitute the instructional staff of the institution. As long as they fail to share common values, except the negative ones of security and careerism, how can such values be put forth honestly in *any* form? Conversely, if the professors held such values and valued their students, those values would be conveyed by a kind of intellectual and spiritual osmosis.

"The Universe is vast," Whitehead wrote. "Nothing is more curious than the self-satisfied dogmatism with which mankind at each period of its history cherished the delusion of the finality of its existing modes of knowledge. Skeptics and believers are the leading dogmatists. Advance in detail is admitted; fundamental novelty is barred. This dogmatic common sense is the death of philosophic adventure. The Universe is vast."

Ludwig Wittgenstein in his book *On Certainty* (which is really about the uncertainty of all of our assumptions about the world) writes: "The difficulty is to realize the groundlessness of our believing." If I understand Wittgenstein (which I am not at all sure that I do), he points out with disarming simplicity how insubstantial are those certitudes on which all our thinking is based. This gentle skepticism was especially demoralizing to the philosophers and social scientists, many of whom were confident that they were on the verge of establishing the scientific credentials of their disciplines.

Everything that can be said about the shortcomings of the various academic disciplines can be said in spades about history, whose muse was Clio, one of nine sisters, daughters of Zeus and Mnemosyne, who presided over poetry, dance, music, the arts generally. It was appropriate that the Greeks named Clio, since they might be said to have invented history.

The sad state that Clio is in is a cause for universal mourning. I believe we could far more readily sacrifice all the social sciences (which in any event have no use for history, as we have indicated) than give up Clio, who is our collective memory and the voice of the unity of the species. The critic Frank Kermode writes, "history is, under all the appearances of change, a unity; the modern is not absolutely new, but a renovation of a classic which the action of time has obscured . . ."

Since history is my "field" and, I dare to say, her study the most essential to sustain a reasonable degree of civilization, I hereby undertake to describe the scandalous abuse she has received in modern times at the hands of her pretended votaries, academic historians. It might well be said that the goal of education is to make students at home in the world by making them at home in history. This, in my view, requires an acquaintance with great historians but, more than that, it requires a familiarity with the whole vast sweep of history. Rosenstock-Huessy has called history "a love-song celebrating the triumph of love over death." The Russian novelist Boris Pasternak expressed a similar sentiment when he wrote that "man does not die like a dog in a ditch, he lives in history."

Testimony to the power of history can be found in every age, from Lord Bolingbroke's observation that history is "philosophy reaching by examples" to Joseph Wood Krutch's lament over the "current obsession with the 'now.' " The translator of *Plutarch's Lives,* Sir Thomas North, wrote of history: "All other learning is private, fitter for universities than cities, fuller of contemplation than experience, more commendable in the students than profitable to others. Whereas, stories are fit for every place, reach all persons, serve for all time, teach the living, revive the dead . . . as it is better to see learning in noble men's lives than to read it in philosophers' writings."

"Indeed," Benjamin Franklin wrote, "the natural tendency of reading good history must be to fix in the minds of youth deep impressions of the beauty and usefulness of virture of all kinds, public spirit, fortitude, etc." Histories of nature and commerce should be read along with those "of the invention of arts, rise of manufactures, progress of trade . . . with the reasons, causes, etc."

The great eighteenth-century parliamentarian Edmund Burke called for a new kind of human partnership: a partnership not "in a trade of pepper and coffee, calico or tobacco. . . . It is to be looked on with . . . reverence, because it is not a partnership in things subservient to the gross animal existence. . . . It is a partnership in all science, a partnership in all art, a partnership in every virtue and in all perfection. . . . As the ends of such a partnership cannot be obtained in many generations, it becomes a partnership not only between those who are living, but between those who are dead and those who are to be born." William James wrote: "Our predecessors, even apart from the physical link of generation, have made us what we are. Every thought you now have and every act and intention owes its complexion to the acts of your dead and living brothers."

Between the great classical historians Thucydides, Herodotus, and Xenophon; the Roman historians Livy and Tacitus; Plutarch, a Greek historian of the first century A.D.; and modern times, there is a kind of hiatus. Gibbon was the greatest historian of the eighteenth century, but the nineteenth century may well be said to have been the Century of History. Great historians abounded on both sides of the Atlantic. Indeed, it might be argued that history was the first field in the world of letters where Americans excelled. The French had their Guizots and Taines, the British their Macaulays and Leckys, but the United States rivaled them in Francis Parkman, William Prescott, John Lothrop Motley, not to mention Henry Adams, George Bancroft, and John Bach McMaster. Parkman wrote voluminously and enthrallingly about the French colonizers of North America; Prescott wrote classic histories of the Spanish conquest of Mexico and Peru; Motley told the story of the Dutch Republics; Henry Adams, the most brilliant of the lot, wrote a seven-volume history of the administrations of Jefferson and Madison; and McMaster wrote a splendid eight-volume history of the United States from the American Revolution to the Civil War.

It is perhaps worth noting that none of the great historians of the nineteenth century had any academic training as historians. Henry Adams taught briefly at Harvard. McMaster, who was trained as an engineer, decided in 1878, when he was on a trip to Wyoming, to write a history of the United States. After the first volume appeared, he was appointed professor of history at Princeton. Motley was a gentleman-scholar and a diplomat. Prescott, who began his career as a lawyer, was virtually blind from a boyhood accident and had to have most of his research material read to him while he wrote in large letters, a few sentences to a page, with a stylus of his own invention.

These historians, along with their British counterparts, were enormously popular. Their vividly written narratives far outranked the novels of the day. In the winter of 1894–95 the Cedar Falls, Iowa, literary club turned its attention to Macaulay's *History of England in the Reign of James I.* In hundreds of similar small town literary societies the works of the aforementioned historians were read and discussed. Such societies were indeed extension schools in which Americans could absorb very substantial quantities of history written by masters of prose style.

It can be said without fear of refutation that in the last half of the last century more Americans knew more history than at any time before or since. By the same token, history was one of the first victims of the new notion of academic scholarship. History must be objective and scientific—ideally, as scientific as physics or chemistry. Vivid narratives, colorful style were no more than impediments, archaic remnants of the age of "romantic," "literary" history. Style was the enemy, because style tended to arouse emotions, and emotions were antithetical to dispassionate reason. Emotions blurred or obscured the facts. Facts—plain, unvarnished facts—they were the responsibility of the trained, professional historian, who talked solemnly of "methodology" and "research in the archives," the latter of which was certainly the practice of the great historians. Soon the new histories—limited of necessity, it was argued, to small fragments of the whole—began to appear, published by university presses in small editions for the instruction of fellow experts in the same field—medieval law, royal land practices in the reign of Charles I, the Wisconsin dairy industry in the 1880s. The monograph, or work on a single limited topic, became the immutable standard in academic history almost at once. Any tendency toward generalization was sternly suppressed. The monograph must be on an "original" topic (which in itself ruled out general narrative history), it must be accompanied by all the approved apparatus of voluminous footnotes, which would often take up a third or more of the text (the general assumption was, the more footnotes, the more scholarly the work) and an extensive bibliography listing all the works that the author had consulted. The monograph was supposed to be exhaustive, exhausting all the "sources" as well as the reader. Ideally, it was "definitive" as well as exhaustive. Once done, it need never be done again. It became a prospective building block ("filling a gap," in August Frugé's words) in a structure made up of similar definitive blocks that, when placed on top of one another, would stand for the final, objective, scientific truth about a particular period of history or a particular topic. The nature of monographic history is perhaps best suggested by a modest sampling. A recent university press catalogue lists under American history *The American Law of Slavery, 1810–1860,* "a Marxist interpretation of the master-slave interdependency . . . a thoughtful analysis of current interpretations of both American history and jurisprudence. . . ." Published in 1981 at $29.00, it is offered now at $11.95. *The Campaign of Princeton, 1776–1777* is, as the title suggests, about the Revolutionary War battle of Princeton. Historians have generally taken the battle of Saratoga as the decisive battle of the Revolution, but the author of this work insists the turning point took place at Princeton a few months after the war began and four years before it ended.

Another monograph is entitled *The Civil Works Administration, 1933–1934.* One year! *The Concept of Jacksonian Democracy: New York as a Test Case,* published in 1961 at $39.00, now on sale for $13.95. *Federal Courts in the Early Republic: Kentucky, 1789–1816.* Not exactly a broad sweep, even of Kentucky history. *Free Masonry in Federalist Connecticut, 1789–1835,* published in 1978 at $28.00.

We also have *Labor in a New Land: Economy and Society in Seventeenth-Century Springfield,* which includes "more than 250 pages on careers, dependency, wages, crop values and population." On the European-history front we have *From Hitler to Ulbricht: The Communist Reconstruction of East Germany, 1945–1946.*

The narrowness of a topic does not, of course, preclude its being a valuable work, but neither does this assure it of any substantial use at all. There is no need to belabor the point. Monographic studies, considering the vast number produced, have contributed astonishingly little to our understanding of our past.

In addition to being, like the dissertation out of which it typically emerged, on an extremely limited and usually insignificant subject, the monograph was (is) required to be dull. It was never stated quite that boldly, of course, but woe to the poor wretch who ventured any glimmering of "style." Theodore Roosevelt, no mean narrative historian himself, chided his fellow historians, most of whom were by now professors, for writing badly and urged them to write well enough to enlist the interest of the general reading public. Roosevelt endorsed thorough research and insisted that there was no conflict between a systematic, scientific approach to history and written history as an art. He would not dispute the fact that "no amount of self-communion and pondering on the soul of mankind, no gorgeousness of literary imagery" could substitute for research. But Roosevelt urged academic historians to strive for "vision and imagination, the power to grasp what is essential and to reject the infinitely more numerous non-essentials, the power to embody ghosts, to put flesh and blood on dry bones, to make dead men living before our eyes."

Roosevelt's exhortation was coldly received. One prominent academic historian, H. Morse Stephens, rejected Roosevelt's advice indignantly: "It is almost an insult to a historian of the modern school to say that his work can be recognized by its literary style. It is not his business to have a style," he wrote. Stephens practiced what he preached; he wrote as dully as he possibly could. A colleague said of him that "when he wrote a sentence that struck him as being especially good, [he] would cross it out and rewrite it."

Woodrow Wilson, a historian in his own right and, like Roosevelt, a member of the fraternity, urged academic historians to write for an audience somewhat larger than other specialists. He suggested, a little rudely, that, since the word "historian" had traditionally signified someone who wrote history that large numbers of people read with profit and pleasure, ideally over generations and centuries, for professors of history in universities to lay claim to the word "historian" was an error. They should be called "historical investigators," since that was in essence what they actually did: they investigated various historical events and problems and tried to state their conclusions as plainly and directly as possible. There was nothing meretricious or improper about that. The mistake was in calling such investigators "historians." Investigators they were; historians most certainly they were not. Needless to say, Wilson's suggestion was ignored. Academic investigators appropriated the name "historians."

One of the odder consequences of the new dispensation is that students are not allowed to read "the great historians." Their work is "pre-scientific" and thus a waste of time. They were "romantic," "literary," pre-scientific figures. They had not been trained in the modern methodologies. Their facts were not always reliable; they wrote so well that the readers were charmed out of their critical shoes. They were not sufficiently analytical. "Analytical" often seemed to mean that, for everything favorable you said about an individual, a historian or a historical figure, you must at once say something negative lest you be thought to be uncritical and not sufficiently analytical. If you could attribute some characteristic of a historical figure to some event in his or her childhood training, some problem with a mother or father, that was reassuring evidence that you were analytical. And of course, as we have noted, writing badly was taken, in some perverse logic, to indicate strength in analysis.

"May not the dominance of the analytical spirit," Sir Richard Livingstone writes, "explain why there are innumerable historical works but very little great history? The modern historian analyses events into their causes—into economic, demographic, geographic facts, into the impact of contemporary thought or the impact of individuals. He provides indispensable materials for a history that is never written. He analyses events and persons and explains them, but he fails to bring them to life. . . . There is a double road to truth, the road of analysis and what we may call the road of intuition, and the first road takes us only part of the way." Livingstone points to John Ruskin's description of Venice as an example of the difference between grasping something factually or practically and penetrating to its inner meaning. When Ruskin studied the Gothic architecture of Venice, he, in his own words, went "through so much hard dry, mechanical toil there that I quite lost the charm of the place. Analysis is an abominable business. I am quite sure that people who work out subjects thoroughly are disagreeable wretches. One only feels as one should, when one doesn't know much of the matter. . . . I lost all *feeling* of Venice." Now, this is an aspect of human experience that the dry-as-dust scholars have trouble coming to terms with. They simply cannot take in that some benefit might accrue to those of limited knowledge who still have the capacity for astonishment and awe. The whole direction of academic studies works to dampen awe. Awe is uninformed naïveté. If the reader is struck in a heap by the power of a poem by Shelley, his instructor may well explain that it is the product of an unresolved Oedipal complex. Poof! The magic is gone. "Analysis," again in Livingstone's words, "deludes us into thinking that we know all about things whose inner reality we miss."

One of the most popular forms of analytical history came forward under the guise of economic determinism. All human history could, it was thought, be explained in economic terms. Economics motivated human beings. Q.e.d. In its more extreme form, the economic interpretation of human history was the dialectical materialism of Karl Marx, but many non-Marxists jumped on the economic-determinism bandwagon. Arthur Meier Schlesinger attributed the cause of the American Revolution to British and American rivalry over the control of colonial trade. Charles A. Beard followed suit by "proving" that the Federal Constitution could be explained as an effort by prosperous merchants and planters to protect their property. In a similar spirit, Beard argued that the Civil War was less a clash over slavery than a struggle between Northern industrialists and Southern planters over profits from cotton.

These propositions had the charm of novelty, or, as scholars preferred to put it, "original work," and for several decades they dominated the academic world, although they were not susceptible to proof in any real meaning of that term. The fact was that they were only able to establish themselves as "the real story" because they were "original" and the original was increasingly confused with the true; because they came forward under the banner of objective, scientific research; because they conformed to the existing intellectual tone or consciousness; and, finally, because, at least in the case of Beard's work, they were engagingly written and, as we have noted, adorned with an awesome scholarly apparatus. Indeed, at the height of the infatuation with the new scholarship there was a general assumption that the validity or "truth" of a scholarly work was in direct proportion to the number of footnotes it contained. Even if nobody, of course, publicly confessed to such an odd notion, there was nonetheless the feeling that, since truth was the by-product of research and footnotes were the visible manifestations of research, the number of footnotes equaled truth. Or, since everything was relative, the more footnotes, the "truer" the work. The fact was that, although style was deplored by serious academics, those works which had the most influence on scholars in a particular field were well written or, as in the case of Frederick Jackson Turner's essay on the role of the frontier in American history, brilliantly written and persuasive not by virtue of footnotes (Turner's essay had, as I recall, none) but by the charm and force with which a thesis was presented.

The appearance of computers gave history-as-science new life. Computers, many academic historians thought, might be just the tool necessary to effect the transition from "history-as-romance" or "history-as-literature" to history-as-science. Soon hundreds of ambitious young historians (and a few older ones) were feeding quantities of data into computers: voting lists, property rolls, statistics on age at marriage and at death, all were grist for the mill. The "New Historians" (there have been half a dozen "New"s since the first appearance of history as an academic subject) were soon referred to as Cliometricians, devotees of the muse, Clio, who were committed to counting and quantifying (they produced miles of charts and graphs). They got grants from foundations, hired researchers by the dozen, and set out to unravel heretofore impenetrable mysteries and destroy long-held illusions. The most spectacular effort along these lines was a large work, crammed with statistics, on the institution of slavery in the American South prior to the Civil War, titled *Time on the Cross* (1974); the authors, Robert Fogel and Stanley Engerman, and their researchers professed to have proved that slavery was a relatively benign institution. It had simply gotten a bad press. Leaving aside the moral issues, *Time on the Cross* demonstrated by charts and graphs that most slaves were happy and well cared for and that slavery itself was flourishing as an economic system (whereas it had often been argued that slavery was coming apart on economic grounds when the Civil War broke out and that it would doubtless have been abandoned for economic reasons within a generation or so).

The authors of *Time on the Cross* were at pains to point out that they were in no sense trying to excuse the institution of slavery. Their findings, which could almost certainly have been reached by less pretentious (and expensive) methods of research, were that there were far more alleviations of the harshness of slavery than present-day historians, in their repugnance for the institution, had been willing to admit. Slaves lived longer, were fed better, had much better medical care and longer life expectancy than industrial workers in the North. Much of the same argument had been advanced by a Southerner, Robert Fitzhugh, in *Cannibals All,* published in 1854. In spite of the hundreds of "man and computer hours" and the mountains of statistics, the authors of *Time on the Cross* ask for their readers' "forbearance": their work should be considered an *"interim preliminary report."* They then add, rather poignantly: "We have come to recognize that history is, and very likely will remain, primarily a humanistic discipline." It is a bit startling, at the end of a work that professes to carry research technique to a new height of detailed analysis, to read such a disclaimer. One has the impression that Fogel and Engerman ended up their ambitious venture with a kind of dazed comprehension that the statistical treatment they had expected so much of had failed them and that they were left with a mass of "preliminary material" that did not yield results that would justify the process itself.

The initial reviews hailed *Time on the Cross* as a breakthrough in the compiling of history, a work that had proved its thesis beyond serious question. Stanley Elkins, one of the most influential writers on slavery and one sharply criticized by Fogel and Engerman, seemed ready to strike his colors, telling a *Time* editor that he would have to revise his own thinking in the light of the "authors' persuasive arguments." The University of Chicago historian Louis Gottschalk went considerably further, comparing *Time on the Cross* to Frederick Jackson Turner's famous essay on "The Significance of the Frontier in American History." The author of a *Time* article went so far as to speculate that *Time on the Cross* would be "the most controversial volume on American history" since Charles Beard created a storm with his *An Economic Interpretation of the Constitution.*

Nathan Glazer, Harvard sociology professor, was almost equally encomiastic. Glazer was overwhelmed by "the awesome apparatus of theory and technology that has been brought to bear on this problem. . . ." Surprising as the authors' conclusions were, "they are not likely to be challenged . . . in view of the enormous work and great ability that have gone into this research effort."

Glazer took the line that the Fogel-Engerman thesis undercut the argument that emancipated blacks emerged from slavery so warped and demoralized by their servitude that they were unable to establish themselves as functioning members of the white society. If they were, on the whole, reasonably well treated under slavery (especially as regards living conditions—food, medical care, shelter, etc.), their failure to "progress" was due to their own inherent shortcomings. What is most notable about Glazer's view is that it reveals a profound ignorance of the conditions that the freed slave faced in the South. It has been estimated that in the post–Civil War era more than twenty thousand freed slaves were murdered by Southern whites, most of them black men and women who showed leadership qualities. The suppression of freed blacks by Southern whites is a story as grim as, or perhaps grimmer than, the story of slavery itself.

Like so many once-acclaimed "building blocks," *Time on the Cross* has already, after a relatively brief fourteen years, begun to crumble away. Rather than converting the unconverted, it has, under closer inspection, revealed so many flaws and unsupportable assumptions that it seems fair to say very few historians any longer take it seriously. But the Cliometricians have hardly been discomfited by the failure of *Time on the Cross;* they have gone back to their drawing boards, or computers, resolute in their determination to devise ever more potent technologies for elucidating the mysteries of history. They are less modest than Fogel and Engerman, who confessed so disarmingly that "history is, and very likely will remain, primarily a humanistic discipline."

In 1982 a volume entitled *Historical Studies Today,* edited by Felix Gilbert and Stephen Graubard, was published by W. W. Norton. It is not an encouraging volume. Three of the articles have to do with "Quantitative History." Others range from the use of psychology in history to urban and local history. A considerable degree of intelligence and learning is displayed, but no coherent picture of the present or future tasks of the historian emerges. The voting weight is clearly on the side of the quantifiers. The "star" of the volume is undoubtedly the historian Emmanuel Le Roy Ladurie, whose skill in extracting a mass of interesting information from French military archives, covering the period 1819–26, dumbfounded his colleagues in England and America and gave additional impetus to quantitative history. Another "star turn" is that of Lawrence Stone, who has invented a new form of historiography which he terms "prosopography," a modified form of "multiple career-line analysis" which investigates "the common background characteristics of a group of actors in history by means of a collective study of their lives."

"The principal causes of [the] proliferation of scientific historical prosopography in the United States," Stone informs us, "has been the great influence of sociology [just what I feared] and political science and the advanced training in the use of, and easy access to, the computer. . . . In addition, the prosopographists are being supplied with data about popular voting at the county level in every election since 1824. . . . A beginning is now being made in collecting machine-readable statistical data for earlier periods of American history and also for other countries." Wow!

In Stone's words, such grand projects "must be carried out by teams of researchers, assembling data on the lines laid down by the director. This material is then studied, collated, and eventually published by the director, to whom alone credit goes." This has resulted in some jealously and resentment among the serfs. "Collective research," Stone notes, "is already fully accepted by the physical scientists as a familiar and necessary process. . . ." But unfortunately historians seem to be more individualistic and self-seeking. They are concerned about things like promotions and become restive at their "peonage," as Stone calls it with disarming candor. Such problems, including apparently a good deal of rather bitter infighting among the quantifiers (or, rather, the "directors" of quantifying) arouse in Stone an anxiety that the modern historian "may retreat . . . into the dark recesses of impressionistic methodology. To make matters worse, there are strong national overtones to the split. . . ." American and French prosopographers, for instance, have an access to computers denied to their English counterparts, a cause, it seems, for a good deal of grumbling.

What is one to say? Perhaps, under the circumstances, it is better to say nothing. I have, after all, a thesis, which is that academic historians are destroying history in any recognizable meaning of that ancient and honorable word. My intention is to call Professor Stone to the stand as a witness for the prosecution.

Although the authors in *Historical Studies Today* have varying (and often conflicting) perspectives, they have a common tone, which is unremitting contempt for anything that might be termed "traditional" history. The author of an article on "political history" is typical. After describing the "new" statistically oriented political history, he rails at the "old political history . . . a corpse that has to be made to lie down." There is "still a danger that political history in the vulgarized form in which it appears in countless popularizing books and magazines may once again invade the real science of history." It must be rebuffed at all costs in "the age of pluridisciplinarity." Pluridisciplinarity? Could the author possibly be joking? No, he is dead serious.

Nothing is mentioned in *Historical Studies Today* about the larger aims of historical scholarship. Nothing about a social role for the historian, nothing about any possible responsibility on the part of the historian to try to communicate with any human being other than another historian. The public is mentioned only as a threat to the purity of scientific history. It would not, I believe, be going too far to characterize the attitude of the "scientific" historians toward those of another persuasion as venomous. There is no disposition to treat historians of basically different (nonscientific) bent as honorable if misguided opponents; they are the enemy, and they and their history must be driven from the field if scientific truth is to prevail; they must be pronounced dead.

While I was writing this book, an enormous work was published with the subtitle *The "Objectivity Question" and the American Historical Professor.* The title is *That Noble Dream.* The author, Peter Novick, a professor of history at the University of Chicago, could hardly have picked a more inappropriate title, for the book is an account of the most scandalous and bitter internecine warfare among American historians over the question of who was more objective than whom. In the name of objectivity, history professors made the most savage attacks on each other's character and intelligence, called each other liars, fools, criminals, and displayed not only a complete and startling lack of objectivity but an absence of decency and compassion as well. Historians considered unorthodox were hounded relentlessly, sometimes to nervous breakdowns and sometimes out of the profession entirely. Novick recounts these Lilliputian if sanguinary conflicts in mind-numbing detail. Mesmerized by the notion that history could be objectively, scientifically recounted, historians clung to the illusion like drowning men, as though their very lives depended on that ignoble dream (or strange infatuation). They believed, almost to a man, that a "professionalized, scientific history would rapidly construct the cumulative and convergent edifice of historial truth," in Novick's words. They called themselves the New Historians and were confident that a "crop of great historians," as one historian put it, would emerge in the aftermath of World War I. The assumption, Peter Novick noted, was that all the little monographic studies would "eventuate in an overarching narrative synthesis." What emerged instead, as Novick recounts it, was an acrimonious dispute between those historians who thought Germany was responsible for the war and those who believed otherwise, some historians going so far as to exonerate Germany entirely. What is also revealed in Novick's book is an appalling degree of anti-Semitism. And, not surprisingly, anti-Catholicism. One eminent historian complained because too many young men of lower-middle-class origins were going into the profession, replacing the gentlemen of an earlier era. John Spencer Bassett, secretary of the American Historical Association, wrote that "Left alone they [these historians from the lower levels] are apt to fall into the dull and dreary habits of amassing information without grace of form and without charm of expression." But wasn't that exactly what they were being trained to do?

That anti-Semitism was epidemic in the profession is evident from a number of quotations in Novick's book. Selig Perlman, one of the first Jews to break the racial barrier (in economics at Wisconsin), was reputed to warn his Jewish graduate students in a "deep Yiddish accent" that "History belongs to the Anglo-Saxons. You belong in economics or sociology." Crane Brinton, professor of history at Harvard, wrote to a fellow historian of a brilliant Jewish student, J. H. Hexter: "I'm afraid he is unemployable, but I'd like to make one last effort on his behalf." Another historian wrote that a young Oscar Handlin "has none of the offensive traits which some people associate with his race." Bert Lowenberg was endorsed by Arthur Schlesinger as "by temperament and spirit . . . measur[ing] up to the whitest Gentile I know." Catholics were barred for different reasons. They believed in God and thus were hopelessly compromised from the beginning. W. H. Mace wrote to Harry Elmer Barnes that "a Catholic cannot teach and be a true Catholic."

Novick ends his mammoth work on a gloomy and indecisive note (the last two chapters are: "The Center Does Not Hold," and "There Was No King in Israel"). He has, he assures us, no inclination to try to predict the course of historical study, either "the indefinite continuation of the present chaos (or some other outcome)." All that he claims for his 629 pages is the attempt to show that "the evolution of historians' attitudes on the objectivity question has always been closely tied to changing social, political, cultural, and professional contexts." We would have granted that long before he compiled this disheartening record of our profession's remarkable power for self-delusion (and rancorous contentions).

One cannot help wondering what Novick himself thought of this beyond the clue given by the title—that the goal of objectivity was "noble." It seems to me, I must confess, to have no nobility about it at all, merely an odd combination of hubris and naïveté. Why did it not occur to the champions of objectivity that their professional behavior was a farcical denial of "scientific objectivity"? There is quite evidently no feeling in the profession, taken as a whole, for the grand sweep of human history, for its drama and tragedy and nobility, only these wretched little squabbles that made C. Vann Woodward, as a young man contemplating a career as a historian, cry out to himself, "My God, is this what I have dedicated my life to?"

The fact is that the whole vast structure of academic, monographic history is based on a false assumption, that assumption being that a definitive work can be done that won't have to be done over again in the light of the unfolding of history. Since history is not a science, it has to be constantly rewritten in response to new events. A general narrative history of the United States in the nineteenth century, written at the end of that century, would, however brilliant, have to be rewritten after the catastrophic events of the twentieth. Take only one instance: slavery and the Civil War. After the civil-rights movement, we could no longer view the role of black people in the same light. The Vietnam War would be another instance. The writing of history is an act of incorporation, among other things. We have constantly to incorporate classes and races and issues to whose significance we have formerly been blind. Among the numerous such issues is, of course, the role of women in our history. Another theme, at present being aired, is the role of religion. Needless to say, with the strong bias against religion evident in the academic world since the turn of the century, historical investigators have ignored the role of religion in American history. This was comparatively easy to do, since monographs by definition deal with only one limited topic. All that was necessary was not to choose religion-related issues as the topics for monographs. The textbook writers, who are, in effect, the researchers with different hats on, followed suit. What students got, in consequence, was a history (or histories) of the United States that left out an element of our past that some impartial observers (like myself) think is the most important element in our history—without proper attention to which our history can't be understood at all. So, under the guise of being objective and scientific, academic historians, when they undertook to write general history in that most depressing of literary forms, the college text, by omitting religion gave their young readers a totally inadequate picture of our past. All of this has nothing to do with whether one is personally religious or not, whether Protestant Christianity is "true" or not. One may have no more faith than a mole or muskrat (gopher, in the West); the centrality of religion in our history is simply an objective fact. It is as specific and concrete a reality as the railroads that bound the nation together with steel rails. A defender of monographic history (and I trust some will step forward in that role) may reply something to the effect: "Academic history has grown far more refined and sophisticated in the questions that it asks and the rather tentative answers that it produces. It has, after all, turned its attention to such issues as the role of women and minorities in general. It is keenly aware of the psychosocial aspects of political developments, of the role of class and gender and racial stereotyping; it is far from the crude materialism that characterized much work in the early decades of the century." Well, true, but that is only to say historical research has followed enlightened public opinion rather than led it. It was not the writers of monographs who inspired Rosa Parks in Montgomery or motivated the marchers on Selma, Alabama. The historians' monographs on racism came after the fact of the civil-rights protests. Even if they had preceded the women's liberation movement, let us say, with powerful monographs, they would have had little effect on public opinion because (1) they would have been largely unreadable and (2) the public was not supposed to read them anyway. Monographs, by their nature, are not prods to conscience, or calls to action; they are almost wholly descriptive. If some small insect-like emotional life is revealed in a monograph, the author may be expected to be rebuked by a reviewer for not being sufficiently objective, for allowing himself/herself to be swept away by gusts of passion.

In any event, the time for an accounting is here if indeed it is not long past. The historical monograph must prove itself as an indispensable contribution to human progress and understanding or else it must give up the ghost and retire from the scene. We, the taxpayers, refuse to be intimidated by it any longer. "Stand and deliver" is our battle cry, "or else sit down and keep a decent silence." Cost accounting can be carried too far, and doubtless, in our society, commonly is. But the appointed hour is now; the accountants are waiting in the vestibule. One of the favorite academic words of the era is "demystify." Ruthless researchers are constantly promising to demystify this or that revered institution or widely held illusion or admired hero. Now the time has come to demystify the monograph and the whole elaborate system that produces it.

It should be noted, almost parenthetically, that the anti-historical spirit of our time extends even to graduate students in history, young men and women who, too impatient to meet history on its own terms, attempt to bend it to their wills. They seem to wish to use history to denigrate both the past *and* the present. They presume to triumph over history by explaining it in terms that suit their ideological requirements. The late Herbert Gutman, a "socialist" social historian, primarily concerned with labor and black history (and author of an important book on the black family), was dismayed by the tendency that he noted in his radically inclined students. They were determined, it seemed to him, "to believe that this [the United States] has always been a culture dominated by the military-industrial complex. Their alienation from the present drives them to reject the past in its entirety. The American past is the unredeeming saga of a mixture of corporate exploitation, all-pervasive racism, and a compliant and corrupted working-class and radical movement. It is almost as though Mayor Daley and the Chicago police landed at Plymouth Rock and as if agents of General Motors dumped the tea in Boston Harbor."

It seems to me ironic in the extreme that the *Zeitgeist,* the spirit of the times, the culture, the devil, call it what you will, was able to use academic history to destroy history, or at least rob it for generations of its potency and relevance. Academic historians clearly had mayhem on their minds, but since it is impossible to kill Clio, I suppose it might better be said that academic history bound and gagged her and locked her in the cell reserved for disturbers of the academic peace. How ingenious to use historians to suppress history! Who would think to charge the guardians with the crime? Indeed, it is only recently that students have come to realize what has happened. In the last decade the number of history majors has declined by 43 percent. Given the nature of the current state of academic history, can we perhaps anticipate 100 percent? That would be a triumph of intelligence over custom. Is it too much to say that it took ten thousand (roughly) professors of history laboring for a hundred years to destroy the classic history that has been a pleasure and an inspiration since the days of Thucydides and Herodotus?

It might be assumed that the field of literature would, in all the array of academic disciplines, be the one most resistant to the claims of science, but once science became the model and measure of things academic, literature departments did their best to be as scientific as the next department. This consisted in the main of close attention to the finest points of critical interpretation. It also meant definitive editions of famous books. In the words of Robert Adams, professor of English, "Mechanical copying machines and word processors made possible the preparation of texts unprecedentedly accurate and sometimes unprecedentedly elaborate. The intoxicating prospect of recording every last variant in every last copy of every edition of an enormous text has had to be qualified by practicalities." But not much. Readers of *The New York Review of Books* have recently been treated to the unedifying spectacle of rival editors of James Joyce's *Ulysses* accusing each other of the most desperate villainies. Both projects have taken years, involved a number of scholarly "peons," and cost hundreds of thousands of dollars. Each claims to be more scientific than the others.

In literature, as in other fields, prestige was enhanced by the securing of large grants, a form of "validation by foundation." In Adams' words, "artful authors started to compile little books of instruction in the craft of plum gathering and grants officers appeared on many campuses to help the retiring, uncourtly scholar get his share of the boodle." One grant encouraged another. The National Endowment for the Humanities kept a respectful eye on the older and more prestigious Guggenheim Foundation, for example. Science aside, literature was in a strong position to respond to the student demand for "particular literary or subliterary modes (science fiction, murder mystery, kiddie lit, comic books, et cetera). . . ." As in history, there were also psychoanalytic, Marxist, semiotic approaches, and, most recently, efforts to adapt structuralism and deconstructionism to literary criticism. The consequence was that in literature, as in history, what was said about a work by critics often became more important than the work itself.

The social sciences were summoned to the assistance of the literature professor to help explain how a particular book was the consequence of "cognitive deviance," a favorite term of the sociologists. Adams protests against the move to deconstruct "all literary texts down to the same meaningless non-propositions. . . ." It occurs to him that "the suspicion may soon arise as to whether in fact departments of literature have any clear notion of what (or how) they are to teach beyond the latest fad."

The application of the notion of science in the field of literature is commonly expressed, in Sir Richard Livingstone's words, by explaining a writer "in terms of his ancestry, his early life, his education, the character of his age, the influences, social, intellectual, and other, which have shaped his outlook and intellect, his subconscious mind, his Oedipus complexes and physic trauma." For example, Coleridge wrote a lyric of fifty-four lines, "Kubla Khan," and an American professor wrote a book of six hundred pages analyzing the poem. Irving Babbitt, the prophet of a New Humanism, wrote that he was told that "the merit of a certain classical scholar [was demonstrated by the fact] that he had twenty thousand references in his card catalogue."

In the anniversary issue of *The New York Review of Books*, Frederick Crews, professor of English at the Berkeley campus of the University of California, surveyed a new subgroup in the world of academic literary criticism. Calling them the "New American-ists," Crews casts a skeptical eye on their critical assumptions. Their immediate intention is to question whether the great figures of what the late F. O. Matthieson called the "American Renais-sance"—Poe, Whitman, Hawthorne, Melville, Emerson, and Tho-reau—are really deserving of the high literary rank that has been accorded to them, or whether they have been grossly puffed up by a kind of elitist conspiracy—in Crews' words, by "an unending chain of interest groups" who have "some kind of vested interest in keeping their reputations alive." The bellwethers of the new, new, new criticism take the line that the writers of the American Renaissance were, witting or unwitting, conspirators in failing to direct their talents toward the gross social injustices so evident in mid-nineteenth-century America—slavery, exploitation of the working class, suppression of the Indians, the inequality of women, etc. Hawthorne is the special target of their barbs, and they are addicted to sentences like the following (in reference to Edgar Allan Poe's famous story "The Fall of the House of Usher"): The story is really about "the fall of the artistic control and unity that Poe feared would accompany modern sensational writings, whose typical narrative patterns he knew to be as crooked as the zigzag fissure that splits apart Usher's mansion." Little Pearl in Haw-thorne's *The Scarlet Letter* "remains the wild embodiment of the antebellum Subversive imagination as long as her parents remain within the amoral value system of nineteenth-century sensa-tionalism."

Another critic of the same school tells us that Harriet Beecher Stowe's *Uncle Tom's Cabin* "misses literary status because its war-ring elements do not *fuse* to create metaphysical ambiguity or multilayered symbols."

To say that most of this is nonsense is perhaps to belabor the obvious. But it finds publishers and readers and is imposed on defenseless graduates and doubtless on undergraduates as well. It is, at heart, a kind of intellectual tyranny in which the critic/tyrant stands at the shoulder of the reader and tells him/her how the actual text must be read. The worst possible mistake would be to assume that the text means what it seems to say.

Frederick Crews ends his discussion of the New Americanists on a note of gloom. The New Americanists understand that in the academic world power can be used to impose one's own views on the wider world. "They will be right about the most important books and the most fruitful ways of studying them because, as they always knew in their leaner days, those who hold power are right by definition."

The problem of the critical approach that Frederick Crews describes as the New Americanism is that it takes all the joy out of life and encourages students, who, from their youthful perspective, have a disposition toward idol-smashing, to think themselves cleverer than they are. The universities, Irving Howe charges, are engaged in "an effort to disintegrate or at least damage the very idea of a classic and to replace it with a hodge-podge of currently fashionable items." But the sin is perhaps more grievous. By challenging classics as to their position on racial matters, let us say, by indicting Melville for his failure to write against slavery, we undermine respect, not just for Melville, but for the past. We deprive ourselves of any genuine connection with the best of what has been done and written. We become foolish and arrogant judges intent on dragging great figures from the past before the bar of the most jejune and superficial opinion and indicting them for not being as humane and enlightened as we are. In David Bromwich's words, the captions for such courses should read: "We're so smart today because they were so dumb yesterday."

The New Americanists have a modest point in the fact that much of the popular literature of the nineteenth century has been neglected. There are any number of interesting social-protest novels, particularly toward the end of the century. There are, for example, the novels of Albion Turgee, most notably *Bricks Without Straw* and, later, *Mervale Eastman, Christian Socialist*. But to take the line that the great writers of the American Renaissance were imposed on the reading public by a reactionary elite is to attain a new level of academic nuttiness.

———

As I pursued my admittedly superficial researches into the current state of the academic disciplines, two names recurred with striking frequency: Jacques Derrida, the French philosopher and creator of deconstructionism, and Antonio Gramsci, an Italian Marxist. It sometimes seemed as if all up-to-date academics were followers of one or the other and, in some of the especially trendy, disciples of both.

Jacques Derrida is a lineal descendant of Nietzsche in that he is above all a destroyer of illusions. The entire Western tradition is to be "deconstructed" in order to expose the shakiness of its unconscious presuppositions. What is left is, in simplest terms, a void, a vast emptiness. There is no way of adjudicating between conflicting systems of values, traditions, and symbols. It is a kind of intellectual pulling of wings off flies. For decades professors have been destroying their students' illusions, their "false consciousness," their naïve adherence to certain obsolete values (religion being one of the most obvious). Now the shoe appears to be on the other foot. Derrida is destroying *their* illusions, especially *their* illusion that they are engaged in objective, scientific investigation of the world. What they are really doing is imposing their own, ultimately baseless, views on their students and their colleagues, and there is no independent, "objective" evidence that their illusions are any better than those of their students; they may well be worse. The students' illusions had at least enabled the students to live a reasonably ordered existence. Undoubtedly there is a vertiginous thrill in looking into the abyss. Derrida may well be the professors' equivalent of a teenager's horror movie, the difference being that the teenager can walk out of the movie house into a moderately real world, whereas it is not yet clear that professors can assemble a post-Derridarian world out of the lumber of the deconstructed one. All we can say is that the human psyche, like the rest of nature, abhors a vacuum and *something* will fill it.

In addition to Derrida, the name I heard frequently, especially from the neo-Marxists, was that of the Italian communist Antonio Gramsci. Gramsci, a native of Sardinia, was a leader in the Italian Communist Party when he was arrested by the Fascists in 1926.

He spent the next eleven years in prison and died there in 1937. During his prison years he wrote voluminously if somewhat obscurely, and his *Prison Notebooks,* in some thousand pages, became the bible of the neo-Marxists, men and women who carried Gramsci's uneasiness about the capacity of the working class to overturn capitalism much further and adopted his thesis that "the whole represents the whole": the overturn of capitalism will not come (or, in Gramsci's view, would not come) until the whole society shares a common culture. Gramsci saw virtues in bourgeois society not perceived by Marx but, more important, he realized the all-pervasiveness of the existing culture and the difficulty of developing the workers' revolutionary consciousness in the face of that intricate cultural dominance. Gramsci thus gave special attention to the role of the Marxist intellectual. No longer was he required to man the barricades or take up the banner of international communism. The triumph of the working class was now a distant hope. Victory could only be won over, perhaps, generations and by an intricate interaction between the intellectuals and the workers. This turned out to be a perfect formula for the rise of a new, denatured (or defanged) academic Marxism. Professors who consider themselves Marxists now appear quite respectable. They do not call for the immediate and violent overthrow of capitalism. They write obscure articles and books analyzing various aspects of capitalist culture with a view to some distant revolutionary event.

In one significant respect the Marxist professors deviate from Gramsci. Gramsci wrote: "The popular element 'feels' but does not know or understand; the intellectual element 'knows' but does not always understand and in particular does not always feel. . . . The intellectual's error consists in believing that one can . . . be an intellectual (and not a pure pedant) if distant and separate from the people-nation, that is without feeling the elementary passions of the people, understanding them . . . and connecting them dialectically to the laws of history and to a superior conception of the world, scientifically and coherently elaborated—i.e., knowledge." Intellectuals have never been very good at this latter function, relating to "the people-nation" or, I assume, to the people of the nation. The academic Marxists do not even make an effort; they are too preoccupied with refinements of Gramsci to pay much attention either to their students or to the world outside of the university. By Gramsci's standard they are, in the main, "pure pedants."

David Gaines mentions a female graduate student he encountered at the Duke conference on "opening the canon" who quoted her "most brilliant professor's opinion that the revolution rather than the curriculum is the issue." Another Marxist professor wrote recently in a campus newspaper: "[T]he US is a capitalist society—based on the exploitation of labor of workers of all ethnic, cultural, etc. backgrounds. . . . [A]nyone who denies that the US is a racist society is either a fool or a knave." The professor offers to debate this issue with anyone "who wants to deepen their understanding of what the US is all about." This seems to me a classic bit of neo-Marxist balderdash. The academic Marxists, who, incidentally, are about the only Marxists left in the world, seem determined to demonstrate their superiority by hating America. If America can be revealed to be hopelessly benighted, and they the first generation of Americans to face this fact fearlessly and proclaim it endlessly, then they are clearly superior to those poor "fools" who think otherwise.

E. P. Thompson, in a review of Herbert Gutman's *Power and Culture,* writes: "What made Herb growl was the limitless capacity of the intelligentsia to write off working-class initiatives with elaborately theorized systems—structures or determinisms—from whose compulsions only they, the intelligentsia, are supposed to be exempt." It was their "strategy . . . to show that all except a small number of initiated theorists, are unfree."

The popularity of Gramsci raises an interesting issue—the revival of academic Marxism. On the University of California's Santa Cruz campus, I am told, there are some forty-five avowed Marxists. Since the "ladder faculty" total 373, of whom approximately 228 are in the humanities and social sciences, where, presumably, the Marxists are concentrated, roughly one-fifth of the faculty in these areas would seem to be Marxists of one brand or another. But before the American Legion sounds the alarm, it should be pointed out that they are quite harmless, if only by virtue of the fact that it is almost impossible to understand what they are saying or writing.

Although it may well be that the percentage of Marxists at the Santa Cruz campus is substantially higher than at many other universities, I know of no reason to assume that Marxists are not numerous on other campuses: academic fundamentalism, Marxist division. One possible explanation for the large percentage of Marxist professors scattered about the various disciplines is that many of them were student radicals in the 1960s and have adopted Marxism as a kind of sop to their consciences for playing the academic game that they criticized so scathingly two decades ago. Seen in this light, our professors' Marxism may give them the comforting assurance that they haven't sold out entirely. In other words, by proclaiming the corruptions of capitalism and the hope of revolution in the indefinite (and presumably remote) future, Marxist professors are absolved of any responsibility for the present state of higher learning. That the universities, as organs of capitalism, are hopelessly corrupt is obvious; it is only what one would expect; it is a "given." The universities cannot be changed or reformed until after the revolution. Meanwhile, more books and articles are needed. The real problem for me is that the Marxists have, in the main, such a dismal, soul-destroying view of the world. One is reminded of Simone Weil's remark: "Culture is an instrument yielded by professors to manufacture professors, who in turn manufacture more professors." It is the closed world of academic fundamentalism.

Before I abandon the academic disciplines to their uncertain fate, I cannot forbear to make some comments on the misapprehension under which most academics-who-would-be-scientists labor in regard to what "real" scientists actually do. The labors of the hard scientists are very different from what the would-be scientists conceive them to be. Whereas the would-be scientists talk about detachment, objectivity, neutrality, the dispassionate treatment of the data, the "hard" scientists and their biographers talk of passion and obsession, of hunches and of inspiration, of insight, excitement, and profound emotion. One thinks of Nietzsche's axiom, "Nothing great is accomplished without passion," and Rosenstock-Huessy's words, "We owe everything to enthusiastic people," "Our passions give life to the world. . . ." "Those who knew Einstein," David Bohm of Birkbeck College, University of London, wrote, "will agree that his work was permeated by great passion." And again: "insight is an *act,* permeated by intense passion, that makes possible great clarity in the sense that it perceives and dissolves subtle but strong emotional, social, linguistic and intellectual pressures tending to hold the mind in rigid and fixed compartments." Einstein himself wrote: "Mysticism is the basis of all true science and the person who can no longer stand rapt in awe is as good as dead." Nietzsche, who alarmed the West by announcing that God was dead, insisted that there could not be any science without presuppositions, that "a 'faith' must be there first of all, so that science can acquire from it a direction, a meaning, a limit, a method, a *right* to exist."

Karl Jaspers writes: "Knowledge comes to life for the real scientist. His extraordinary patience and toil become enflamed with enthusiasm. Science becomes the principle animating his whole life." This was a fact that I noticed in trying to recruit scientists for my college. The best scientists, older men of established reputation, impressed me as having an innocence and a purity of spirit that I assumed came from the dedication that Jaspers speaks of. They had a kind of transparency that I deduced came from the singleness of purpose and joy in their labors and that much attracted me. I met many vigorous and lively individuals in fields other than the sciences, but none gave off quite that sense of focused energies and personal wholeness.

James Trefil, a physicist at George Mason University, writes in *The Dark Side of the Universe* that the important scientists are rarely "hard headed, show-me individuals who believe something only after it has been demonstrated to a fare-thee-well in the laboratory." Rather, "beauty, elegance, and simplicity play a much bigger role in the way scientists think than people suspect." An idea must bring with it "a brightening of the soul" if a true scientist is to accept it.

The academic world has ignored the simple fact, apparent to

the most unsophisticated citizen, that there is no pure "objectivity" in the world. There is, and should be, fairness, judiciousness, what the French call *mesure,* but no one can be entirely free of personal views and biases, and the most dangerous individuals are those who believe that they can be. When the Nobel Prize–winning physicist Werner Heisenberg put forward his famous "uncertainty principle"—in brief, the argument that even the toughest-minded scientist in his most carefully controlled experiments brings to them his own predispositions and alters the "object" of his investigations simply in the process of observing it—most scientists accepted Heisenberg's theory. It did not, in any event, affect very directly their own researches, which had to be validated by being repeatable by other scientists using the same data and the same methods. But it was otherwise with the so-called social sciences and even with the ill-fated humanities. They continued to behave as though there were such a thing as "objectivity" and, moreover, that the only subjects admissible in the academy were those that were measurable, quantifiable, and unentangled with messy emotions and transitory enthusiasms.

Perhaps we should leave the last word on the subject of science to Sir Richard Livingstone: "Science," Sir Richard writes, "goes steadily about her work, revealing as she does it, the greatness of man, and if we misuse her, the blame is ours. . . . All that we need are the firm standards and clear philosophy of life, which distinguishes evil from good, and chooses good and refuses evil. . . . Any great new force that comes into the world is revolutionary; and for the moment upsets and confuses the minds of men. That was as true of Christianity as it is of science; it too was a disruptive force in the world. . . . [A] history of the world might almost be written in terms, first of the discovery of great truths, and then of their exaggeration." The time has clearly come to place science in its proper relation to traditional wisdom.

17
WOMEN'S STUDIES

"In theory, my instinct rather turns to the woman than to
the man of the future. In modern society, the man and his
masculinity are at disadvantage. The woman . . . is only
beginning her career. What she will become is known only
to the Holy Virgin. . . . A branch of her sex is sure to break
off as an emancipated social class."

—HENRY ADAMS

Since we are discussing the academic disciplines, it is, I think,
appropriate to discuss a new one—Women's Studies.

The strife of the late sixties and early seventies had barely sub-
sided when militant feminists made their move. They declared,
with considerable justice, that male attitudes and prejudices (or
simply indifference or incomprehension) had penetrated to the
very heart of the university. It was evident in hiring practices, in
policies of admission to graduate study, in the nature of research
itself, most conspicuously in the social sciences, most notably in
psychology. The militants demanded courses designed specifically
for women: women's history, women's psychology, sociology from
a female perspective, even biology. There must be courses on
women literary figures and departments of women's studies. And
these must, of course, be taught by women. What most feminists,
focused on achieving a fairer share of the existing academic pie,
failed to take into account was the degree to which men had made
the university a place singularly uncongenial for women. This was
a problem that went well beyond giving proper attention to women
in the curriculum. It had to do with many of those issues that we
have been discussing throughout this work, among them the impersonality of the university, the fragmentation of learning, the

lack of contact between teachers and students, the absurdly extended time needed to acquire the necessary Ph.D., the emphasis on often sterile research—the list could be considerably extended. The things that the rebellious students listed as glaring deficiencies in the universities were, in the main, things that were thoroughly uncongenial to women-as-faculty as well as to female students. The problem was that to admit that the male-created, male-dominated atmosphere of the university was inhospitable to women would be to accept, at least tacitly, the notion that women were different from men, had different emotional needs and a somewhat different perspective on the world, and this many of the feminists were unwilling to admit. Their case was based, in large part, on the argument that there were no substantial differences between men and women. Those traits that appeared to differentiate the sexes were the consequence of "culture," not "biology." But the bottom line was still that women had to come into the university on male terms. Their entry simply served to fragment learning further. To the already bewildering array of courses were added female versions or counterparts or supplements. Such courses as "Brazilian Women Poets of the 19th and 20th Centuries" took their place beside "Peasants and Artisans in French History," "Topics in Chicano History," "Black Women Novelists."

In a period of confusion about the nature of higher education, a militant group that had a strong sense of its own imperatives was, I suspect, bound to exert a disproportionate influence. For one thing, the militants had, as their prospective constituency, roughly half the student body—that is to say, all women students. Although by no means all of the women on any particular campus are ardent feminists, most can be rallied to the cause by any indication of discrimination or less than equal treatment in all matters having to do with the curriculum and the quality of campus life in general as it affects women. The university had barely recovered (if indeed it *has* recovered) from the body blows delivered by the "student rebellion" of the sixties before the women's movement began to call into question the male-oriented character of virtually all the academic disciplines. This was an argument difficult to rebut, because it was, in large measure, true. In no field in the social sciences and the humanities had women, their accomplishments, and their needs been adequately attended to. The male custodians of the academic world were thus attacked where they were most vulnerable. Most of them being individuals of reasonably good intentions, they set about—under, to be sure, severe pressure— to remedy the situation. They began to employ women, and most of the women they employed were militant young women who talked constantly and unnervingly of the "gender agenda," which, if it did not call for taking charge of the cloisters themselves, called for "equality," an equality in which it seemed that some programs were more "equal" than others and that women's studies were the most equal of all. The result has been a bewildering proliferation of courses concerned with the special perspectives of women on everything under the academic sun, most of them taught by women, many of whom are unabashedly hostile to men in general, if not to their male colleagues.

At the University of California, Santa Cruz, of the twenty-three instructors (all ranks) listed in the catalogue as participating in the American Studies program, eight are women. The male members of the board or department teach over a wide range of topics. Six of the eight women instructors list as their "fields" "women's history," "women's studies," "U.S. sexual history," "women's and labor history," "feminist theory," "American feminism," "women and social policy."

In history the situation is much the same. There is a course on "Women in American History," and one on "The History of the Family," in which it seems safe to assume women figure prominently. There are courses on "European Women's History," "U.S. Women's History in Comparative Perspective," "Race, Class and Gender in California History."

Sociology has its share of women's courses, taught, of course, by women. "The Sociology of Love" covers "(1) how the experience of love is constructed/shaped by the individual, social structure, conventions, ideology; (2) functions of love for the individual/society; (3) how love varies by gender/social class; (4) mythologies of love. Emphasis on romantic heterosexual love and its historical development in Western culture." One can't help wondering whether that's not dissecting love to death?

Sociology also offers "Women in the Courts," as "litigants, lawyers and judges. The nature and consequences of gender-based stereotypes, myths, and biases imbedded in the law. . . ." Of the six women instructors in sociology, four list "gender" as one of their major concerns—i.e., "women and work," "sociology of gender," "gender and justice." There are also courses on "Sexual Politics of Medicine," and "Sociology of Women" (in all fairness, it must be said that there is also a course on the "Sociology of Men").

Anthropology has seven women instructors out of eleven (again of various ranks), of whom five list among their major concerns feminine-related topics—"Evolutionary and cultural perspectives on sex roles," "sex roles," "anthropology of women," "sexuality."

Although women's studies do not have a department *per se* at Santa Cruz (a number of women students and faculty fought hard for one), they have a Women's Studies Program, which brings together all the instructors on campus from various disciplines who share an interest in such studies. The list comes to forty-six, including two men. The courses from which a student majoring in Women's Studies may choose include "Asian American Women," "Women and Radical Social Movements," "Women in Changing Asia," "Seminar on Women Artists," "Women in Latin American Literature and Society," "Latin American Cinema," "Great Adulteresses and Others," "Feminist Reading, Lesbian Writing," "The Human Body in Cultural Perspective," "Biology in Culture and Sex Roles," "Sexual Politics: Lesbian and Gay Liberation," "Gender and Politics," "Language and the Sexes," "Sexual Politics of Medicine."

In addition to the courses given in various departments on some aspect or another of women, Women's Studies offers seventeen courses on its own, including "French Feminism: Texts and Contexts."

In other words, by my rough calculations there are approximately eighty courses offered on the campus of the University of California, Santa Cruz, whose principal focus is on women. Virtually all of these courses are taught by women faculty members. There are two things that might be said here. The older notion of "objectivity" has gone by the board completely in Women's Studies. There is no pretense that the instructors have objectivity or even impartiality or "judiciousness" as a goal. The courses are, with doubtless notable exceptions, unabashedly "sexual politics." Women have, in effect, seized control over a substantial part of the curriculum of the Santa Cruz campus. Relatively few men take the courses taught by women and reflecting their "gender" concerns. (I was told that a course entitled "Introduction to Feminism" had 750 students enrolled of whom only ten were men.)

There are certainly positive aspects to the new "counter"-education run by women for women. There are strong moral imperatives: there is the drama of the good girls versus the bad guys. There is passionate conviction as opposed to the bland neutrality of much of the rest of the curriculum. My impression is that women teachers take a far more personal interest in their students/recruits than do their male counterparts. The older ones play a warm, supportive, mothering role for immature and uncertain young women. I suspect the atmosphere is not dissimilar to that of women's colleges in the late nineteenth century, places like Mount Holyoke, Smith, Wellesley, Bryn Mawr. Indeed, it is as though two different institutions occupied the same campus. One institution, the University of California, Santa Cruz, Male Division, is a more or less conventional university campus where the traditional pieties still prevail (or the ghosts of them): science, objectivity, scholarship above all, students if not as enemies at least as impediments to the "real," the serious work of research. The other campus, existing in uneasy juxtaposition, is the University of California, Santa Cruz, Female Division. This is basically a novelty in higher education, as we have noted. All pretense of objectivity (that precious icon of the modern university) has been cast aside. There is an air of excitement, of discovering new truths, a unity of spirit and purpose, an exhilaration largely missing in the "other campus."

It is difficult to overestimate the importance of women in undermining the academy's notion of "objectivity." First off, women were able to demonstrate to any but the most obtuse male that virtually all the standard academic disciplines were at the very least deficient in their attention to the role of women. If there was objective truth, and if the practitioners in various fields were, as many of them believed, approaching it, albeit slowly, how was it that they had left out roughly half the race—and, as some thought, the more important half? Women scholars had once been warned away from the academic study of women on the grounds that, as women, they couldn't be sufficiently objective about other women (just as black scholars were not so long ago warned away from studying the problems of blacks on the same grounds: as blacks, they couldn't be objective in regard to their own race). What was laughable was that it never occurred to white males to question *their* objectivity. In any event, it became increasingly difficult to persist in believing in the religion of science and/or objectivity. Moreover, if the objectivity myth was finally and irrevocably laid to rest, what, indeed, was it that scholars *were* doing? That question has become harder and harder to answer—hard even to pose.

The point I wish to emphasize is that none of this could have happened (at least in the extreme form that it has) if the demoralization of the academic world was not already far advanced. The real question is how well this curriculum will serve those it is intended to serve—its female students. It seems to me that they deserve something better. They, after all, have to go out into a world where men and women must confront the task of repairing already strained relationships. We cannot exist as an armed camp in the war between the sexes with all the other urgent problems that beset us. Will courses in the depiction of women's roles in Latin-American films be of much use in solving the problems that face our society?

But, then, of course, it might as well be asked: will a conventional major in psychology, history, and anthropology or economics be much use, with those fields as fragmented and disorganized as they are? By accelerating the process of fragmentation, already far along, Women's Studies may force a re-evaluation of the whole of higher education.

Only rather dimly aware of the development of Women's Studies and basically sympathetic, I find myself astounded by the reality. I have been inclined to take the "long view"—this is a passing aberration; the pendulum has swung, as pendulums do, too far the other way; time will bring a better equilibrium. Easy enough for me to say (or think). I left the campus fifteen years ago, when these matters were just distant rumblings. Now I am not sure. It may very well be that Women's Studies, in their most extreme and imperialistic form, have become institutionalized, and we will have to live with this strange transformation for years to come. The alternative is a fight that, in the present demoralized state of the university, no one has the stomach for (except the aging warriors of the National Association of Scholars).

Whatever one may think about the validity of Women's Studies, the existing situation (one that I assume is reflected in a lesser degree on other university campuses) is clearly out of hand. I don't know of any theory of education that could be evoked to justify such an imbalance. The effect on male students of this internal armed feminist camp in the midst of a more or less traditional university is a topic on which one can, at this stage, only speculate. It is hard to believe that the situation is a healthy one. Granted that there was much to be done to redress the balance, to give a fair accounting of the essential role and remarkable accomplishments of women in history, surely things have gone too far. The image that women students carry away with them on graduation must be of a world hopelessly divided into exploiting males and oppressed females. It is one thing to say that women should have their proper place in all disciplines and departments of a university and another to turn over the enterprise to the most militant of their sex.

The point at which the feminist ethic makes contact with the larger "We're so smart today because they were so dumb yesterday" ethic is in the common conviction that the past has been an unrelieved record of wickedness and oppression. If this were so, and if men were in control in history, then it is men who are to blame for history, and history is, to paraphrase James Joyce, "a nightmare from which we must awake." It is, I believe, a basic feminist Marxist assumption that when we awake it will be to a world where the gender issue has somehow disappeared and women, if not in charge, will be virtually indistinguishable from men at all levels of our common social and political life. Thus, I suspect, the morale of women students is, generally speaking, much better than the morale of their male counterparts. They are the last utopians; they have revived the dream of a better, more humane society, not to be achieved this time by science or reason or objectivity, but by the keener sensibilities and nobler character of women.

18
REVIVING
THE SPIRIT

"Fools act on imagination without knowledge; pedants act on knowledge without imagination. The task of a university is to weld together imagination and experience. . . . It is the function of the scholar to evoke into life wisdom and beauty which, apart from his magic, would remain lost in the past."

—ALFRED NORTH WHITEHEAD

I began this work with a chapter on the current state of higher education. I then attempted to give an account of how we got to where we are. The crisis of the university is, as the reader of this work will know by now, nothing new. Nor are my criticisms. When I was in graduate school forty years ago, I read Alfred North Whitehead's words, and they have buzzed in my head ever since. I know them almost by heart. "To my mind," Whitehead wrote, "our danger [in the academic world] is exactly the same as that of the older system [the scholasticism of the late medieval period]. Unless we are careful, we shall conventionalize knowledge. Our literary criticism will suppress initiative. Our historical criticism will conventionalize our ideas of the springs of human conduct. Our scientific systems will suppress all understanding of the ways of the universe which fall outside their abstractions. Our ways of testing will exclude all the youth whose ways of thought lie outside our conventions of learning. In such ways the universities, with their scheme of orthodoxies, will stifle the progress of the race, unless in some fortunate stirrings of humanity they are in time remodeled or swept away."

There seems to be no gainsaying that the conventional academic disciplines are unraveling at an astonishing rate. As they do, they all face essentially the same problem: what are we to do? What is our discipline after all about? All the professors in the land can't put Humpty Dumpty together again. The center does not hold; there is no king in Israel.

The first and most destructive disease of our time is "presentism," that tireless lust for the new. Dean Inge wrote, "a man who marries the spirit of the age soon finds himself a widower."

Specialization is another common disease of the spirit—that is, excessive specialization at the cost of any capacity for generalization or any awareness of the unity of life.

Knowledge for its own sake, rather than knowledge that ripens into wisdom or that serves larger ends—this is another common disease of the spirit.

Then there is relativism, which denies any moral structure in the world, any absolutes, any finalities. Everything is relative, of equal importance or unimportance.

Throughout this work we have taken note of what I have called "academic fundamentalism." You cannot indefinitely omit one-half or more of human experience without paying a heavy price.

Then, finally, there is simply the brute fact of size, the disease of giantism. True learning is clearly incompatible with immensity. Formalism, lifeless routines, bureaucratic obtuseness, coldness of heart, and impoverishment of spirit are the inevitable consequences of excessive size.

One of the most striking consequences of presentism is the swelling power of greed. If there is nothing but the transitory present, the impulse to seize and devour everything in sight is irresistible. Greed then becomes truly monstrous. Not simply greed for money (although there is plenty of that, both inside and outside of the academic world) but greed for experience of every kind in every form—greed for sex, for drugs, for "things," for baubles, for transitory pleasures and exotic places, greed for any titillation of the senses.

John Jay Chapman insisted that the emotions of youth in every vigorous society should be fed upon the great works of the past: "songs, aspirations, stories, prayers, reverence for humanity, knowledge of God—or else some dreadful barrenness will set in and paralyze the intellect of the race. . . . To cut loose, to cast away, to destroy, seems to be our impulse. We do not want the past. This awful loss of all the terms of thought, the beggary of intellect, is shown in the unwillingness of the average man in America to go to the bottom of any subject, his mental inertia, his hatred of impersonal thought, his belief in labor-saving, his indifference to truth. . . ."

At the end of the nineteenth century, the fever of specialization became all-consuming. Any sense of larger unities was lost. The means became the end. Mindless activity was valued for its own sake. "Culture," Alfred North Whitehead wrote, "is activity of thought, and receptiveness to humane feeling. Scraps of information have nothing to do with it. A merely well-informed man is the most useless bore on God's earth. . . . There is only one subject-matter for education and that is Life in all its manifestations." Instead, we offer an array of subjects to our students, "from which," again in Whitehead's words, "nothing follows." "The spirit of generalization should dominate a University." And again: "The function of a University is to enable you to shed details in favour of principles. . . ."

Jacques Maritain has written: "The overwhelming cult of specialization dehumanizes man's life. . . . This represents a great peril for democracies, because the democratic ideal more than any other requires faith in and the development of spiritual energies—a field which is over and above specialization—and because a complete division of the human mind and activities into specialized compartments would make impossible the very 'government of the people, by the people, and for the people.' "

Salvation by knowledge is the message of the modern age. Knowledge is something to be "used." Knowledge does not mature into wisdom or lead to action but exists independently, on its own terms. In the words of Sir Walter Moberly: "If you want a bomb the chemistry department will teach you how to make it, if you want a cathedral the department of architecture will teach you how to build it, if you want a healthy body the departments of physiology and medicine will teach you how to tend it. But when you ask whether and why you should want bombs or cathedrals or healthy bodies, the university . . . must be content to be dumb and impotent. It can give help and guidance in all things subsidiary but not in the attainment of the one thing needful. In living their lives the young are left 'the sport of every random gust.' But for an educator this is abdication. . . . We have paid the tithe or mint and anise and cummin, and have omitted the weightier matters of the law, judgment, mercy and faith."

There must always be a reciprocal relationship between knowledge and experience. Blaise Pascal enjoined us to think as men of action and act as men of thought, and no more essential axiom has been uttered. To act in useful ways and to create beauty in the world are two of humanity's deepest impulses, and it is to those impulses that we owe virtually every good and beautiful thing in the world beyond God's original bounty.

Then there is relativism. Everything, we are told, is relative. There are no clear moral standards. The good is whatever we enjoy (applied most notably to sexual experience); the "bad" is whatever causes pain or unhappiness to others (a better definition, to be sure, than that of the "good"). Peter Berger points out that the past, in consequence of the "advances" in the social sciences, is "relativized in terms of this or that socio-historical analysis," which is to say, in effect, that we need take nothing in the past very seriously since, relative to what we know today, it can be seen to have been "wrong." The flaw in this argument, as Berger indicates, is that the "*present* . . . seems strangely immune from relativization." But, he argues, the fact is that, among the more perceptive individuals, the realization is growing that "relativizing analysis, in being pushed to its final consequence, bends back upon itself. The relativizers are relativized, the debunkers are debunked. . . ."

What we are talking about in essence are "systems of belief." The scientist and, equally, the pseudo-scientist have their own beliefs, held to quite as doggedly as those of any Christian or Muslim fundamentalist. William James wrote to Helen Keller: "The great world, *the background* of all of us, is the world of our beliefs." Every effort to relativize the world runs aground on this most basic fact. So we are not talking about "facts" versus "faith," or the "truth" versus "belief"; we are simply talking about different kinds of belief. James, for one, believed that one truly knew more through love than through "scientific detachment." He was deeply conscious of "the difference between looking on a person without love, or upon the same person with love. . . . When we see all things in God, and refer all things to Him, we read in common matters superior expressions of meaning."

Throughout this work we have been concerned with the relationship of the academic world to "the world of the spirit." "The essence of education . . ." Whitehead wrote, "is that it be religious. . . . A religious education is an education which inculcates duty and reverence. Duty arises from our potential control over the course of events. . . . And the foundation of reverence is the perception that the present holds within itself the complete sum of existence, backwards and forwards, that whole amplitude of time, which is eternity."

We have argued at some length the consequences of the academic world's excluding a major portion of human experience in the name of science. This is what I have called "academic fundamentalism." The question, then, that confronts us is how to break the stranglehold of science and, more specifically, pseudo-science on the academic world. Jaspers wrote that science "fails in the face of all ultimate questions," and Wittgenstein likewise reminded us that science leaves "the problems of life . . . completely untouched."

The truth is that science needs religion in order to survive. Toward the end of her life, Hannah Arendt wrote: "What has come to an end is the distinction between the sensual and the suprasensual, together with the notion, at least as old as Parmenides, that whatever is not given to the senses . . . is more real, more truthful, more meaningful than what appears; that it is not just beyond sense perception but *above* the world of the senses." Arendt points out "that once the suprasensual realm is discarded, its opposite, the world of appearances as understood for so many centuries, is also annihilated. The sensual, as still understood by the positivists, cannot survive the death of the suprasensual."

Whitehead's solution to the disposition of science to take over the world was that we should "urge the doctrines of Science beyond their delusive air of finality." In other words, push science to prove its claim to have the last word about the world and thus demonstrate its inherent limitations. This, in a real sense, is what Jacques Derrida and Ludwig Wittgenstein have shown.

Finally, we come to the simple, if formidable, issue of size. Writing of the American universities, at the end of the century, Laurence Veysey, author of *The Emergence of the University,* noted that, "while unity of purpose disintegrated, a uniformity of standardized practices was coming to being." Intellectual fragmentation and bureaucratic centralization were to be the main themes of the university for the upcoming century. The laws of institutional life are that all institutions, large and small alike, and the large more rapidly than the small, tend first to defensiveness and rigidity, then to decadence. So far as there are any "laws" governing human affairs, the law of institutional obsolescence seems most immutable. In traditional societies, institutions may have a comparatively long and useful life before they become impediments to the ends they were established to achieve. This process seems to be far more rapid in "new," "open," "democratic" societies and is certainly observable in the American university. One of Smith's "laws" is that, when the organizational structure of an institution of higher education is indistinguishable from that of a major corporation, the spirit dies. Bureaucratic obtuseness stifles all real creativity. Huge institutions become muscle-bound, slower to respond to stimuli than the dinosaur. Committees proliferate; the effort required to accomplish the most modest reforms is out of all proportion to the results. No community is possible where a thousand or more faculty are surrounded by twenty or thirty thousand students. It is all too unwieldy. One cannot contemplate the issue of academic giantism without thinking of William James' famous reflection: "The bigger the unit you deal with, the hollower, the more brutal, the more mendacious is the life displayed.

So I am against all big organizations as such, national ones first and foremost; against all big successes and big results; and in favor of the eternal forces of truth which always work in the individual and most unsuccessful way, underdogs always, till history comes, after they are long dead, and puts them on the top."

The principal (perhaps the only) argument for huge campuses of from ten to forty thousand students is greater efficiency in terms of research facilities, specifically libraries and science labs. It is also sometimes argued that one university of fourteen thousand is more efficient than, say, seven of two thousand (which I suspect is at the upper limit of human efficiency). I believe that the argument for size/efficiency is without substance. Undergraduates do not need large "research" libraries. In addition, the means of securing books by interlibrary loan have become so refined that even quite modest libraries have access to an extraordinary range of specialized works. Beyond that, smaller institutions could share certain kinds of laboratory facilities, as many, in fact, do. If we can deflate the pretensions of academic research, as indeed we must, the question of research facilities becomes much less of an issue.

If we were to agree that real education is virtually impossible in the huge modern universities in which some 75 percent of undergraduate students today receive their inferior educations, we would still be faced with the fact of bricks and mortar. The universities, top-heavy bureaucracies that they are, cannot readily be dismantled or broken up into smaller units. In the "experimental period" following World War II, many universities established "colleges" within their boundaries. The University of California, San Diego, and the University of California, Santa Cruz, both attempted to base undergraduate life on colleges that would, in the aggregate, make up a university. These efforts, promising as they were in many respects, failed, largely because the colleges were in competition with the entrenched disciplines represented by departments that ate them alive. Their existence, transitory as it was (the bricks and mortar remain), serve to remind us that the vast, impersonal universities so hostile by nature to true learning can, after all, be broken up into more human units. All that is necessary is the will to do so.

In the second chapter of this work, I postulated two opposing kinds of consciousness—the Classical Christian Consciousness and the Secular Democratic Consciousness. I argued (and argue) that the greatest achievement of the Classical Christian Consciousness, a consciousness characterized by belief in natural law and original sin, was the Federal Constitution. After that remarkable accomplishment, the fruit of two thousand years of political speculation, the Classical Christian Consciousness lapsed almost at once into a primarily conservative and reactive mode. The Federalists, authors of the Constitution, found control slipping from their hands and frequently expressed their dismay at what seemed to them an excess of democracy. The creative residue of the Classical Christian Consciousness was what I have called the Protestant passion for redemption (of the United States first and then of the world). That passion motivated every important reform movement of the nineteenth century, from abolitionism to temperance to the women's rights movement to Dorothea Dix's prison and asylum reforms and, finally, to the Populist Party, the most radical political movement in our history.

Much as the Constitution was the fruit of two thousand years of the Classical Christian Consciousness, Johns Hopkins was the American fruit of the Secular Democratic Consciousness, or, perhaps more specifically, the Enlightenment. The Enlightenment had been inspired by the dream that the rational mind might take charge of the progress of humanity. Science and reason would join to banish ignorance and superstition. Education would be the means by which those two, combining forces, would redeem the world from ignorance, superstition, and religion and usher in a new, more just and rational social order.

Johns Hopkins made the era from 1876 to 1900 a time when, in Josiah Royce's words, " 'twas sweet to be alive." To believe that Americans and, to a degree, the human race stood on the threshold of a new age of universal reform was, of course, intoxicating. Those involved in that incandescent moment felt, doubtless much like the Puritans under the leadership of John Winthrop, who dreamed of being "as a citie uppon a hill . . . that all those who come after might say 'let us be like those of New England.' " The Massachusetts Bay Colony had started with the avowed intention of reforming all Christendom. The Founding Fathers, heirs of the Classical Christian Consciousness, had the same exalted conviction that they were inaugurating a new age, Novus Ordo Seclorum, in the phrase they chose from Virgil for the Great Seal of the United States, "a new series or order of the ages begins."

The secular monks and acolytes of the newly founded "religion of the university" were acting in the same spirit. It was a time, brief and brilliant as a flash of lightning, that illuminated the American social landscape and threw light into every dark corner of our society. Not only was the movement for universities with their graduate studies given an irresistible momentum; the entire curriculum was reshaped in the same instant. If America was to be saved from violent, revolutionary upheaval, it was, most assuredly, to be done by dedicated scholars laboring in their studies and laboratories, under the aegis of science. There was no one else capable of such an emergency operation. The institutional churches were moribund, paralyzed in large part by the social issues that cried out to be solved. The politicians were hopeless relics of an earlier era. It was only the professors who could save America (and the world) from anarchy and chaos. The new curriculum was laid out specifically in terms of the pressing social issues; if the economy was staggering from one devastating depression to another, a group of professors and students under the rubric of "political economists" must direct their attention to a solution. If class antagonisms threatened to explode into open warfare, sociologists must search for a solution. If what was perhaps the most unnerving development of all, the collapse of religion, left a fearful vacuum in the lives of many people, the study of the soul or psyche under the banner of psychology would help to fill that vacuum. If politicians were to be made the reluctant agents of change in a democratic society, politics must be made into a science; hence "political science" claimed a central place in the new curriculum. Anthropology was the study of the evolution of living forms. It drew its rationale from Darwinism and traced the evolution of the species from the most primitive cellular forms to the astonishing complexity of human beings. Moreover, it ranked the races of the world in terms of their evolution from lower to higher, a "scientific" procedure fraught, as it turned out, with dangerous implications.

The first generation of graduates of Johns Hopkins fanned out into the cities of America, armed with the results of their studies. They joined forces with such urban reformers as Tom Johnson in Cleveland (Frederic Howe was a volunteer there) and Golden Rule Jones in Toledo (Brand Whitlock was Jones' aide and successor). Milwaukee was captured by reform-minded socialists. Walter Lippmann, a graduate of Harvard, went to work in Buffalo for another socialist mayor. Robert La Follette recruited professors at the University of Wisconsin to draft blueprints for his progressive politics.

The vision of a society redeemed by scholarship suffered two sharp setbacks. Attached as it was to Progressive Party politics— in the East to the political fortunes of Theodore Roosevelt, and in the West to Midwestern progressivism à la La Follette—it experienced its first serious disillusionment when Howard Taft and the conservative wing of the Republican Party denied Roosevelt's bid to be once more his party's standardbearer in the election of 1912. The defeat of Progressivism was a heartbreaking setback. If your vision of the world is that of steady progress, progress "on and up," as Noël Coward put it cynically, and that hope is suddenly and unexpectedly overthrown by a resurgence of politics-as-usual, your reaction will understandably be one of despair. The response of those progressive spirits inside and outside of the academic world may have been a measure of their inexperience and naïveté (most of them were, after all, comparatively young men and women), but it was no less poignant. Brooks Adams, who was far from a wild-eyed radical, assumed that the election of 1912 marked the defeat of reform politics and the virtual inevitability of revolution if the stranglehold of capitalism on American life was to be broken. In Adams' words, "at Chicago [the site of the Republican convention] capitalists declined to even consider receding to a secondary position. Rather than permit the advent of a power beyond their immediate control, they preferred to shatter the instrument [the Republican Party] by which they sustained their ascendancy."

The retreat of the university from its original vision of placing "the mind in the service of society" coincided, then, with the defeat of the Progressives in 1912 and the onset, two years later, of the European war. As we have noted, conservative trustees and reactionary legislators made clear to university professors what they considered to be the limits of free inquiry when it threatened to encourage (or turn into) crusades for social reform. The crusades were over, gone as suddenly as they had appeared, leaving behind a vast academic bureaucracy and the modern "disciplines" to mark their relatively brief passage. Having achieved the university, the Secular Democratic Consciousness declined into decadence. It turned inward and became an end in itself. Highly specialized and ritualized activity called, rather pretentiously, "scholarship" dominated the scene.

The pattern was strikingly similar to that of the medieval university, which rose out of the needs of students, attained a brief glory, and then sank into the long twilight of scholasticism, where the original mission was forgotten and scholarship became, as it has today, an end in itself, producing increasingly meaningless refinements.

Jacques Derrida has destroyed the basic assumptions of analytical philosophy, as Wittgenstein destroyed logical positivism, but he has done far more than that: he has destroyed the underpinnings of the modern positivistic, "objective," scientific consciousness. He has buried the last lingering hopes of the Enlightenment-Darwinian-Marxist, rationalist consciousness (for he has drawn attention to the fact that it is, for all practical purposes, dead), and it is this fact that has attracted to him the more troubled laborers in all the academic vineyards. He is the bearer of frightening news that we are unable to resist.

There is a strange irony in the Derrida phenomenon. In France, Derrida associated himself very strongly with that nation's student rebellion of the 1960s, an upheaval similar in many ways to that which took place in the United States. It does not seem too far-fetched to assume that his philosophical assumptions are directly related to the events of those years. In other words, Derrida became, in a sense, the philosopher of the students. Or the philosopher whose critique of the received wisdom of the academy was inspired by his sympathy with the charges of the students against the universities.

It is by now fairly clear that the signs of decadence in the academic world that students professed to see in the tumultuous sixties have only accelerated in the years since then. Whether Derrida's philosophy was a direct or an indirect outgrowth of his experience of the rebellion, it has been an acid eating away at the dominant structures of the academic world, French, English, and American. He has quite literally "deconstructed" higher education and left us with the question of how we are to regain our moral and intellectual equilibrium.

Will the teachers teach? If they will, can they? What will they teach?

Can the terrible flood of mediocre monographs-for-the-sake-of-being-promoted be dammed (be damned); of journals for the same purpose be reduced to some manageable, rational number?

Can a more humane and sensible system of tenure be worked out? Or should the whole system be abandoned?

Will the academic fundamentalists give up their "scheme of orthodoxies" and allow some light and air into their closed minds?

"Civilization can be saved only by a moral, intellectual and spiritual revolution to match the scientific, technological and economic revolution in which we are now living," Robert Hutchins wrote. "If education can contribute to a moral, intellectual and spiritual revolution, then it offers a real hope of salvation to suffering humanity everywhere. If it cannot, or will not, contribute to this revolution, then it is irrelevant and its fate is immaterial."

A new consciousness representing a synthesis of the two prior consciousnesses, the Classical Christian (thesis) and the Secular Democratic (antithesis), must take shape. I do not presume to say just what form this new consciousness will take. I am confident that it must include the enduring elements of both traditions, powerfully reanimated and enthusiastically reconstructed. Ortega y Gasset reminds us that a generation *in form* can accomplish more genuine reform than centuries of lackluster effort. And that historical change can take place with startling swiftness—*vide* Mikhail Gorbachev and glasnost. But so strong is the hold on our minds and imaginations of what *is* that to make any substantial change in the way we think about the whole process of education will require, in David Bohm's words, "an energy, a passion, a seriousness, beyond even that needed to make creative and original discoveries in science, art, or in other such fields."

INDEX

INDEX

Free Speech Movement, 162, 165–66, 232

Freneau, Philip, 30

Freud, Sigmund, xii, 238

Friedman, Milton, 250

Frugé, August, 177, 182–83, 184–85, 186–88, 261

Gaines, David, 143, 281

Galer, Roger, 62

Gara, Michael, 242

Geertz, Clifford, 234–37

Gellner, Ernest, 255

general education, 140–42; Western Civilization programs and, 142–51

George, Henry, 52, 78, 248

Georgia Commonwealth, 228–29

German scholarship, 44–46, 49, 54, 68, 81, 110, 254

Gibb, Sir Hamilton, 112–13

Gilbert, Felix, 268

Gilman, Arthur, 97

Gilman, Daniel Coit, 54, 59, 60, 100–1

Gitlin, Todd, 3–4, 157

Glazer, Nathan, 267

Godkin, E. L., 79

Goldman, Emma, 69

Goodman, Paul, 152–53

Goodrich, H. B., 86–87

Gothic architecture, 5

Gottschalk, Louis, 267

Gould, Jay, 73

grading system, 13, 219

graduate studies, 61, 68, 70, 73, 74–75, 85, 138, 244; instituting of, 49–60

Gramsci, Antonio, 247, 279–81

Grand Theorists, 230

Graubard, Stephen, 268

Graves, John Morton, 90

Great Awakening, 25–26

Great Strikes (1877), 51–52

Greenberg, Richard, 4

Grinnell, 68, 228

Guggenheim Foundation, 276

Gunnell, John G., 243–44, 246

Gunton, George, 78

Gutman, Herbert, 274, 281

Haessler, Carl, 127

Hall, G. Stanley, 57

Handlin, Oscar, 271

Hannah, John, 158

Hare Krishnas, 168–69

Harper, William Rainey, 58–59, 76–77, 181

Harriman, Florence, 128

Hart, Albert Bushnell, 71

Harvard University, xi, xii–xiii, xiv–xv, xvi, xvii, 14, 26, 31, 34, 37, 39, 42–43, 44, 57, 59, 73, 82, 83–84, 85, 97, 102, 106, 109, 110–11, 113, 116, 128, 129, 133–35, 141–142, 153, 156–57, 165, 178, 206, 217, 218, 219, 230, 232, 242, 253–54, 259; corporate alliances of, 12; founding of, 23–25; graduate program instituted by, 50; Press, 118–19; undergraduate experience at, 70–71, 72, 75

Haskins, Charles Homer, 57, 129

Hawes, Gene, 181–82

Hawthorne, Nathaniel, 277

Hayes, Rutherford B., 51

Heidegger, Martin, 247, 255

Heisenberg, Werner, 284

Henderson, Lawrence, 134

Herron, George, 68–69, 228–29

Hexter, J. H., 271

Hickman, Harry, 17

high schools, 43–44, 64

Historical Studies Today, 268–70

history, 148, 224, 231, 253, 257–75, 287; constant rewriting of, 272; economic determinism and, 264–265; internecine warfare over objectivity in, 270–72; literary style of, 260, 262; monographic, 260–262, 270, 272–74; in nineteenth century, 259–60; power of, 258–259; quantitative, 265–70; religion omitted from, 272–73

History of American Socialisms, The, 225

Hitchcock, William, 215

Hobson, J. A., 76

Holmes, John, 85–86

Holmes, Mary, 215

Holmes, Oliver Wendell, 47

Hooker, Richard, 27, 28

Hoover, Herbert, 87

Hopkins, Johns, 50, 54

Horowitz, Irving Louis, 250

Howe, Frederic, 54, 55–57, 72, 79, 88, 128, 129, 136, 159, 244, 302

Howe, Irving, 278

humanities, 9, 253–84, 287; *see also specific disciplines*

Hunt, Frazier, 135

Hurston, Zora Neale, 234

Hutchins, Robert, 16–17, 61, 74, 132, 148, 171, 196, 201–2, 251–52, 304

Hutchinson, William, 178

Huxley, T. H., 100

INDEX

Merrill, Isabel Trowbridge, 93
Meyer, Marshall, 156–57
Mezes, Sidney Edward, 129
Michigan, University of, 69, 78–79, 91, 97
Michigan State University, 158
Miers, Earl Schenk, 182
military, 1, 10–11, 13, 157–59, 163
Mill, John Stuart, 47
Mills, C. Wright, 230, 232
Mitchell, S. Weir, 239
Moberly, Sir Walter, 9–10, 201, 223, 295–96
Moley, Raymond, 136
monographs, 180, 190, 260–62, 270, 272–74
Monsanto Company, 11
Moon, Reverend, 169
Morison, Samuel Eliot, 24
Morrill Act (1862), 61, 64
Motley, John Lothrop, 259
Mount Holyoke College, 89–90, 91, 94, 98, 289
Mumford, Lewis, xvi
Munsterberg, Hugo, 71
Murray, Henry, 242
Murray, Nicholas, 180
Muscatine, Charles, 253

National Aeronautics and Space Administration (NASA), 1, 10
National Association of Scholars (NAS), 18–19
National Enquiry, 183–85, 188–89
National Liberal Reform League, 102–103, 107, 226
National Science Foundation, 250
natural law, theory of, 28–29
natural selection, 46–48, 53
Nebraska, University of, 62
neo-Marxism, 279–82
Nevada, University of, at Las Vegas, 15
New Age philosophy, 167–68
New Deal, 136, 151, 245
Newman, John Henry, 199
New Student, 131
New University Conference, 159–61
New York Review of Books, 275, 276–77
New York Times, 4, 12, 18, 193, 241
Nichol, Donald, 215
Nietzsche, Friedrich, 279, 282–83
normal schools, 18
North, Sir Thomas, 258
Northern Iowa, University of, 194–95
Northwestern University, 80, 97
Novick, Peter, 270–72
Noyes, John Humphrey, 224–26, 249

Oakeshott, Michael, 113
Oberlin College, 40–41, 88, 95–96
O'Connor, Flannery, 1
Oklahoma, University of, 14
Old Faiths in New Light, 99
On Certainty, 257
On Demand publishing, 185–86
Oneida Community, 224–26
Order of Saint Crispin, 51, 52
Origins of American Scientists, 86–87
Ortega y Gasset, José, 108, 140, 147–148, 151, 196, 199–200, 201, 305
Otis, James, 28–29
Out of Revolution, xvi, 172
Outward Bound, 206–7
Owen, David, xii
Oxford, 23–24, 81, 112–13, 133, 154

Page, Walter Hines, 57
Parkman, Francis, 259
Parsons, Talcott, 230
part-time instructional staffs, 7–8
Pascal, Blaise, 296
Passing of the Saint, 229
Pasternak, Boris, 258
Peirce, Charles Sanders, 50, 253
Pembroke College, 97
Pendleton, Ellen Fitz, 92
Pennsylvania, University of, 27, 211
Perfectionism, 224–26
Perlman, Selig, 271
Ph.D. degree, 13–14, 60, 68, 108–14, 196
Phelps, William Lyon, 212, 213
Philosophical Investigations, 242–43
philosophy, 102, 134–35, 253–57, 303
Pieper, Josef, 208
Pilgrims, 23
Plato, 207
Poe, Edgar Allan, 277
political science, 243–48, 249, 268, 301
Populism, 5–6, 52–53, 68–69, 300
Porter, Noah, 100
Positive Philosophy, 223
post-modernism, 3–4, 5
Powderly, Terence, 52
Powell, Jack, 110
Power and Culture, 281
Prabhupada, A. C. Bhaktivedanta, 168–169
practical education, classical education vs., 31–35, 37–38, 42, 43, 55
Presbyterians, 26, 28
Prescott, William, 259–60
presentism, 148, 294–95

INDEX

Trefil, James, 283
Truman, David, 158–59
Truman, Harry S., 142
Tugwell, Rexford Guy, 136
Tulane University, 97
Turgee, Albion, 278
Turner, Frederick Jackson, 265, 267

Uemura, Tamali, 92
Ulysses, 275
Uncle Tom's Cabin, 143, 144, 277
undergraduates: added to universities, 59; experience of, 69–75, 156–57
unions, 51, 52
Unitarianism, 27, 87
university: as academic community, 17–18, 209; as capitalistic institution, 12, 13–14, 76–85, 125; modern, emergence of, 49–60
University College London, xiii–xiv, xv
University Crisis Reader, 157
University Microfilm International (UMI), 186
university presses, 180–87, 190–92, 260
Urey, Harold, 205
Uses of the University, The, 153–56, 157
utopianism, 224–26, 228–29

Vanderbilt, Commodore, 57
Vanderbilt University, 57, 96
Van Hise, Charles R., 64–67
Varieties of Religious Experience, The, 104, 144
Vassar, Matthew, 90
Vassar College, 90, 98
Veblen, Thorstein, 57, 81–82, 84, 85, 137
Versailles Treaty (1919), 129–30
Veysey, Laurence, 114–15, 298
Vietnam War, 157–59, 161, 220, 221, 243, 272
Villard, Oswald Garrison, 71
Voegelin, Eric, 37

Wald, George, 161–62
War Between Science and Religion, The, 99, 100
Ward, Lester, 98, 102, 226–27, 229
Washington University, 11
Wayland, Francis, 38
Wealth Against Commonwealth, 52

Weber, Max, 48, 232
Webster, Noah, 32, 33–34
Weil, Simone, 282
Weld, Theodore, 40, 41
Wellesley College, 90–92, 93, 98, 289
Western Civilization programs, 142–51
Wheeler, Benjamin Ide, 72–73, 75
White, Andrew D., 58, 75, 80, 96, 99, 100
White, William Allen, 124, 126
Whitefield, George, 26
Whitehead, Alfred North, xiii, 5, 111, 134–35, 200, 210, 217, 254, 257, 293, 295, 297, 298
Whitlock, Brand, 302
Whitman, Walt, 144, 277
William and Mary College, 14, 25, 26, 32
William and Mary Quarterly, 189–90
Will to Believe, 103–4
Wilson, James, 116–17
Wilson, Woodrow, 54, 73, 75, 124, 126, 127–28, 133, 136, 217, 262–263
Winthrop, John, 301
Wirth, Louis, 201
Wisconsin, University of, 57, 61, 62–63, 64–67, 69, 79, 80–81, 85, 97, 127, 271, 302
Wittgenstein, Ludwig, 242–43, 257, 297, 298, 303
Wohlstetter, Roberta, 113
women, 37, 41, 67–68, 121, 124, 272; coeducation and, 95–98
women's colleges, 67, 88, 89–95, 98, 131, 207, 289
women's rights movement, 40, 41, 273, 285–87, 300
women's studies, 285–92
Woodward, C. Vann, 272
Woolson, Alba, 89
Wordsworth, William, 49
World War I, 126–27, 130, 270–71, 303; peace process after, 127–30

Yale University, 17, 25, 26, 37–38, 39, 73, 80, 93, 100, 128, 131, 134, 140, 162, 212, 213; Law School, 136; Press, 181; Report of (1828), 37–38
Young Communist League, 135–36

Ziskin, Jay, 241